The Truth Within
A Humanist's Memoir

by Leonard M. Cachola

First edition

ISBN-10: 1726252558
ISBN-13: 9781726252553

Printed by CreateSpace Independent Publishing Platform

The events and situations depicted in this book are true to
the best of my memory based on journal entries.
Some of the names and details have been changed to
protect the privacy of the individual.

Prologue

March 10, 2005

I was up and alert as soon as the alarm went off at 6 a.m., putting on loose-fitting clothes as requested by the hospital. Just as we had planned, I gave my next-door neighbor Carrie a wake-up call. After her groggy voice answered the phone, I caught a glimpse of her long, dark hair through her window while she stumbled around half-awake looking for all the contact information she needed.

Several minutes later, I heard a knock. When I opened the front door, I found myself staring down at a foot-tall pink teddy bear with "I love you" embroidered across its belly. I gingerly took it, revealing a woman on a mission. Part of me wanted to save myself the embarrassment of lugging that display of affection around the hospital for the next few hours, but I embraced the sentiment and clung to that bear as if it were my only friend in the world.

We sat there on my mattress and watched the clock tick well past our appointed pickup time until my boss' wife Imelda showed up at the front door. As we rode to the hospital in silence, the dark of the city passed by us in a blur.

When I checked in to the hospital, I asked to have a testosterone test done, but was given the run-around because I needed doctor approval first. Dr. K had arrived early, but I didn't know where he was and hadn't thought to ask him about the test beforehand. It would have given us a baseline in case of more extensive treatment later that might affect my testosterone levels.

I had to have that test. I had to.

"You look like you're going to cry," Carrie said.

But I didn't. I wouldn't.

When we arrived at the pre-op room, the nurse took my blood pressure and pulse. Once that was done, I changed out of my civilian clothes and into the vulnerability that comes with wearing a hospital gown.

The anesthesiologist and several nurses came by the pre-op room around 11 a.m. to administer the IV. A brief burst of intense pain in my left hand indicated the IV was in.

Once the nurse was certain the medication and anesthesia had taken hold, they placed me on the gurney to wheel me away. With escorts clad in green scrubs guiding me, I gleefully floated through the hospital corridors and into the operating room. When I arrived, I overheard a nurse say Dr. K was running 15 minutes late. A voice in the back of my mind was worried the painkillers and sedatives might wear off before he arrived. "Make sure I'm not awake and alert when you cut me open!" I wanted to plead with a scream, but I was too high to say anything intelligible at that point. Once Dr. K arrived, they put me under. I lasted a whole ten seconds before my world went black.

Early Years

Eight

I was changing channels on our wood-paneled 13-inch Sony television hoping to find cartoons to watch, but the only programming on at 6:45 a.m. on a Sunday morning in 1980's Houston called for salvation from a higher power. "All you have to do is believe and the Lord will wash you of all your sins and grant you eternal glory," the old white man in the pastel blue three-piece suit said before I flipped the channel. Other than my parents teaching me the Lord's Prayer, it was the closest I came to eternal salvation at eight years old.

Dad was asleep in his bedroom after taking Mom to work as a nurse's aid that summer morning. Once Dad woke from his slumber, he began his Sunday morning ritual by taking a shower, then getting dressed in his tennis whites and sweats. He then cooked us bacon and eggs with buttered toast for breakfast. After we were done eating, he filled up his red plastic jug with a gallon of water, packed his tennis rackets and a couple of fresh cans of tennis balls into a duffle bag, then loaded everything into the trunk of his enormous, bright silver Ford Thunderbird. Since we didn't use it all the time, it was a treat to ride in the cavernous interior of the Thunderbird with its slippery smooth, red vinyl. It may not have been the real leather of a Benz, but it was close enough for us. We then made the half-hour drive over to the huge, sprawling rec center on Houston's west side so Dad could get in a couple of tennis matches. A self-taught player, Dad had won dozens of trophies displayed in our living room with great pride.

When we went through the lobby at the rec center, Atari's *Missile*

Command arcade game captured my attention with its colorful cabinet beckoning me to play hero. Dad gave me a roll of quarters and left me there while he went to play tennis with his friend. After inserting a quarter into the machine, I wildly thrashed at the trackball while mashing the trio of fire buttons in an attempt to protect my cities from missiles showering from above. Every time I cleared the screen of those missiles, a new wave rained down quicker than the last until all my cities were reduced to rubble, bringing my feats of heroism to a disappointing end. Not wanting to give up after only one game, I continued putting in quarters to keep playing hero until I finished off the roll.

With the roll of quarters done, I walked over to watch Dad play tennis with his friend, a middle-aged white man with a mustache. After watching a few rallies, I walked over to Dad's duffle bag and picked up the old wooden tennis racket he brought as a backup to the fancy aluminum one he was using. I grabbed a couple of balls, then walked over to hit against the practice wall, just as I had seen Dad do when he was waiting for his friend to show up. I would love to say I was brilliant with long sustained rallies against the unyielding wall, but the ball bounced past me more times than I cared to count.

After tiring myself from chasing down the ball, I wandered the grounds until Dad finished playing with his friend. He then spent a few minutes hitting with me on the court until it was time to go home, grab some lunch, and pick up Mom from work. I had fun spending time with him doing something he enjoyed, and I was glad he didn't mind I wasn't coordinated with a racket.

"Leonard, I thought we were playing Smokey and the Bandit," Kevin whispered so he wouldn't wake my mom in the other room, one of three bedrooms in our single-story brick home with its distinctive pink mortar. It was one of those warm summer days in Houston where the sweltering heat and humidity drove us to remain sheltered inside our air-conditioned home. My next-door neighbor Kevin, the youngest kid on our block, had Asian eyes and could have passed for my cousin if it weren't for his light colored hair and white skin contrasting my black hair and brown skin.

"We are. We are playing Smokey and the Bandit meet the Shogun Warriors and Godzilla," I beamed. I pressed down the button on the large yellow and blue armored action figure, shooting plastic missiles at the black toy car with the gold firebird painted on its hood in Kevin's hand. We were playing on Plywood Town, which was made up of a bunch of plastic toy buildings placed on a 4x4 piece of plywood I had hand-painted roads and empty plots of land on.

Kevin groaned.

"Look, I just wanted to change things up," I said in an attempt to bring peace so we could get back to some serious playing.

"I could change things by going home," he mocked.

"You just want to go home so you can play with your Intellivision," I said.

"I would rather play Hot Wheels like we said we would," he said with disdain.

"All right, have it your way," I said to appease his demands because it was more fun sharing my toys with someone than keeping them to myself.

When we resumed our battle through Plywood Town, I cornered Kevin's Bandit with my sheriff, a tank, an ambulance, and anything else I could grab within arm's reach. When Bandit refused to surrender, they all opened fire.

"Ha! You're dead!" I gloated as I turned his Firebird upside down.

"No, I'm not. Bandit is just sleeping," he boasted.

"Uh-uh. We agreed when we turned the cars upside down, they were dead," I said in an authoritative manner. Well, as authoritative as an eight-year-old could be.

"I don't like being dead. You can't do anything anymore," he said with a pout as I continued moving my vehicles around Plywood Town while refusing to let him move his. "What do you think happens when we die? Do you think we go to heaven or hell?" he asked while picking up his Firebird.

"I have no idea," I told him, "but whatever happens will happen to me first since I'm older."

"As long as we're still best friends, I don't care what happens," he replied.

"Deal," I said while nodding in agreement.

Later that evening, I was guiding my Hot Wheels cars from one destination to the next in my playroom when, without warning, the door slammed open, causing me to bolt upright, fear and dread coursing through my veins. I looked up and saw Dad looming in the entrance, belt in hand, still dressed in the light-colored dress shirt and dark-brown slacks he wore to work as an office clerk at the local phone company; his war face with its furious eyebrows, angry eyes, and bared teeth ready to charge in. He may not have been a tall man, being average height for a Filipino, but to my eight-year-old self, he was plenty big. I scrambled for the far corner of the room to get away from the belt, wreaking havoc on Plywood Town as I did, but there was nowhere to run or hide. Within seconds, Dad barreled across Plywood Town with his belt raised, crushing the good citizens who had survived my panicked scramble across the town. I tried covering myself but there was little protecting me from the stinging pain of Dad's angry blows to my back.

"Why are you so stupid?" he yelled over and over again with the fury of a man possessed by demons. "Why?!?"

I didn't answer him because I didn't know why he was angry. Did I forget to put away my toys from the living room? Did I wake Mom since she was sleeping in the other room? Or could it have been the broken window shade now hanging from the window, easily visible from the street? It didn't matter what I had done. All that mattered was Dad in the room pounding me with his leather belt. I cried and wailed from each blow while crouched down in the corner, hoping it would all come to a quick end.

After Dad calmed down and left, I got up and surveyed the damage to Plywood Town. Cars had been tossed around as if a tornado had torn right through the middle of town, parts of buildings were strewn all over the place, and the golden train circling the town had derailed. I reached over and righted the train, then began rebuilding the town so my friends could return to their beloved community.

Eleven

In the summer of 1982, my family moved to a two-story, four-bedroom home in a quiet suburb outside of Houston. After the move, my parents purchased a 3-foot-tall marble statue of the Virgin Mary and placed it in the center of a huge landscaped star in front of our home. That was the closest Dad ever came to talking about God. Although moving had put distance between Kevin and me, my parents still owned the old home next door to Kevin's family and would rent it out. I would go back with Mom and Dad over the course of a weekend and help fix up the place if the house needed repairs between tenants.

On weeknights, Dad would drink hard liquor for hours on end while seated on the living-room couch, the TV tuned to channels he received from the twelve-foot satellite dish looming in the backyard over his vegetable garden filled with eggplant, tomatoes, and peppers. Sometimes, if it were late enough, he would fall asleep in front of the TV with Mom at his side. My mother was slightly shorter than my father and had a petite figure and yellow skin. She wore large, round glasses that made her look young for her age and had long, dark wavy hair that went down her back. Every now and then, Dad would turn his attention on me when I was present. Whenever he spoke through that drunken haze, he would tilt his head down like a bull ready to charge, his intense, dark eyes piercing right through me.

"You need to work hard, boy," he would say with a slur. "If you don't work hard, you won't make any money. And if you don't make any money, then you'll be nothing but a stupid bum. You hear me, boy? You'll be a BUM."

"I hear you, Dad." I didn't care for the method he chose to deliver his message, but it was nice to know he cared about my future.

Whenever the television diverted Dad's attention back to whatever sport he was watching, he would yell at the television whenever a player would make a mistake, no matter how minor. "Oh, bullcorn. What's wrong with you? Don't you know how to play? I don't know why any of you get paid so much money." I hated being around him when he was like that. Instead of subjecting myself to his rants, I preferred retreating to my room to watch TV, play video games, read comics and books, or draw.

Sometimes, he would storm up the stairs to my room, his stomps reverberating through the entire house before he burst into my room with his full war face on. He would swing the door wide open, slamming it against the wall, bringing me to attention.

"What's wrong with you, boy?!? Why are you so stupid? You think you're so smart, but you're stupid," he would say. The more he called me stupid, the more I despised the way he made it sound as if I should never have been born.

If I answered back, he would raise his hand as if he were going to hit me. I knew what he was capable of and that was enough to keep me quiet and obedient. I eventually learned any attempt at answering back was the worst thing I could do. Life was more peaceful when I waited for him to calm down in hopes he would go back downstairs without incident to take his anger out on the TV.

Many of Dad's tantrums were soon followed by trips to stores to buy things I wanted, like comic books and video games for the Atari 2600 game console my parents had given me one Christmas. If anything, I learned if I did something bad, I could get rewarded with something I wanted.

What I wanted was stories like the imaginative ones depicted in comic books Dad bought me at comic book stores we frequented—stories where heroes with special powers reigned supreme. These stories made me wish I had special powers so I could be strong and powerful. At the same time, my desire to succeed to spite Dad's calling me stupid gave me the discipline to create my own art. My early works were attempts to mimic the mini-books that came with Atari games. These books were full of fantastical art depicting realistic scenes far exceeding the limitations of the simplistic 8-bit games themselves. Once I started putting together my own comic books, Dad would take me to his work and make copies for me to give to classmates. I always loved when he did that because it showed he cared.

Fourteen

It was a cold, cloudy mid-March Sunday morning in 1987 when Dad dragged my fourteen-year-old self out of the comfort zone that was my bed to hit the hard courts. We were heading over to the local high school for a round of tennis, much as we did every Sunday for the past six years after dropping Mom off at her nursing job. None of Dad's friends or their children were there this day due to the chilly weather and strong winds.

For our practices, Dad would hit the balls all over the court while I chased them down with my racket. My body would surge with adrenaline with each step while I ran from one side of the court to the other, knocking those balls back to the other side with authority. When Dad's basket of tennis balls reached empty after the area behind him became littered with the balls I pounded over there, I would go to the other side of the court, help Dad pick them up, and start all over again.

During our practices, my making a mistake was always an adventure with Dad. "You're so stupid!" he would yell at the top of his lungs as he slammed the balls at me with the fury of a man consumed by the desire for his son to be the success he wasn't. One ball for an errant backhand that faded into the net, then another for the forehand that went two inches too wide, followed by a third for the overhead I whiffed at, then several more to blow off steam. I may have been able to use my racket to deflect the painful sting of those yellow bullets, but I couldn't escape the idea I was too stupid to live up to Dad's idea of tennis perfection. He wanted me to become a rich and famous tennis player like his idol Jimmy Connors, whose bowl-shaped haircut graced my head from childhood until I gained a faint glimmer of style my junior year in high school. Whenever I made a break for the exit to get away from those fast-moving projectiles and Dad's relentless insults, the high fences lining the courts trapped me there like a caged animal. Knowing he became more violent if I ran or fought kept me in line. It wasn't all bad, though. Dad would always start up the grill and cook his delicious barbecue ribs, chicken wings, and burgers to reward me for a week's practice.

This practice, however, was different. Dad was calmer and more understanding than usual with the stiff wind pushing the balls around mid-flight making them difficult to hit. The only sounds heard from either of us in the midst of all the wind were our shoes squeaking with every change of direction on the hard courts, our rackets giving off a light ping sound when they made contact with the ball, and the balls making a satisfying THOCK every time they bounced off the court.

When we returned home after two hours of practice, I noticed the blinking red indicator light on the answering machine telling us there were awaiting messages. Since we received a lot of messages from telemarketers, we usually ignored the light.

After we put away the tennis equipment, Dad fixed me something to eat, then we drove over to the hardware store to pick up a few things before heading out to pick up Mom. The rest of the day proceeded as normal, with me and my parents trimming the plants, pulling weeds, mowing the yard, and tending the garden, then they cooked dinner while I played in my room, the answering machine still blinking away, ignored and neglected.

When I woke up to the radio the next morning so I could get ready for school, I was about to hit the snooze button on my clock radio when a familiar name stopped me cold.

"Kevin _____ of Steeplechase Road was accidentally shot and killed yesterday by a playmate. They were playing with the gun when it went off."

I bolted upright in bed wide awake with the realization my fourteen-year-old self was no longer invulnerable like the superheroes in the comic books Kevin and I used to read together when we weren't playing with Hot Wheels. With those two sentences, the finality of death was no longer something that happened after Kevin and I had grown old and gray; it was something that could happen anytime and anywhere. When I went down and played back the messages on the answering machine, there was a familiar but frantic voice on several of the recordings.

16

"Where are you, Leo?" Kevin's dad Curt said, addressing my father. "I need to talk to you. Something bad has happened to Kevin," he said in a broken down, grief-stricken voice. That's when it hit me, I may have lost my best friend, but Curt had lost his only son. I couldn't imagine what he, his wife, and Kevin's older sister, Annie, could be going through.

I went to school that day because my parents didn't want me to miss any classes and I didn't dare cross Dad because I didn't want the belt, but all I could think about the entire day was Kevin shot up and bleeding to death from his wounds.

A few days later, my parents took me to Kevin's wake. I walked past the mourners in the seats, most of whom were unfamiliar to me, and approached his coffin alone. Staring at Kevin's lifeless face, his collar hiding the neck wound that felled him, I wanted him to wake up and tell me he was okay and ready to play again just as we had for years, but he just laid there at peace with his eyes closed while tears rolled down my face. How could he be so stupid and irresponsible, playing with a gun like that? Then again, maybe he had nothing to do with it at all. Maybe it was God teaching me a lesson that life is precious and sacred. It made me wish God had picked a more peaceful way of saying that other than taking away my best childhood friend. How could God be so cruel?

"Don't worry, Leonard. He's in a better place," his sister Annie, who was a year older than me, told me as she came over in an attempt to console me. She was wearing a long, black dress with her long, dark silky hair tied back. Although I was thankful for her words, her telling me Kevin was in a better place did nothing to stop the fact he was dead and wouldn't be coming back.

For the first several Sundays after Kevin's passing, all I wanted to do was stay in bed and sleep. Going out to play tennis so I could put up with Dad's tantrums seemed pointless in the face of death. If I wasn't having any fun at it, why should I bother?

"C'mon, boy. It's time to go," Dad would say when he came to wake me for tennis practice.

"Not today, Dad. I don't feel like going."

It took Dad several weeks to figure out I had no intention of returning to playing tennis with him. One night, Dad came home and had his usual round of whiskey and vodka—plus whatever else he had stocked in the wet bar he had installed. I was downstairs sitting on the couch watching some sitcoms when Dad started speaking.

"Hey, boy," Dad said in his loud, gruff voice, slurring his words as he did. Like most nights, Mom was busy fixing dinner in the kitchen, which I dared not enter so I wouldn't go into a sneezing fit from my allergies. My parents were having their usual, steamed rice and chicken adobo, while Mom had fixed me up some spaghetti and meatballs to appease my Americanized palate.

"Yes, Dad?" I asked, doing my best to come across as pleasant and easy-going so I wouldn't arouse his anger.

"When are you going to play tennis with me again?" he asked.

"I don't want to anymore."

"Why not? Don't you want to make lots of money?" Dad said.

Dad liked to talk about how I would make a lot of money if I played tennis as a pro, but I found it difficult to believe he thought I could become a successful tennis player when I had never won a local tournament. Plus, the odds of me making the high school team were slim to none. All of my friends had gotten bigger and stronger and hit the ball harder with better accuracy while I was still the shrimp of my class from not having hit puberty yet.

Worse, whenever I played a tennis match with friends, family, at tournaments, or even for fun, I would worry about how stupid I was while allowing the searing sun, gusts of wind, and stinging sweat getting into my eyes irritate me like an itch that refused to go away no matter how much I scratched it. Smashing my racket into the ground and loudly grunting my displeasure became regular antics to drive the irritation away. My parents saw my tantrums as a lack of discipline deserving punishment instead of an outward expression of how much I wanted to quit playing tennis.

"Well, what are you going to do then?" Dad asked, his voice rising as he did.

"I don't know yet."

"You don't know, huh? You're so smart and you don't know?" Dad mocked. "Well, boy, you know what," he continued. "You're being stupid. You can make millions playing tennis. You know that? Millions."

"I know, Dad, but I don't want to play anymore," I said, uncertain this was the stance I wanted to take.

"Well, I'll tell you what you're going to do," he said, his eyes going wild while his nostrils flared.

"YOU'RE GOING TO BE A BUM! THAT'S ALL YOU'RE GOING TO BE. YOU THINK YOU'RE SO SMART AND ALL YOU'RE GOING TO BE IS A BUM! YOU HEAR ME?!? A BUM, YOU STUPID BOY."

18

Mom took interest and asked what the problem was. Well, I'm guessing that's what she was asking because I didn't understand a word she was saying in Tagalog, nor did I want to. Once they started yelling at each other, I slipped away and headed upstairs to the comfort of my room. Once there, I turned on my Commodore 128 and loaded up *M.U.L.E.*, a game about the economics of colonizing a planet, because it gave me the opportunity to dive into a world where I was in control of my life.

After the yelling stopped, I could hear Mom's sad sobs reverberating up the stairwell and into my room. I turned off the computer, then crept downstairs to make sure she was okay. When I arrived on the ground floor, I saw Mom sitting at the breakfast table, crying. Across the room, Dad sat on the couch with his glazed eyes transfixed by the large, wood-paneled 20-inch television in front of him, drink in hand.

"I'm sorry, anak," she said, calling me 'child' in Tagalog. "I'm sorry. I'm sorry he yelled at you. Do you hear me? Just do as he tells you to, anak. okay?" Mom said through the tears.

"Okay, Mom," I said before returning upstairs and back to my game. When Mom came upstairs to my room, her eyes still red from the tears, she told me to go to sleep. I did as she said, but as I lay there in the darkness, I decided to never play tennis again no matter what Dad asked of me.

College

So Strong

My first year-and-a-half of college comprised of me making the long commute to the University of Houston, attending my requisite freshman and sophomore classes, then going home to do homework and work part-time at the local pizza place as a delivery driver. For work, I used the old silver hatchback my parents handed down to me with 119,000 miles on the odometer after I received my driver's license at 16 years old.

To get away from Dad's nightly tantrums, I would stay out late with the cooks, delivery drivers, and one of the assistant managers, Chris, a former army technician who had moved from the Bay area to live with his brother's family. A well-groomed man of average height and build with a regal Italian nose and blue eyes, Chris and I connected on our love of new wave music, like New Order, The Cure, and Depeche Mode. He expanded my music knowledge by introducing me to the progressive rock of Pink Floyd, the punk musings of The Sex Pistols, the beautifully written trash rock of The Replacements, and many more bands.

The first couple of times I stayed out late, Mom would stay up and wait for me to come home, but the more I stayed out, the looser my parents' restrictions became since I was now over 18. Sometimes I would arrive home from work or school late to find Mom fast asleep on the couch with Dad upstairs in the bedroom, indicating they had a fight. On the nights I wasn't working, Dad was his usual drunken self.

One night during my first semester in college, I came home early from work to find Dad sitting at the dining table, alone.

"Your mom. Do you know where she is?" he said as he looked up from his drink, his blood-red eyes filled with sadness.

"No. I've been at school and work all day. How would I know?"

During their fight the night before, Dad accused Mom of cheating on him, which was impossible since she never went anywhere without him. Mom called the police when Dad grew violent, but the police didn't do anything since she wasn't physically harmed and Mom didn't bother pressing charges. I guess she decided to take matters into her own hands and left without saying a word.

"Nobody knows. Not your auntie. Not her family. Nobody," he said. Evidently, he had been making frantic phone calls the entire day after she didn't show when he went to pick her up from work.

"If she doesn't come back, we won't be able to afford the house or your schooling," he said with the regret of a man who had made a big mistake. Listening to his words, I never realized how tight their budget was. Visions of having to drop out of school and move to God knows where had me questioning whether or not staying with my parents had been a good idea after all. What was I going to do without a degree?

"I want to burn down this house," he said with menacing bitterness.

In my mind I could see Dad and me running from the house as it became engulfed in flames, approaching sirens wailing in the distance. It was a future I hoped would never come to pass.

When I returned to work at the pizza place the next day, my mother called on one of the lines.

"Are you okay, anak?" she asked after one of the 'phone girls,' who had a look of concern on her face, handed me the phone.

"Yes, Mom. Where are you?" I asked.

"You don't need to know that right now. I just want to know that you're all right," she said in a worried tone.

"I'm fine, Mom," I said with little emotion.

"Good. I don't want you to worry about anything, anak, especially your school. I will take care of it. Don't you worry." I took a few deep breaths to calm down while everyone watched with looks of concern on their faces. It was like the whole store had stopped to listen to what I had to say and see how I would act. Mom's confidence relieved me of my fears over my future and made it easier to sleep that night.

As the weeks wore on, Mom kept Dad in the dark over where she was and what she was doing, choosing to give him the silent treatment to punish him. At first, she was pretty sure she wouldn't come back, but her will dissolved the longer she stayed away because she was worried Dad might do something bad to me. She didn't know what that might be, but my reassurances failed to convince her nothing would happen. As a result, I knew there was a good chance of her returning. Part of me found this disappointing because I was cheering for her to stay away from Dad, but another part of me wanted my parents together because it was less stressful than worrying about their tiffs affecting my education. Knowing she was wavering gave me the leverage and confidence to convince Dad to wait for Mom's return.

"You're so strong," he said. It was the first time he ever said that of me, though I was perplexed what this sudden shift in my relationship with Dad meant. Was I now the man of the household? Having never been independent, the thought of me heading anything was inconceivable.

After six weeks away, Mom came back, more out of concern for my well-being than wanting to be with Dad. I was just happy to see our broken family back together.

After she returned, Dad became less temperamental and would tell me he loved me, which was awkward for me after having him call me stupid for most of my life. He still drank alcohol but left me to my own devices. Knowing how volatile his temper was, I wasn't sure if this drastic shift in attitude would last, but I accepted it as the new normal of our relationship.

Comic Strip

"Hey, Leonard! How have you been?!?" Trina shouted with the enthusiasm of running into a long-lost friend when we ran into each other in the fall of 1992 at the UH Satellite. The Satellite was a small food court and recreation center located in the northern part of the campus.

I was surprised Trina, who stood a little taller than my 5-foot 9-inch frame and had shoulder-length wavy brown hair, recognized me considering how long my dark hair had grown since I had last seen her. I had stopped having my hair cut after years of Mom giving me bowl cuts like Dad's idol, US tennis star Jimmy Connors. It was my way of rebelling against my parents while living with them. Mom would ask in protest to cut my hair the way she used to, but I refused because I was stubborn like that.

"Pretty good. Just busy with school and work. You?"

"Same," she said with a smile. There was a grunt from the guy she was with. "Oh, this is my new friend, Shannon," she said. "Shannon, this is Leonard. Leonard was classmates with my friend Teresa last year."

"Pleased to meet you, man," Shannon said as he shook my hand. Shannon was slightly shorter than me and had short, brown hair in a crew cut. He wore glasses, a Guns N' Roses T-shirt, and spoke with a drawl.

"Ugh. I don't get these comics at all. They're so bad," Shannon said after looking at the school paper we brought with us. I didn't think the strips in *The Daily Cougar* were as bad as Shannon was saying. Both *A Little Moore* and *Harrison* were subversive and funny, though uneven. *Erin's Closet* was inventive and philosophical while moody in its nature, but dense and difficult to read. There were a couple of other strips too, but neither were memorable.

"Leonard, I remember you started working on your own comics. Were you able to get any done?" Trina asked.

"I had some ideas, but nothing concrete. Do you think I should try again?" I asked.

"Of course!" Trina said.

"Yeah, I'd love to see your work," Shannon said, backing Trina up.

With that, I spent the next several weeks taking the characters I had previously sketched and put them in random joke situations in a comic strip I named after The Smiths' album *Strangeways, Here We Come*. When I showed the comics to Shannon and Trina, they laughed and encouraged me to do more. When I posted the comics on the bulletin board at work, it was a different story.

"This is crap," my friend Chris said. "You have no sense of character relationships, you can't draw, and, worse, you're not funny." It hurt to hear someone I respected speak so ill of my work. Then again, maybe it was what I needed to hear so I could improve.

But it wasn't all bad. Some of my other coworkers liked them and encouraged me to do more. While my friends' opinions mattered, the real test was sending submissions to syndicates and applying at *The Daily Cougar*. I put several weeks' worth of strips together then sent them off to several syndicates. I also stopped by the *Cougar* offices and met up with the editor in chief. Mike was a dark-haired, fair-skinned male in his mid-20s with a mustache and glasses wearing a button-down shirt, slacks, and dress shoes.

"Sorry, we don't have any spots open," he said after looking over my work. "You can try again before the spring semester starts."

Over the course of the next few weeks, I received rejection notices from all the syndicates I submitted to. *Strangeways* was a failure.

When the spring semester rolled around, I was rejected again by *The Daily Cougar* due to space considerations. There wasn't an opening and nobody was leaving or getting kicked off.

Failing again to land a spot on the *Cougar*, I tried a different approach for a comic strip. Set in a high school newspaper called *Strange News, Print!* took characters from *Strangeways* and added new ones, including a woman hell bent on protesting anything she found objectionable to her beliefs, a ghost called 'The School Spirit,' and his best friend, Death, aka Carl. I wanted to immortalize my experiences of working as a cartoonist on my high school newspaper with all its fun and frivolity in the newsroom while putting together the best paper we could.

"Hey Leonard, did you notice something missing from the paper today?" Shannon asked during one February lunch.

"No, what?"

"One of the comics is missing. Now's your chance. Go apply again," Shannon said. He had a point, just because I was rejected twice didn't mean I should quit. Over the next couple of weeks, I put together a new packet to submit to *The Daily Cougar*, determined to get in with *Print!*

"You again, hm," Mike said when he saw me drop off my comics in the submission box in the *Cougar* office, located in the central courtyard of the Communications building, a short walk from the Satellite.

"I noticed one of the other comic strips was missing in the paper," I said with uncertainty.

"Yeah, he was too busy with school and had to drop out. Let me see what you have there."

I handed the comics over to him.

"These aren't bad, but does it have to be set in high school?" he asked.

"No, I can easily make it about college."

"Yeah. Make it about college, change the name, and you're in. *Print!* doesn't do much for me. "

I said the first thing that popped into my head. "How about we call it *Strange News*?"

"Sounds good to me. You start Monday."

I went home that night terrified because I had no experience working on a daily comic strip other than writing and drawing a few weeks' worth of strips. Regardless of what I thought, it didn't matter. I had a job to do.

New Car

Sitting at the stoplight on the highway feeder road, I was trying to see past the "For Sale" letters painted on the windshield of the sporty used Toyota when a gray Mustang pulled up next to me. It was the summer of 1992 and the old family hatchback had been spending an excessive amount of time with Teddy, the family mechanic. The stop and go nature of pizza delivery driving had taken its toll on the ten-year-old car.

With the hatchback on its last legs, Dad suggested I shop for a used car as a replacement. I wanted something youthful, sporty, reliable, and dependable while being affordable for someone working a minimum wage job plus tips. This particular Toyota had more miles than I wanted and came with a musty smelling, worn-out interior.

The Mustang revved its engine a few times, loudly showing off its free-flowing exhaust. I decided to play along by revving up the Toyota a couple of times in response. I wasn't going to let some Mustang intimidate me. I pressed the clutch in and put the car in first gear in anticipation of the light turning green. I had managed not to stall the first two used cars I had driven earlier that day and was feeling pretty good about my shifting. It had been a week since Chris took time out of his schedule to teach me how to drive his manual transmission red hatchback to help prepare me for buying a car.

When the light turned green, the Mustang and I took off from the light, my heart racing from the adrenaline rush. Determined to get ahead, I managed to get through first gear okay, but when I shifted to second I could hear the gears grind as the car sickeningly bucked back and forth. I put the clutch back in quickly, but the damage to my ego had already been done as the Mustang easily pulled away.

The Mustang waited for me to catch up, then the young man at the wheel rolled down his window and yelled, "Learn how to drive a stick, dumbass," then laughed as he took off. Embarrassed by my poor shifting prowess, I drove away slowly, listening carefully for any funny noises. Hearing nothing out of the ordinary, I drove the car back to the dealer lot, dropped the car off, then continued my search. I looked at several other cars over the next few weeks but never found one in my price range that didn't cost me more money to fix than keeping the old hatchback and all its problems.

"You're wasting too much time looking at used cars," Dad said, fed up with how long it was taking me to find a car. "Why don't you look for a new car? Your mom and I will help you pay for it."

With Dad's blessing, I test drove several brand-new cars. After reading *Car and Driver*'s annual Ten Best issue, I decided on a small Nissan sports sedan because the magazine gushed over how its handling could teach its owner the thrill of lift-throttle oversteer, whatever that was, and provide years of fun. While I was at work one night in September of 1992, my parents negotiated for one on the lot. A couple of days later, I picked up the car and proudly drove it home, my first-ever stick shift.

The Interview

For Christmas of 1992, my parents bought me my first Windows PC. Over the next few months, I read several books on graphics and multimedia to see how a PC could be used as an artist's tool. If I hadn't been such an avid reader of *The Daily Cougar*, I would have missed the tiny classified ad that ran in the summer of 1993 advertising the desktop publisher position at the *Cougar*. Excited at the opportunity to get paid to learn programs enabling me to use a computer as a creative outlet, I filled out an application and turned it in.

"Oh, hey, I've seen you around the office before. You're one of the cartoonists," Stan, the production manager, remarked during my interview the next day. Stan was a lanky figured T-shirt and jeans kind of guy who wore a dark-blue Astros baseball cap and a pair of Chuck Taylors. He spoke in a nasal voice with a distinctive twang and had a pronounced neck crane from having spent a lot of time hunched over doing screen printing and working in paste-up on the newspaper. He wore large, square glasses that fit the shape of his face well. "It's good you're on staff because you're familiar with all the craziness." It was a relief to know my knowledge of the late nights, tight deadlines, and conflicting personalities gave me an in.

"What's your major?" Stan asked.

"I'm a graphic design major, but I've been looking for another major," I said. I was looking for something to satisfy my parents. After all, they were still paying for my schooling. And my car. And my computer. The mental list of what they were paying for made me feel unworthy of such generosity.

"I'm getting a BFA in printmaking," Stan said. "Just a fair bit of warning, we don't do much design here. This is all about production and deadlines.

Are you okay with that?"

Knowing from high school I was better technically than creatively combined with my desire to learn the software made it a no-brainer on how to reply.

"Yes, I'm good with that."

"The hours are from 6 p.m. until we put the paper to bed. That will be as late as 1 or 2 a.m. the first couple of weeks. After that, we'll be able to get out earlier once you get used to the job."

I took a deep breath and realized this was going to be a lot of late hours, but it wasn't much different from working at the pizza place, where our prime working hours were evenings from 6 p.m. until 11 p.m. Knowing I would be learning software programs that could lead to more work after I graduated from college would make all those late hours worth the effort. "I don't have a problem with that," I said. "It sounds fun."

"Good, I'm glad you said that because this job is both easy AND fun," Stan said with a smile. "Say, what kind of music do you listen to?"

"Alternative rock. New Order, The Cure, Depeche Mode, The Smiths, R.E.M., The Replacements, plus Pink Floyd, Rush, that sort of stuff."

"Great, me too. Do you like baseball?"

"Yes, I have been following baseball since the Houston Astros went to the playoffs in 1986." My fondest memories of my first season following baseball were Astros pitcher Mike Scott's no-hitter to clinch the National League West title and the epic playoff battle between the Astros and Mets in the League Championship Series that ended with the Astros losing the series in extra innings in Game 6.

"You've seen *Bull Durham*, right?"

"Yes. Great movie."

"Yeah, well, I'm like Annie in that I worship at the house of baseball. I listen to every Astros game on the radio while I'm working. Are you okay with that?"

"Sounds great."

"Perfect. You start on Wednesday."

My first couple of weeks on the job, Stan taught me how to lay out the paper on the Mac, use the scanner to digitize photographs submitted by the staff photographers, use the waxer and X-acto knife for doing paste-up, and all the other technical minutiae that came with the job. After that, he let me lay out a few papers on my own and I picked it up easily. By the end of the summer, I resigned from the pizza place and said goodbyes to all my coworkers. I was on a new path and there was no turning back.

Bible Study

In the spring of 1994, I wrote my first editorial column for the *Cougar*, a tribute to a comic my friends had derided during my freshman and sophomore years: Travis Baker's *Erin's Closet*. When Travis arrived at the *Cougar* office later that day, he yelled, "I HATE IT!" when he saw me, which was unusual because Travis never spoke to anyone when he was in the office. I would have believed him if it wasn't for the huge grin on his face when he said it. The editor in chief liked my writing enough to keep me on as a regular columnist on top of doing my comic strip and editorial cartoons, which I started doing in the fall of 1993.

Later that same year, I wrote an editorial column about the time Mom left Dad because of his alcoholic ways. I became more relaxed and at ease after writing it. It was like a huge weight had been lifted from my shoulders. Most of the attention from readers was positive, though some criticized me for airing private family matters public.

"Hi, I was looking for Leonard," a tall, muscular guy asked one of the staff after I arrived at the *Cougar* the day the editorial ran. Curious, I walked over to listen to what he had to say.

"I wanted to tell you I was touched by your column that ran today," he began. "I am here to invite you to join in on a Bible study group at 1:15 p.m. tomorrow. Do you think you'll be able to go?"

"Hm…" It sounded like a sincere invitation. Though I wasn't certain Christianity was how I wanted to relate to God, I didn't think it would hurt to stop by and hear what they had to say. "I'll probably be able to make it."

"If you do, I will definitely see you."

"Okay."

The Bible study meeting took place at a University Center meeting room. There were a few dozen students there when I walked into the well-lit room. I took a seat in the back, curious as to what they had to say. Many were there looking to the Bible in a search for meaning in their lives by learning about Jesus Christ and his disciples. A couple of audience members even introduced themselves as agnostic. It was nice to see people present who admitted not knowing. The keynote speaker pulled me aside after he noticed I was there, which caused several attendees to whisper among themselves after they recognized me from the mug shot that ran next to my column in the paper. I guess long-haired Filipinos are rare enough to easily get noticed.

"I searched high and low for a religion," he started. "I chose Christianity, but refused to adhere to a specific denomination because of all the hypocrisy from practicing Baptists and Catholics alike."

It wasn't the first time I had heard about Christianity's hypocrisy. Chris and Jeff, his good friend and verbal sparring partner, used to argue about it all the time when we were hanging out after hours at the pizza place. They didn't like how the church would talk about helping the poor, yet take in millions of dollars from the same poor to build elaborate cathedrals. I didn't like listening to Chris and Jeff fight about the hypocrisy then and didn't like listening to it again in a room full of strangers. Besides, I didn't need conflict in my religious life because I had enough at home. So, I left the room, unconvinced Christianity was for me.

One of the guys from the Christian group tried contacting me a couple of weeks later. I didn't return his inquiries because I was too swamped with my work for the paper on top of the homework I was doing for my classes. He eventually ended his efforts.

Changing Majors

"Leonard, you need to finish school. We are not going to keep paying for you to go to school if you have no plan to graduate," Dad told me one night during the fall semester of 1994. "You can't keep working for little money forever." Mom agreed. With my grades slipping in graphic design class, I was not going to be a candidate for Block in a timely enough fashion to graduate. You needed to complete two years of Block to graduate with a BFA in graphic design at UH and I was nowhere near qualifying after four years of college.

"Why don't you major in English literature?" Dan, a fellow *Cougar* staff member, suggested one day. Dan was a scruffy-looking reporter who wrote for the sports section and was majoring in English and journalism. He had large brown eyes, short brown hair, neatly trimmed facial hair, and liked wearing *Star Wars* T-shirts.

"You have a real knack for writing and analysis and an English lit major would fit you well." I wasn't sure what kind of work I would be able to do with a major in English, so I was skeptical it was a good idea. "Your column writing is your real strength, not cartooning."

Several other friends at the *Cougar* agreed with Dan's assessment and the more I thought about it, the more it made sense. Paper writing in English and art history classes had been my strength during my first two years of college and my column writing for the *Cougar* was an extension of that.

The challenge was convincing my parents this was a good thing for me.

"I thought you were going to do graphics," Dad said when I told him I was changing majors.

"I can do graphics once I graduate, but English is where my strength is. Do you remember what happened when I tried business and engineering?"

"Do you think you can make a living after you graduate?" Dad asked, understandably skeptical.

"I can do all sorts of stuff: I can teach, go to law school, or go into another field with some job training. It'll be good for me," I said, regurgitating the arguments for being an English lit major Dan and other friends had told me. "If all else fails, I can do graphics production just as I do at the newspaper now, or I can become a cartoonist, or a teacher, or, well, anything I want."

"How long will it take you to graduate?"

"A year-and-a-half."

"You'd better be right, boy. You'd better be right," he said in a threatening manner.

When the fall semester came to a close, I went ahead and changed my major. The goal was to graduate by Spring of 1996 and would require I take a full load of English literature and foreign language courses for the rest of my time in college.

In Charge

In February of 1995, Stan quit the *Cougar* after eight years, leaving me in charge of production on top of reading a couple of novels a week, writing papers in all my classes, plus a daily comic strip, editorial cartoons once or twice a week, and a weekly column. The closest I had come to being in charge of anything at a job was when I ran dispatch for a couple of months at the pizza place, which involved me assigning pizza deliveries to each of the drivers. Here, I would be in charge of two production artists.

On my first day in charge, I was cutting up printouts when my X-acto knife hit a rough spot on the cutting board and rode up into my left middle finger.

"OW!"

I looked down to find I had sliced off a sliver of my finger, causing blood to start squirting out. Great. My first day in charge and I almost take off my own finger. Bobby, the assistant editor who looked like a rock and roll version of Santa Claus, rushed over as soon as he heard me scream in pain, his experience as a medic in Vietnam coming in handy at the right moment.

"Did you get any blood on the printouts?" he asked, showing where his priorities were.

"No. Of course not," I said, annoyed he would even think such a thing.

"Good."

He went over and grabbed the first-aid kit, pulled out gauze, and applied pressure. Once the bleeding stopped, I went back to work. I wasn't going to let a little thing like a sliced finger stop me from doing my job.

The Last Summer

Toward the end of the spring of 1996, Cheryl, the newly elected *Cougar* editor in chief, announced the editorships with me as the summer photo editor. She was familiar with my photography from having taken photos around campus with me for fun that semester. I had enjoyed a couple of photography classes when I was a design major and liked to keep my skills up by continuing to take pictures. This position was on top of working night production for the paper, though I had to give up cartooning and column writing to do it. After several years of doing both, the photo editor position would be a welcome change in my routine. With only one class left to earn my degree, this would be an easy summer for me academically.

As the photo editor, I handed out assignments to my small staff of photographers and took on any assignments the staff weren't available for or needed help on. I put a heavy emphasis on getting action and reaction shots while maintaining tight crops and pushing for atypical angles.

During one press conference with a state senator, I decided to shoot the senator from behind his back as he spoke. The assistant editor hated the resulting photo because it didn't show the senator's face, but Cheryl thought it was eye-catching and different. They reached a compromise on running it because I had the presence of mind to take a standard mug shot of the senator, which they ran below the main photo.

Another photo of mine featured Republican presidential candidate Senator Bob Dole. I framed the picture so that a video camera took up two-thirds of the frame, dwarfing Senator Dole. Again, the assistant editor hated the composition because it made Senator Dole look like an afterthought, but Cheryl loved it because it grabbed your attention and directed you right across the frame to Senator Dole.

These two examples were indicative of the subjective arguments the editorial staff had over my work. Cheryl and the assistant editor were such polar opposites in their opinions it was a wonder they compromised on anything I presented them. Yet, they did on much of what I submitted. Working for them proved a valuable lesson on the subjectivity of the decision-making process of editors when weighing the needs of the reader with those of the staff.

The biggest event I covered that ran in the paper was a Democratic presidential candidate fundraiser for Arkansas Governor Bill Clinton at a hotel in the Galleria, the largest and busiest shopping mall in the Houston area. Despite being relegated to the press area in the back of the large conference room and having too short of a telephoto lens, I snapped a shot of Governor Clinton at the end of the fundraiser. He looked like a glowing angel who had descended into a sea of black suits worn by attendees.

When my fun-filled summer of photography came to a close, so did my time at UH. All I had to do now was figure out what to do with the rest of my life.

Duck Tale

First Dance

While I was visiting a friend working in the music department at a local Barnes and Noble bookstore one mid-August day in 1997, a young female customer with her jet-black hair done up like classic pin-up model Bettie Page walked up to the music counter and asked if they had any swing music.

"Do you swing dance?" I asked while my friend who worked behind the counter looked to see what he had in stock.

"I do," she said.

"Where?"

"Club Chicago on the west side. It's not much to look at on the outside, but it's amazingly cool on the inside." She went on to describe spots she frequented around town, including ones with lessons. "Here's my e-mail address. What's yours?"

"L-C-A-C-H-O-L-A@..."

"Hey, wait, I know you!"

"You do?" I didn't recognize her.

"Yeah, you're the one who used to write columns for the *Cougar*! I used to read you all the time!" Ever since I started writing the column for the *Cougar*, I had been having a lot of these happy coincidences at various spots around town. "My name is Tanya. It's nice to meet you in person."

I wondered if she wanted to go out sometime.

"I just graduated with a degree in French and am about to leave for France to teach high school English."

Ah. Oh, well. At least I got an e-mail address out of it. More importantly,

I had the name and address of a local club to go to with Angelique and our friends. Earlier that summer, Angelique had been e-mailing me about the exciting Los Angeles swing dancing scene. She was there teaching creative writing and asked if there were places to go swing dancing in Houston.

Angelique and I had met through an online dating site in the spring of 1993, though we never dated. When we met in person after several days of online chats, she resembled her online handle, Elf. She was a short, attractive long-haired brunette with fair skin and exquisite fashion sense. She was a lot of fun to be around with her outspoken and opinionated personality combined with a sharp wit and keen, observant eye.

Angelique and I cemented our friendship during my last two years at college when we took several English classes together after I changed my major. After Angelique and I graduated, we hung out together Wednesdays at McGonigel's Mucky Duck, a pub with a warm wooden decor and many Irish and Celtic decorations adorning the walls. Wednesday was open mic night, where musicians would go up on stage and practice their various folk instruments.

Another regular event Angelique invited me to join was Movie Night Mondays at Chuck and Ashley's place. Chuck, a tall, lanky bespectacled fellow with a fashionable collection of dress shirts, hats, and vests, would pick double features based on connections he had found on the Internet Movie Database. It wasn't unusual for Chuck to show David Lynch's depiction of a dark suburban underworld in *Blue Velvet* with the science-fiction epic *Dune*, not because they were both David Lynch films, but because they both starred Dean Stockwell, one of Chuck's favorite actors. Ashley was an illustrator with a steady, quiet presence and enviable fashion sense. She wore long, dark flowing dresses that went with her long, dark hair that constantly covered her bespectacled eyes. She and Angelique were the best of friends and inseparable. Finally, there was *X-Files* Night at Tim's. He was another friend of Angelique's who was a big fan of all things science fiction. Tim had short, dark hair, narrow eyes, a round face, average height and build, and liked to wear a long brown coat reminiscent of one worn by Doctor Who, the main character of the British science-fiction television series of the same name about a time-traveling hero who traverses time and space in a phone booth.

After I told Angelique about the local swing dancing scene and Club Chicago, we made plans to go.

Friday, August 22, was one of those typical warm, muggy late summer nights in Houston where you would step outside after a shower and have to come back in for another shower five minutes later. Angelique had invited Chuck and Ashley to come out swing dancing with Angelique's friend Nicole, who was worried about not having a partner. Nicole was a short woman who looked like a cross between Sherlock Holmes and Velma from *Scooby Doo* with her vest, tie, thick glasses, and short, dark hair. "Don't worry, Tanya said you won't need a partner since we'll be switching partners during the lesson," I told Nicole. Ashley winced with worry after hearing that. Angelique comforted her with a hug. Chuck and I just shrugged at each other. Everyone was dressed sharp, but comfortable. Even if the night turned out to be a bust, at least we all looked good.

I knew where the club was since I had scoped out the location earlier that day, so Chuck, Ashley, and Nicole followed me and Angelique. "Keep your speed down, there are people following us," Angelique reminded me as I pulled out of her parents' driveway in my Acura. I had purchased it after my beloved Nissan, which I drove like a hooligan at every opportune moment, was totaled while helping move my old college friend Shannon's family to a rural home near Texas A&M. The biggest problem for me was buying a new car instead of moving out of my parents' place where I was still living. Because the rent my parents were charging me was cheaper than moving into my own place, remaining with them allowed me to put money into savings for first and last month's rent plus three months' living expenses.

Not wanting my heavy right foot ruin the evening by leaving everyone else behind, I went ahead and did as Angelique said. When we arrived at the warehouse marked with a small exterior sign proclaiming itself 'Club Chicago,' Angelique began laughing maniacally. The exterior of the warehouse with its rusted metal paneling, worn wooden planks, and tall weeds looked as if it had been plucked out of some old horror movie. "Geez, I hope this place looks better on the inside than on the outside. I wonder what horrible thoughts are going through Ashley's mind now," she said as Chuck and Ashley pulled up in their Honda.

"I heard it's much cooler on the inside," I told Angelique and the group, putting full faith in Tanya's judgment.

After we each paid our admission, we walked in at 7:45 p.m. I fell in love with the huge parquet floor, the movie-theater style seating at the edges of the floor, the large balconies, and the wall-spanning backdrop featuring a silhouette of the Chicago skyline at night that glowed with city lights. "How popular did Tanya say this place was on Fridays?" Angelique asked. There was only one couple dressed in vintage garb sitting near the edge of the floor in the entire place. After we did our walkaround, we took our seats in the chairs adjacent to the floor while Nicole made a beeline for the bar by the entrance.

When the music started, the couple got up and started doing what looked like the lindy hop, which I recognized from a recent Gap commercial that had been airing on television. It was both fascinating and frightening at the same time. Fascinating because they looked as if they were having fun as they danced in sync to the music, broadly smiling as they did. Frightening because it meant I would have to learn how to lead another human being in a dance I knew little about.

Once the couple began teaching the lesson for the evening, I found I lacked any sense of coordination: I stepped too far back. My hands and arms weren't synced with my body. I couldn't follow directions.

Angelique took note of my nervousness: "Len, stop being so hard on yourself. You're trying to learn something new."

Over the course of our first hour there, the couple, who announced themselves as members of the Houston Swing Dance Society, taught us basic 6-count East Coast swing with a few turns. "That's plenty to have fun with," Angelique reassured us all.

Once the lessons were done, Ashley, despite her initial apprehension about switching partners, was out on the floor more than any of us, having picked up the steps with ease. Angelique and I danced together a couple of times, but I still wasn't getting it.

"I'm going to need more practice if I'm going to get this right," I said at the end of one of our dances.

"We all will," Angelique replied.

"This is fun, but it might be a bit much to do every week."

"I agree," Angelique said. "But we should definitely come back."

"Yes, definitely."

Angelique and I went swing dancing three more times over the next couple of weeks, inviting more of our friends along. I was hoping all those years of tennis would shorten the learning curve, but dancing with a partner added a level of complexity tennis hadn't prepared me for because it required me to be creative when leading a partner through a dance. It's a difficult process if you don't know many moves because you have to vary up moves to keep it interesting. Determined to get better, I started going on my own to the Club Chicago lessons to learn new moves and improve my skills, dancing with whoever was willing to put up with me, which was easy. All I had to do was put forth an effort and ask for a dance.

The Binder

When I arrived at the Mucky Duck the night of October 3, I was carrying around a binder containing a couple hundred pages worth of comic strips I had done for *The Daily Cougar*. Some of the regulars were curious as to what my artwork was like beyond the sketches I drew of the other patrons at the pub while hanging out with Angelique and the gang, so I brought my homemade compilation to show them.

Normally, I would be playing chess and having a Newcastle brown ale with Wynn, a skinny guy with a big laugh whom I had met at Chuck and Ashley's. He had short brown hair, a Romanesque face, expressive eyes, thick eyebrows, and a slight limp in his confident walk. An English lit major with a love of Dr. Seuss, he would flatter me with compliments in an attempt to get me to go bed with him. I would humor him by hanging out with him, but would never oblige his advances. One day, he took it upon himself to teach me how to play chess and we started arriving early at the Duck on open mic Wednesdays before all our friends did so we could get a couple of rounds of chess in.

As I walked into the pub, I took note of an attractive blonde at the bar whose eyes followed me as I made my way across the room. She had her long curly hair tied back in a ponytail and looked out of place in the laid-back atmosphere of the Duck with her gray and black corporate attire.

Several of my friends were having a round of beers and enjoying the musicians taking advantage of the open mic. Eric, an information technologist whom I knew from my English literature classes, was there with Nicole and Tim. I gave the binder over to Diehl, one of the regular musicians who was too young to drink, and he looked through the comics. "Wow, you did all these? These are great!" he said as he flipped through the pages. Once Diehl finished, he passed the binder to the next person. Everyone else was already familiar with my comics from reading the paper at school, so they glanced through the binder. As they did, the blonde at the bar kept leaning forward to get a better view of what was in the binder.

Nicole and Tim shifted their conversation to a script Tim had started to write when Angelique arrived with Chuck, both looking as if they were dressed for a nice night out on the town. Angelique took one look at the table and declared "I want to move over to the penalty box." Angelique and Chuck then made their way over to a booth next to the bookcase on the far wall from the stage. Tim, Nicole, Eric, and I got up and followed her while the blonde at the bar watched us get up and move over.

Who was this beautiful young woman and why did she keep staring at us?

After we seated ourselves, I stood up, looked over at the blonde, and said: "I am going to hate myself if I don't do this, so I might as well summon up the 30 seconds of bravery and do it." Angelique and Nicole both looked at me as if I had lost my mind. I strode over to where the blonde was seated at the bar, our eyes locked on each other.

"You can't be having fun here all by yourself," I said without averting my gaze.

She gave me this broad smile, the first I had seen from her all night, and said: "Sure I am, I'm having lots of fun listening to the music."

"Well, you're more than welcome to join us over at the penalty box."

Her eyes brightened with glee as she got up and followed me over to the box. When I arrived at the box, all my friends looked up at me, confused as to what was going on.

"Everyone, this is…" I turned to the blonde.

"Amy," she said with a smile, her eyes shining in the dim lighting of the Duck.

"… Amy!"

"Hi, Amy!" everyone said in unison.

"Amy, this is everyone."

Angelique and Nicole were giving me a look of 'what the hell is going on?' as we made room for Amy. She sat down and looked over at my binder at the table.

"I need to satisfy my curiosity. What IS this?" she said, pointing at the binder with her delicate fingers.

I took the binder and handed it to her. "Yeah, I noticed you looking at it earlier. Here. It's a book of comic strips I did in college."

"Smooth," a surprised Nicole said to an incredulous-looking Angelique.

"What do you think? Are they any good?" I asked Amy after she read a few pages.

"Yes, they're very funny."

"Thanks."

She was quiet and shy. Much different from Angelique and the rest of our outgoing gang. I noted she didn't have a ring on, though she did have on a pair of large, beautiful earrings that looked as if they were handmade.

"So, Amy, where are you from, and what do you do?" Playing 20

43

questions when first meeting someone isn't the best way to get someone interested in you but is an opportunity to learn their story.

"I'm from Vermont and graduated from school with a degree in accounting. I don't like my job and will be leaving in December."

"Why did you come to Houston?"

"I don't want you to get the wrong impression of me, but I came here because of someone special. We're not together anymore."

"Oh. Sorry to hear that." I decided not to press too much on why she and this special someone weren't together because it sounded like a touchy subject. "What are you going to do after you quit?"

"I don't know, but I would like to have a job outdoors."

"I wouldn't be able to work outdoors, I have bad allergies."

"I do too, but I do like going camping. I camped at the Renaissance Festival every weekend last year."

"Wow, I've never been camping."

"Never? You should go sometime, it's fun!"

Her large, brown eyes brightened as she smiled. She looked pretty in the low light of the Duck.

"Your hair smells wonderful," she said as she leaned in and took a whiff of my long, dark hair that went down to my belt line. With Amy so close, my body tingled with excitement. "What do you put in it?"

"Thanks. Head and Shoulders," I replied. I worried I was being too straightforward with my answer because I didn't come across as playful and charming as I wanted.

"Hey, Len, are you coming out to the Beans show this Saturday?" Angelique asked from across the table.

"Of course." Amy had this look of intense curiosity on her face. "You're invited to come with if you're interested," I added.

"What is it?"

"Beans Barton and the Bi-Peds is this eclectic rock band who dress in crazy costumes when performing. They've been around for years. The coolest part is when Beans does abstract oil paintings on stage. He auctions them off for charity at the end of the show."

"Sounds fun. I would love to go."

"Great. Would you be up for dinner with me beforehand?" I asked.

"Yes, I would like that."

We exchanged numbers before talking more and learned we were both 25 years old. We were the last of our group when Amy decided to leave well past midnight. I let her walk out of the Duck without walking her to her car.

44

I worried I had made a mistake there.

"So, who was that?" Mindy, one of our regular waitresses, asked. Wynn had been trying to get me to ask Mindy out because he enjoyed the stilted way we interacted as if we were stumbling around in the dark in our flirtations with each other. She was a tall woman with blonde hair that came down to her chin, large blue eyes, and a long nose like tennis star Steffi Graf. Every time I saw Mindy, I had a difficult time taking my eyes off her because I found her physically attractive. I never asked her out because she had both a young son and a boyfriend.

"Amy."

"Amy? What kind of a name is Amy?"

"Um..." I almost asked 'What kind of a name is Mindy?' but thought better of it. "I don't know." Wait a minute. Was Mindy jealous? I narrowed my eyes at Mindy, who gave me an intent look. "Ugh, I can't believe you," I said in disgust.

She giggled.

"So, what does she do?" she asked after she stopped giggling.

"She's an accountant, but she wants to be an artist."

"That doesn't make any sense."

Huh? "What do you mean?"

"Artists become accountants, not the other way around. She's no artist." I didn't agree with Mindy on that count, but couldn't vouch for Amy since I had only just met her. "Well, she seems like a nice person. See you next Wednesday."

"Yeah. See you."

Kind of Blue

It took me three days and three phone calls to get in touch with Amy. I left messages the first couple of times, but she didn't return my calls. When I got ahold of her the day we were supposed to go out, we made arrangements for me to pick her up for dinner after I got off work, then head on over to the guitar bar near Amy's apartment.

I worked as a pre-press technician at a family owned printing business. My primary duties included scanning photographs into the computer and outputting film to be used for printing. Working pre-press was valuable experience for someone who was thinking of going into graphic design because you gained an understanding of how to deliver digital files that give the printer few, if any, costly problems. It wasn't creative work like I did at *The Daily Cougar*, but it did pay the bills.

I arrived on time at Amy's and, just as I did, the rain that had been falling in heavy sheets the entire week began to lighten up. It was dark and there wasn't much light for the driveway leading up to the garage above which Amy lived. I tried my best not to step in the mud covering the driveway as I made my way from the street to the wooden steps located left of the garage leading up to the second floor. I proceeded up the steps with caution, then tapped on the door, but the only response was from a mewing cat. I could see through the drawn curtains the lights were on inside and knocked again with more confidence.

I heard footsteps approach and Amy opened the door. "Hi, I just got home," she said as she let me in. She had on a long-sleeved white shirt with black corduroy pants and black shoes. Her hair was tied up in a ponytail like the first night we met.

"So, this is my place," she said as she led me past the small living/bedroom room, dining room, and into the kitchen. There was some jazz music playing in the background.

"I like the music. Who is it?"

"That's Miles Davis' *Kind of Blue*. Do you like jazz?"

"I like this," I said with a nod as she smiled.

A skinny black cat came up and brushed against my leg.

"That's Kitty. He's got a habit of rubbing people's legs because he's shedding." Kitty began rubbing my leg as if on cue. Kitty? Who names their cat Kitty?

"How old is he?"

"Two."

She looked at me and smiled, then said: "I want to clean my face before we go."

"Okay," I replied as she went into the bathroom.

I walked over to her small bookshelf to check out her book and CD collection, which contained albums by Enya, Bob Dylan, Ziggy Marley, Neil Young, Philip Glass, and several others. There were books about Taoism and yoga, plus several self-help and self-healing books. Strewn about the apartment were various herbs, small paintings, plus drawing and watercolor paper. There were two closets full of clothes, while her bed consisted of a mattress on the hardwood floor.

I tried walking over to the kitchen. "Ow! Hey!" Kitty, who had been rubbing me, had bitten me. Not friendly, cat. Taking the hint, I went back to the dining room and waited.

After several minutes of waiting, a happy and calm Amy came out of the bathroom.

"Ready?" I asked.

"Yes, let's go."

She let me out of the apartment, then we both walked down the stairs before heading into the darkness of the driveway. I could barely see with what little ambient light there was and tried my best not to step in any of the mud puddles in the driveway. Amy laughed and confidently walked past me.

"The car is over to the left. It's the black Acura," I said from behind her.

"Oh, I like Acuras. I want to buy one someday. I looked at getting a Jeep the other day, but it was so expensive."

"Yeah, cars are expensive," I said as I unlocked the passenger side door. "I'm in a pizza mood. Does that work for you?" I asked as I let her into my car.

"Yes, that sounds great."

We made our way over to a pizza restaurant whose warmly lit, dark wooden decor reminded me of the Duck. Walking through the narrow passageways was like walking through a labyrinth. We took a seat at a cozy, intimate booth, where the table was lit by candle, then looked over the menus.

"Do you want to split one? These look pretty big," I said, nodding over to the neighboring table.

"I don't eat meat, but we can split one."

"I'm going to get mushroom and pepperoni on my half. How about you?"

"I'll take black olives and tomatoes."

After we placed our order, we continued our conversation.

"Tell me more about Vermont. Do you miss it?"

"Sometimes. I miss the changing of the seasons and all the colors of the leaves there, but I like the temperate climate here."

"Would you ever go back?"

"I don't know. I have more of a future here than I did there, but I would like to eventually live in a log cabin."

She had this longing for a more simple life I found attractive because it

47

would be a nice change of pace to live a relaxed life away from the bustling city.

After we finished our pizza and paid the bill, we went outdoors to find rain pouring down like mad. We waited on the front porch for several minutes until it stopped. After the rain died, we made our way over to the Beans show. After we paid our admission, I showed her a couple of Beans Barton's impromptu oil paintings on the wall that he did on stage. They were bright, warmly colorful abstract pieces that could be anything you imagined them to be.

"These are great," she said as she proceeded to stare at them with the same wonder I had when I first saw them.

I saw Eric seated across the way in T-shirt and jeans. I waved at him and he waved back.

"Hey, Amy. Do you want to take a seat?" Eric asked.

She looked at me, smiled, and nodded. We then went over and sat next to Eric. He then leaned toward me.

"I'm happy to see you two are getting along," he said into my ear.

"Me too."

Chuck and Angelique came by after, looking sharp as usual.

The Beans show was its usual wild mix of performance art and rock show. During Beans' lengthy set piece when he does his painting, Amy got up and joined me on the dance floor. As she did, a sharp, piercing scream cut right through the loud music. I turned my head toward the scream in time to watch a man collapse into convulsions. As I did, Amy pushed past me and began comforting the man, then accompanied him to the back room. Not knowing what else to do, I took a seat with the others while Beans continued with the show.

"Is Amy an EMT?" Angelique asked.

"I don't think so," I said with uncertainty.

"I think she might be an EMT," Eric chimed in.

"I don't know," I replied.

"Either way, she's really cool, Len," Angelique said with a smile.

I had to agree.

A half hour later, the show was over and Amy came out of the back room looking exhausted.

"Could you give me a quick backrub?" she asked me.

She sat down in front of me and I obliged her request, happy to have the opportunity to touch her, even if it wasn't sexual.

"Are you an EMT?" Angelique asked.

"Yeah, what you did was really cool," Eric added.

"I agree. Do you have any training?" Chuck asked.

"No. Nothing," Amy replied, sounding more relaxed than when she came out of the back room. "I did what came naturally," she said with confidence.

Just as she finished, Beans came out for an encore. Amy joined us out on the dance floor, looking rejuvenated and happy to be back in our circle of friends.

After the show finished, we made our way out into the night air.

"Will we see you again, Amy?" Angelique asked.

"Yeah, we would love to have you come out again Wednesday," Chuck added. Eric agreed.

"I don't know yet. We'll see," she said as she smiled at me. I couldn't wait to see what she meant by that.

When we arrived back at her place, it was well past 2 a.m. I parked my car in front and looked over at her. My eyes drifted down to her lips as she returned my gaze with a look of expectancy.

"Do you mind if I walk you up to your apartment?" I asked, not wanting the evening to end.

"Not at all."

We got out of the car, then walked across the driveway and up the stairs to her place. She put her key into the door and jiggled it a few times to get it to open. She gave me a sheepish look while her cheeks turned red with embarrassment.

"Come on in," she whispered.

We sat down on her mattress, which had several throw pillows set up in the shape of a couch, then admired each other in silence. She had a hint of a smile on her face.

"You know, I don't normally ask people out of the blue to join us," I started nervously.

"Thanks for inviting me," she said, her smile growing wider. "Would you like to listen to music?" she said.

"Sure. What do you have?" I asked, grateful for a break in the mood.

We got up and went over to her bookshelf and looked at the CDs.

"How about Miles Davis? He's already in the player," I suggested.

"Okay," she said with a smile. After she hit play, we returned to our spots on her mattress.

"You know, you're very pretty," I said while admiring her slender curves and the way her eyes sparkled in the low light of the room. It wasn't the most poetic phrase, but an honest one. Was it too honest?

"You're pretty, too," she said, her smile growing larger and more beautiful.

I leaned in toward her, hesitated, then she came forth and our lips met. The room then melted away as seconds became minutes, then minutes became hours.

Three days after our first date, I went over to Amy's after I got off work. I brought my old 13-inch Sony color television I used to play video games on so Amy would have a television to watch. When I arrived, I went ahead and put it on her table so she could figure out where to place it later.

She was dressed in a short-sleeved shirt and jeans, her long hair tied back in a ponytail as usual. I took a seat next to her on her bed.

"Your friends are all very happy," Amy started.

"Some of them have been through bad relationships over the past year and like hanging out together because it takes their mind off their troubles."

"I'm glad to see I'm not the only one who has been through a bad relationship," she said with a look of surprise.

"Oh? Is that how you arrived in Houston?" I wanted to know more about her beyond being with her physically.

"I'm not sure I want to talk about that. I don't want to scare you away," she said with a worried look.

"It doesn't matter how you got here, it matters that you're here now," I said as her face softened with a smile.

"I was working as a waitress back home when I met this guy and his group of friends, much like you and your friends. He was visiting from Houston and we had several nice, long conversations before he returned home. We kept talking over the phone but would forget what we were talking about because he was going through cancer treatments. I came down here to be with him because he was lonely and had no friends in Houston. I didn't bother packing anything, I just had to be with him."

"He must have been special," I said, looking her over as I did. Would she do the same for me if I were in the same situation?

"You're special," she said as she leaned over and kissed me.

The next night, I met up with Amy at the Duck, then stayed over at her place to hang out. One night became two, then three, then almost every night over the course of the week.

Sometimes, we would watch films such as Louis Malle's *Au Revoir Les*

Enfants or Krzysztof Kieslowski's *Blue*. Other times, we would chat until we tired ourselves out from a long night of sharing. She talked about ex-boyfriends and family, while I talked about my friends. Once we were done chatting, we then fooled around on her bed until the wee hours of the morning, falling asleep in each other's arms until her alarm went off. She would then leave for work, while I returned to my parents' place. Then, we would start the cycle all over again the next day.

The next weekend, we went to the Renaissance Faire together, holding hands and kissing at every opportunity. Being with her brought a joy to me I had never known. "When I look into your eyes, I can see forever," I said, imagining a happy future with this woman.

A week later, we traveled to Austin to go camping but ended up staying inside my friend Shannon's home because we were ill prepared for a cold front that dropped temperatures to near freezing. Lying there in the dark bedroom, far removed from any city lights, we declared our love for each other. Was it too soon to speak of that four-letter word after only a couple of weeks of being together? It didn't feel like it.

We began talking about moving in together. It was all happening so fast.

The next Saturday, Amy and I went shopping together and went into a nearby adult bookstore. When we returned to her place, we talked about what we had seen there and later that evening fulfilled one of my fantasies.

Then, Amy didn't show up the next week for Chuck's Movie Night, Tim's *X-Files* Night, or Duck Night. She just didn't feel like going.

"Is everything okay between you two?" Angelique asked at Duck Night. "She's starting to miss out on outings with us."

"As far as I know everything is okay." I suspected she was missing on outings because we had been staying up late every night for the past several weeks now. It made me wish our work schedules were better aligned since she worked days while I worked evenings. I figured she was just being sensitive to her own needs. "I don't think it's too much of a problem. She knows how to take care of herself."

"If you say so, Len," Angelique said, unconvinced.

"Do you want to know what true love is?" Mindy said as she came over with our drinks.

"What's that?"

"My man has a tattoo of my name on his leg. THAT'S true love, baby," Mindy said with a proud smile.

I wasn't sure if it was true love, but it did make an impression.

The next night, Amy and I went swing dancing at Club Chicago, but we didn't have any energy, nor were we enjoying each other's company. Was it something I did or said? When we arrived back at her place, we gave each other a massage, but it was as if there were a great weight on our backs keeping us down. Could the six straight weeks of late nights be catching up with us?

While at work the next day, Amy gave me a call.

"I'm going to go out with Beth to a club tonight." Beth was her best friend in Houston whom she spoke positively about, one of the few people she ever mentioned to me. "I'm not sure when I'll be back."

Wait. Does that mean I'm not coming over tonight? But I stay over every night.

"Also, I'm thinking of staying at art school all weekend long to work on a project for class."

Um. Weren't we supposed to spend the weekend together at her place? I didn't vocalize my question because it was all happening so fast.

After work, I went for a drive around town through the various neighborhoods. I didn't have a destination in mind. I just wanted some semblance of control over something. Anything. Was she losing interest in me? If she was, then she wouldn't have called. What would happen if she met someone new at the club? Would she take him home with her and have him sleep over instead of me that night?

I stopped by a nearby grocery store and picked up a newspaper to find the club she was at. I scanned the entertainment listings, found where the club was and made the drive over. When I arrived, I parked at a restaurant across the street and walked up to the door. The bouncer searched me for weapons, then let me in when he didn't find any. I paid my admission and walked into a dimly lighted room filled with young adults wearing baggy pants and heavy makeup. The unfamiliar reggae music filling the room was a far cry from the alternative rock and new wave dance music I was familiar with. I made my way through the smoke-filled club, scanning each face for Amy, but I didn't see her. Maybe she had already left?

I made my way to the back, and out into the cold, night air. There were several small groups including one gathered around a barrel looking as if they were something out of a shantytown. In another, there was a head of long, curly hair that reminded me of Amy's. I walked up to her, not having a plan for what to say, then looked to find it wasn't Amy. I then turned around and found myself staring at the familiar face I had been spending almost every day of the last six weeks with. A strong sense of regret and desire to

52

run for the exit hit me like a wall of bricks. I shouldn't have come, I thought.

I walked over to her as she spoke with a woman who must have been Beth. Amy smiled as she continued chewing her gum.

"How are you doing?" I asked.

"Good. Did you just get off work?" she asked.

"Sorta."

"Hi, I'm Beth," her friend said, she could have been Amy's sister with her blonde hair and similar petite figure.

"Hi. Leonard," I said as we shook hands. "Don't worry, I was just leaving," she said as she made her way back into the club.

Amy didn't take her eyes off me as she kept smiling. "Do you want to come back to my place?"

"Sure." I was relieved she asked because it meant I didn't have to, plus it made being there and wanting to be with her less awkward.

"You don't mind that I showed up, do you?" I asked, curious as to why she hadn't admonished me for wanting to see her.

"No, not at all." That was a relief. "I was looking for an excuse to leave," she said as we walked to her car. After she dropped me off at my car, we drove back to her place, where I gave her a massage.

It wasn't long before we went to bed. Instead of cuddling with each other as we had done previously, Amy just turned her back to me and went to sleep. As she did, I laid there and stared at the ceiling, feeling more alone than if I had been by myself.

Turning Point

I awoke in Amy's apartment to a cold, gray Saturday morning. Inside, it was nice and toasty from the gas heater that kept the winter chill at bay. Amy stirred as if awake, but then went back to sleep.

Was she still planning on spending the weekend at the art school as she had said? Or was she going to spend the weekend with me exploring fantasies of us together as we had planned? If she did, she made no indication of her intention. In fact, she wasn't in much of a hurry to get out of bed at all.

Hours passed as I drifted in and out of sleep while lying there in bed with her, yet she made no move to get up.

When noon rolled around, Amy turned and stared up at the ceiling while I watched her, uncertain of what to do.

"Morning."

"Hi," she said, but without the winning smile she usually greeted me with.

"What's up?"

A long silence followed.

"I've been thinking a lot this week," she finally said.

"About what?"

"How I've been distancing myself from everyone."

"Why?"

"I'm fearful of everyone."

"Does that include me?"

"Yes."

That didn't sound very promising.

"Do you want me to leave?" I asked. It sounded like the logical thing to say, even if it wasn't what I wanted to happen. What I wanted was for us to be together the way it was before. Carefree. Intimate. Fun.

"No. I don't want you to leave."

Nothing but the faint hissing sound of the gas heater running was all I heard for several excruciating minutes.

"When I was a kid, my father used to take me to go play tennis. We did this for years," I said to break the silence.

"That's great."

"Not really. He would explode whenever I made a mistake. Playing with him was like being in a waking nightmare."

Amy sat there in stunned silence with a shocked look on her face for a couple of minutes before speaking. "I used to feel strong and whole, but there was this man whom I spent long hours talking to about my family, but I lost touch with him. When I tried getting back in touch with him, I found out he had a heart attack and died."

I wanted to hold her and tell her everything would be all right.

"His death left me broken and unable to care for myself. I thought I could. I really did, but I can't. I used to be more in tune with my needs, but not anymore."

Was my being there impeding her healing process? Would she have been more down without me there?

"I'm having doubts about you moving in. Just thinking about it makes me feel closed in. Trapped."

"Do you know what I do when I'm feeling down or alone?" I said in an attempt to be helpful while changing the subject.

"What's that?"

"I draw."

"Like the comic strips you showed me?"

"Anything, really. It could be your plants over there across the room," I said with a gesture, "or even the old man on the back of that magazine over there." I grabbed a pencil and a sketchbook she had lying around the apartment, then showed her how to do a blind contour drawing, where you draw a subject without looking down at the page until you are finished. She watched with fascination as I talked myself through the process.

"Oh, I like him. He could be representative of birth, growth, and death," she said, a smile returning to her face. "This is going to be perfect for my art class final." With that, she began sketching the man's face on a drawing pad she had nearby. It was the happiest she had looked in days. It filled my heart with joy to see that I helped get her to that place.

The gray day of Saturday gave way to a sunny Sunday. With the sun shining through the leaves surrounding Amy's apartment, she was fun, flirty, and sexy again. It was as if the conversation of the previous day were a distant memory.

When it came time for me to head off for work, she packed up her laundry basket and followed me to our cars. Mine was parallel parked in front of hers on the street. The air was cool and crisp while the trees overhead covered the street with their thick, dead leaves.

I got into my car, started it up, checked my side-view mirror, and pulled out well ahead of an approaching car several lengths back.

As I reached the stop sign at the end of the street, I looked in my rearview mirror and noticed Amy's car was stopped and blocking the road for some weird reason. I didn't think much of it as I turned onto the next street and made my way to work.

Being the only one in the office was like being in exile from the world. It was just me and 200 photos to be scanned into the computer on the drum scanner. I cursed myself for not coming in to work the day before, but there was no way I was going to abandon Amy.

At six, the phone rang. There was only one person who would be calling at that hour.

"Hi," I said.

"Hi," the familiar voice replied. "Um. I was in an accident."

"What? Where? Are you okay?"

"I'm fine, but the car isn't. It was right on my block. I was watching you when I pulled out. There was an Olds Cutlass coming right up behind me as I did. They tried to swerve to miss me, but they were going too fast and hit me. They knocked off the bumper and crumpled both headlights and the hood."

That explained why her car looked funny when I saw it in my rearview mirror.

"I take it *X-Files* Night is out?"

"Could you come over instead? I want you here with me."

"Okay, I'll head right over after I finish up at work."

When I arrived at Amy's, her car was parked out on the street, its front end looked a complete mess. Fixing it would cost more than the econobox was worth. In the backseat, Amy's laundry had gone untouched. When I walked into her place, the dishes had gone unwashed, and the cat's drinking water needed to be filled. We sat down in front of the TV and watched episodes of *The Simpsons*, *King of the Hill*, and *X-Files* before she started drawing with a peaceful intensity I had never seen of her previously.

"Am I doing this right?" she asked.

"You're doing fine," I said. It was tempting to correct her drawings, but I didn't want to limit her self-expression. She kept drawing while I went on about my fantasies of us together. I couldn't tell if she was listening to me by the intense concentration on her face.

"Any ideas about what you're going to do with the car?" I asked.

"I was thinking of getting another used car," she said. "I would have to get a loan, but I don't have good credit."

I considered co-signing her loan since I had good credit, but I thought that was far more than I needed to do since we weren't married. My parents would have never approved of me helping out a woman I was dating without marrying them first. I went over and laid next to her while she continued drawing for several minutes.

"C'mon, take a break," I said in a flirty voice while I gave her a gentle nudge. She didn't budge at first, but then, in one quick motion, she rolled over and pinned me down with a naughty grin. I guess she was listening to me after all.

Falling

With Amy's car rendered useless, I drove her everywhere she needed to go whenever I came over: to work in the morning, to her art class, out shopping at The Galleria, to a job interview, and any place else she required.

Although she didn't make it to Movie Night, Duck Night, or *X-Files* Night, we did go to a party at a former coworker's place, who related her EMT experience to Amy, who was smiling and having a good time at the party, but her mood changed on the drive home. "I'm jumpier now when you drive," she commented after I made a quick turn on the way over to her place. She would have never said that before the collision.

When we arrived at her place, I put away some art supplies while she curled up on the bed and started crying. I tried comforting her, but nothing I did or said worked. It hurt to see her that way. It hurt even more knowing there was nothing I could do to help.

One minute, she would be happy, as if nothing was wrong and everything was great, then the next minute, she would be quiet and withdrawn, not willing to talk about anything, sometimes on the verge of tears.

"I don't mean to be like this around you because I like you. This is how I am at work, though. My manager likes to learn about our weaknesses, then uses those weaknesses against us. It makes me ill to be around him," she confessed at one point.

"Try sending her flowers, that cheers anyone up," a coworker suggested the next day. It worked as well as I hoped when Amy called me up at work after receiving the flowers the next day. I could hear her smile through the phone, but a voice in the back of my mind thought sending her flowers was a move of desperation and hoped Amy couldn't see that. Later over at her place, she spoke a mile a minute about her day, mostly about her coworkers. It was a relief to hear her open up, but I suspected it wouldn't last.

I spent Thanksgiving with Angelique at her parents' place. Amy and I acted as if there were nothing wrong between us, then went back to her place. She then spoke of her family as she withdrew from my touch. The next morning, she was happy and cheerful with the sun shining through like the first time I was at her place—as if the past three weeks had never happened.

We started looking at lofts and studios the next day. "Our studio," she emphasized. "I want to own my own business and we need a space for that.

I think we should share an apartment with another couple, though." I could see us together in a space for the two of us, she as a masseuse working on clients, while I would be working on my writing and comics.

Just as I would start envisioning a new life together in a new place, she would talk the next day about making space for my computer and home theater equipment in her tiny apartment. Then, just as I would become comforted by the idea of moving in, she would talk about moving to another city, like New York or LA. Anywhere but Houston. Her ideas kept changing so fast, I had a difficult time keeping up. It was all so dizzying.

On December 12, I went over to Amy's and she looked happier than I had seen her in weeks. "I know now what I want to do—what I HAVE to do. I want to go to massage school so I can help people on a level I am comfortable with." I thought about how she comforted the man who had gone into convulsions at the Beans show. It all made sense now.

She then enthused at length about Jamie, an actor attending the High School for Performing and Visual Arts she met.

"We talked about spirituality and emotions as if we had known each other our whole lives," she said with a huge smile. The joyous way she spoke of Jamie made me sad and full of longing for her.

"You're physically sensual and creative and I like that, but it isn't me," she said, then continued talking well into the night about miracles, the power of the mind over the body, and how she lacked the words to express what it all meant.

As she spoke of her growing spirituality, a topic I knew little about and had no interest in, one unspoken thought hammered through my head: "Where does this epiphany of yours put us?"

I didn't have to wait long to find out.

The Mountain

December 14, 1997.
4:45 a.m.
I had to get out of my parents' house. I had only been there a day, but it was long enough for my parents to ask why I was home instead of with

58

Amy. I told them she was sick but didn't tell them I needed space away from her to think more clearly.

I stepped out into the winter chill, my breath visible. It was still dark out, one of those beautiful clear nights where you can see the stars through the bright city lights, even with a full moon. I thought about Amy and how much she would appreciate it.

I got into my car and drove slowly up and down the many streets Amy and I had been shopping for homes two weeks previous, talking of a life together. I thought about heading up to the airport to people watch, but decided against it and went back to my parents' place.

When I arrived home, it was 6:45. I went upstairs, turned on my computer, and proceeded to play *Quake 2*, a first-person shooter you played on the Internet with players from around the world, to get my mind off Amy.

With the afternoon sun happily shining through the windows, I decided to go ahead and give Amy a call.

"Hi."

"Hi."

"What'cha doin'?"

"I'm reading a book on acupuncture. There is a story about a man who went through brain surgery and he was given acupuncture instead of anesthesia and literally walked away from the operation. Can you believe that?"

"Wow, sounds amazing," I replied without feeling.

"I'm strongly against the use of any anesthetic because it does terrible things to the body."

It was obvious she had been thinking about this for a while.

"What have you been up to?"

"I went for a drive. Up to Montrose, through the Village, West U, then back to Montrose and up north."

"That's a long drive. What were you thinking about?"

"Just random stuff."

"No, not just random stuff. What were you thinking? What were you feeling? I want to know these things," she said with urgency in her voice.

I didn't know how to articulate what she was asking of me.

"How's your car?" I said, switching the subject to something I was more comfortable with.

"I found out repairs on my car would cost over $2000 and the junkyard would only give me $200 for it. Jamie took me to see a Volvo yesterday. The owners are going to let me drive it for a week to see if I want it."

"That's great," I said faintly.

"Do you realize we never argue about anything?" she asked with assertiveness.

Why would I want to argue? I got enough of that talking to Dad. At least, that's what I should have said. Instead, what came out of me was a whole lot of nothing.

"I used to argue all the time with my ex. I found out a lot about myself even though it was a violent and frustrating relationship."

I wasn't sure what to say to that, so I switched subjects. "What time should I pick you up for the Christmas party tonight?" We had been planning on going for weeks.

"I don't want to go tonight. My body feels small. It just doesn't feel right."

Small? What's that supposed to mean?

She continued, "How important is this to you? Because all I'm getting from you are sighs and silence. I didn't invite you to my holiday office party because it was superficial and didn't mean anything."

There was a firmness to her voice I had never heard before. I didn't feel strongly enough about the issue to make an argument of it. Was she baiting me into one?

"Look, if we were REALLY compatible, if you REALLY took an interest in me, you would participate in the martial arts with me together whenever I call, but that's not how it works out."

I was unable to respond to her as she grew more and more confident.

"This move into healing people. This is what I REALLY want to do. Going out with you gets in the way of being able to climb a mountain and if I never climb that mountain, then I'm going to be miserable for the rest of my life. And that's why I can't commit myself to a relationship right now."

Did she just say what I think she just said? I laid myself down on the floor in my room and stared up at the ceiling. I thought of the clear night sky I had admired earlier and of a future that would never come to pass.

"What are you doing?" she said after several seconds.

"Staring into blank space."

"What are you thinking about?"

I could have said so many other things at that moment. How what she was doing with her life was fantastic and how I wanted to be there by her side cheering her every step of the way. How beautiful I thought she was, both inside and out. How much I valued our time together and looked forward to a future with her, deep in the woods on a mountaintop, happily raising our 2.5 kids.

Instead, what came out was this:

"I need to come over and get my stuff."

2:55 p.m.

It was one of those clear, bright sunny days in Houston where you could see for miles. The exact opposite of our first date. When I arrived, her mattress was blocking the door.

"This is a problem," I said as I walked in.

Amy was dressed in a T-shirt and jeans. As she moved the mattress away from the door, I gathered my stuff. First, we moved the TV to my car, then I came back and picked up the VCR, my CDs, drawing board, pencils, razor, and toothbrush. Once those were packed up, I looked around to see if I had forgotten anything.

Her cat came over to me. I knelt down, gave it a rub on the head, leaned over, and kissed it.

"Bye."

I looked over at Amy, sitting at her breakfast table, the acupuncture book placed face down. She had a sad smile on her face.

I walked over to the door, took one look at her, the kitchen, the living room, and the bedroom. This was almost my home. Our home. The dream of being together as a couple so close and yet so far.

"So, this is it, huh?" I said.

"What do you need it to be?" she asked.

"I just need time alone," I struggled to say.

"Alone," she repeated sardonically.

I took one more look around the apartment with the sun shining through the west windows, then locked the door and closed it. I walked down the steps and driveway, then over to my car, holding my head high as I did. After I got back into my car, I broke down into a mess of sobs.

On the Move

The following Monday, I was sitting in front of the drum scanner at work in my high chair when the traffic manager dropped off a project for me to do. Staring at the job ticket with its dull, menial task, I could see this job was nothing more than an endless sea of job tickets with only two assignments: scanning images and outputting film. That was it. No drawing. No design. No writing. No cartooning. No collaborating with writers or editors as I had done at the *Cougar*. Not even conversations with other artists. None of that.

I thought of Amy and how she hated her job as an accountant because she thought it de-humanizing and had decided to follow her passion for helping heal people. What was my passion? Was I living the life I wanted? Was I hanging out with friends who had my best interests at heart and could help me get where I wanted to go? Did I even know where I wanted to go? Was this job going to get me anywhere other than a cramped office with no windows and nobody to talk to? I had to get out of there. Not the next day, week, or year, but right then and there.

I got up and walked over to the other side of the building to the owner's spacious office. With its large desk and huge windows behind Bob, dressed in a three-piece suit like usual, his office was a stark contrast to my cramped production area with the uncomfortable high chair and no windows. I rapped lightly on the door frame.

"What's up?" Bob asked, looking the part of the self-made businessman he was. I must have looked a sight standing in his office with my long, dark hair, dress shirt, and jeans.

"This isn't working out," I told him without hesitation.

"What's wrong?"

I thought of Amy's passion for healing. "I don't love what I'm doing."

Bob took a deep sigh and lowered his reading glasses. "I understand where you're coming from. I was hoping you would learn to love printing the longer you stayed, but I can see now that isn't the case."

"You're not angry with me?"

"No. Getting angry will only force you to leave sooner."

Oh. That was good to know.

"Listen," he continued, "I need a month or two to find someone to replace you. In the meantime, please use discretion when talking to anyone else about you leaving the company. In other words, don't tell anyone."

"Okay." Relieved, I went back to my office and continued working, both excited and terrified over what I was going to do with my life. My parents were going to kill me for quitting.

With the end of my relationship with Amy, I decided to spend more time with Angelique and her friends, but without a future with Amy to look forward to my life was on pause. Being with Angelique and her friends was fun with all our various scheduled outings together, but it wasn't getting me anywhere in my career and I didn't have a creative outlet as I had in cartooning and column writing for the *Cougar*.

Hope for a brighter future arrived during the weeklong break between Christmas and New Year's when Angelique encouraged me to show my sketchbook full of drawings of people at the Duck to Ashley, who was in town taking a break from attending animation school in LA. "These are great," Ashley said as she flipped through my sketchbook. She gave me an issue of *Animation Magazine* that included an article on animation schools. I read through it and learned there were people who made a living drawing all day collaborating in a creative work environment, just as I had at *The Daily Cougar*. It sounded like heaven.

"It was brave of you to quit your job," Ashley said. "Be strong. You can do this. I believe in you. You can pursue a career in animation. If you decide to go to animation school, I will vouch for you."

"Yes, you should definitely do it," Angelique said in agreement.

The idea had been planted and it was now a matter of following through with it.

After I sent my application to the animation school in late February, I went with my parents in March to the Philippines to visit my parents' hometowns. I then spent a couple of weeks at home before heading off to Europe for a seven-week trip. I started off in France, then went over to Germany, down to Austria, Italy, up to the Netherlands, down to Spain, and ended my trip in Paris. I used up a total of 35 rolls of film between the two trips, taking pictures of everything from friends and family to architecture and street scenes.

When I returned home in early June, I was surprised to find I hadn't received word from the animation school on the status of my application. When I called several days later, I learned they had never received my application. Bruce, the owner and head of the school, told me to go ahead and send in a new portfolio, but without references this time.

On June 11, I finished up my portfolio and overnighted it to the animation school. I called them up the next day and Bruce asked me a couple questions:

1) How was I going to pay the tuition? and 2) Where did I learn to do my animal, figure, and face drawing? I told him 1) I would be paying for school through work and with help from my parents, and 2) I learned some of my skills in school, but also on my own through books. "There's great potential in your work," he said. "Give me a call when you arrive in LA."

It was 11:15 p.m. on Thursday, June 18, when my parents and I pulled up to a small, light blue one-story house Dad owned in LA. There were no lights on when we arrived. Was anyone home? Were they even expecting us?

After we parked our vehicles in front, Dad walked up to the door and knocked. A middle-aged Filipino man wearing a white T-shirt and shorts answered. He looked like a rounder version of my father. After a brief conversation, the man, whom I later learned was my uncle, nodded and gave orders inside. Minutes later, several dark-haired, brown-skinned male teenagers dressed in polo shirts, jeans, and slippers came out of the house and unpacked our vehicles while Mom and I took a tour of the house. As we did, a couple of teenage females and young boys in their pajamas scrambled to empty out a bedroom for me in the back of the house. Watching them work made it obvious they either didn't know we were coming or hadn't been told. Either way, I was too tired to find out.

I counted eleven people living in the three-bedroom house including two adults and seven kids ranging in age from five to eighteen, plus two significant others. I also counted three roosters in cages on the back patio who wouldn't stop crowing. With all my stuff now occupying one bedroom, my uncle's family were now crammed into the other two bedrooms. In the family room, they placed several blankets in the form of makeshift beds in front of the TV. With so many people in such a cramped space, I regretted taking away a bedroom from the family, but it was hard to complain about a free room.

Though my eyes were bloodshot and body weary from two days traveling cross country, I dug out my pillows and blankets so I could sleep on the couch the family left in my room, excited my life in LA was now beginning.

The next day, we made the drive to a two-story bank building in downtown LA for a 3 p.m. appointment with Bruce. Built at the turn of the century, the huge columns adorning its facade reminded me of those old banks featured in prohibition-era heist films. We parked across the street and entered the bank through the garage. Once inside, we walked into a small room with drawing stations, where there were several students hard at work. We asked them where we could find Bruce. A petite Asian woman dressed in black leather with long, black hair and purple highlights approached us from across the room.

"Hi, I'm Mara," she said with a warm, toothy smile and naturally tanned skin.

"I'm Leonard, and these are my parents," I said as we all shook hands.

"Oh yeah, you're Ashley's friend," she said with a look of revelation.

"Yes, we have an interview with Bruce at 3 p.m."

"Great. I'll take you to him."

Mara then escorted us through the enormous main hall and past the teller stations to Bruce's office, which was next to the main entrance. We entered and found Bruce at his desk on the phone. With his short, black curly hair, thick mustache and beard, he looked friendly and welcoming while coming across as confident and firm. If you looked closely, you could see the twinkle in his eye signaling a visionary with a dream and a will to fulfill it. After my parents and I took seats in front of Bruce, Mara exited the room as Bruce began his pitch.

"I looked at your work and it's pretty impressive. Our program here is a one-year vocational training program for aspiring animators with a heavy emphasis on life drawing geared toward building a portfolio and demo reel to get artists such as yourself into the industry. We want our students to succeed and have placed many artists in animation studios around the city."

"We want 10-12 motivated people and only take the best and most dedicated to animation into the program. This is to be treated like a job. Tardiness, alcohol, and drugs are a no-no. This is a no-nonsense program and a lot of hard work, but fun. What I always find amazing is watching the improvement in portfolios because of the dedication of the students and intensive nature of the program."

I liked it was a program geared toward jobs and career and knew my parents liked that as well. This would be money well spent.

"Hi, Bruce," a female voice said from the entrance behind us. "I heard you were interviewing Leonard so I decided to stop by." I turned around and there was Ashley. It was nice to see a familiar face in a new surrounding.

"Hi, Ashley, could you bring in your portfolio to show to Leonard and his parents?"

"Sure, I'll be right back."

A few moments later, Ashley walked in with her huge, black portfolio, placed it on a table in Bruce's office, and opened it flat so we could all see.

"WOW!" my parents both exclaimed as Ashley flipped through the pages, which were full of life drawings and special-effects work. There was a dedication to the craft in her work that was both intimidating and awe-inspiring. Seeing the results of a year-and-a-half of intense drawing, I wanted to hit the same level of craft Ashley was showing in her work because I wanted to see the same reaction my parents were having looking at Ashley's work. I wanted to be great.

"With all you've seen and heard, Leonard, do you think you can handle it?"

"Yes. Most definitely yes."

The Big C

Neighbor

"I can do it," I said when the topic over whom to hire as the photographer for the upcoming Thailand Film Festival came up at a Festival Graphics company meeting in August of 2004. It was an opportunity my 32-year-old self couldn't pass up. For my bravery, I received quizzical looks from fellow staff members since they had no idea I had any photography experience. "I used to be photo editor for my school paper," I said with confidence to ease their minds. They returned my confidence with a healthy dose of skepticism on their faces.

"We'll talk later, Leonard," Edward said in his distinguished accent. I gave Edward a nod in agreement, then he and the rest of the staff continued with their plans for the upcoming festival.

When I didn't find work as an animator after graduating from animation school in 1999, I landed a job as a production artist for a small advertising agency specializing in the cruise industry. I liked the work I was doing but hated the long hours without overtime pay. After I was let go in December of 2002, I freelanced at various spots around LA for several months until I was hired as a production artist for Festival Graphics in May of 2003 to work for Edward, who also served as art director. The main project we worked on was the Thailand Film Festival program book, which contained articles about the participating filmmakers with synopses and stills for every movie and event in the festival.

Edward wore large, circle-rimmed glasses on his distinguished nose and had a warm smile complementing his deep jowls. He had an average figure for a 60-year-old and walked with a slow, steady gait.

Since he couldn't work a computer himself, Edward would sit behind me for hours while taking great joy in having me digitally flesh out his verbal directions. It was like having a back-seat driver who knows nothing about how to drive giving you precise directions on how to get where you're going, only to have him change those directions on a whim, then telling you to go back where you started because he liked it better there. The reasons I stayed were the ten-minute commute and the opportunity to work in Thailand as a production artist for two weeks out of the year. However, due to budgetary constraints the previous year, I was unable to go to Thailand to work at the festival. When the opening for a photographer at the upcoming festival came up during our staff meeting, I saw it as an opportunity to go.

Upon completion of the meeting, I returned to my desk and pulled up my personal website full of photos from both my European and Philippines trips as well as *The Daily Cougar*. Edward came by as he usually did when he wanted to do design work and caught a glimpse of my photos on the monitor.

"Are these yours?" he asked.

"Yes," I said with a nod.

"Show me more," he said as I clicked through my photos from Europe, offering a brief explanation of each one. I would then wait for Edward to acknowledge when to load the next photo, an intensely focused look on his face I wasn't sure what to make of. When I finished going through the photos, Edward sat back in his chair and took a deep breath.

"You've got a great eye, Leonard. This is exactly what I'm looking for, especially the ones you did for the newspaper. I'll let you know by the end of the day."

Listening to Edward's positive words sent a tingle of excitement down my spine. Had my gamble worked? Since it wasn't our busy time of the year, I had nothing to do but dream of Thailand while watching the clock tick by until quitting time. Once my shift ended, I went straight over to Edward's office to see what his decision was.

"Tell me, Leonard. How long did it take you to do those photos?"

"No time at all. I take pictures as I go."

"Well, congratulations, you're going to Thailand."

I bounded out of the office with glee and went to bed that night and dreamed of the upcoming trip to exotic Thailand as the staff photographer. If the shoot worked out well, I could use my work as a basis for a new career. I went ahead and purchased a digital single lens reflex camera with several lenses I might need, then learned to use the camera by taking pictures around the neighborhood every night after coming home from work.

One bright, mid-October Saturday morning in 2004, I was walking out to my car in the lot behind my apartment building when a disembodied voice interrupted my morning plans.

"Are you the one who plays the guitar?"

Looking around the communal driveway of my apartment building, I couldn't find the source of the sweet-sounding Southern twang calling to me.

"Down here."

I looked beyond the curb to my right at the laundry room of the apartment building next door, located several feet below because of the incline of the hill both buildings resided on. I found myself staring into the large, brown eyes of a young woman dressed in jeans, a pink T-shirt, blue denim jacket, and white platform shoes.

"I hear you play on your doorstep through my window. You play beautifully," she said, her sincerity massaging my ego.

"Thanks," I replied. I had to bite my tongue to avoid revealing I had only been practicing scales and chords I recently learned instead of playing any actual music. Best not to destroy the illusion I was any good.

I had been playing out on my doorstep every day for two months in an attempt to learn a musical instrument that wasn't a recorder or kazoo as I had in elementary and junior high schools. So, meeting someone who enjoyed my playing after such a short amount of practice time was a real surprise. I credit Frank's beautiful-sounding classical guitar more than my actual playing for attracting attention, though. Frank was a finger-style guitarist who resembled a shorter version of actor Peter Sellers. He moved from Massachusetts to LA to be with his wife, Christa, an aspiring storyboard artist whom I was good friends with from animation school.

"Hi, I'm Carrie," she said with a grin as she reached up to shake hands.

"I'm Leonard. What do you do?"

"I'm a porn actress," she said without hesitation. Her frankness over her career choice threw me for a loop. I had been in LA for six years and met several aspiring actresses through the swing dancing scene, but this was the first time I had encountered someone who worked in the adult entertainment industry.

"Right on," I replied with too much enthusiasm over a new experience.

"I'm looking to start my own escort business and need a photographer to help build my website," she continued. Her casual tone made being an escort sound equivalent to any other profession you mentioned in polite conversation, like a doctor, lawyer, or teacher.

"Oh, hey, I'm a photographer." I was thinking my experience of going out and taking pictures of the local nightlife in addition to my upcoming trip to Thailand as the Festival Graphics staff photographer was enough to qualify me as a photographer.

"Do you have a business card and phone number?" she asked, the sincerity in her voice toughening up.

"I do."

Not wanting to turn down an opportunity to earn income, I reached into my wallet and handed my homemade card to her.

"How cute! Did you draw this?" My card featured Otis and Iris from *Innies and Outties,* a webcomic I started as a hobby in 2000 to keep my drawing skills up after graduating from animation school. It was about the adventures of a pair of latchkey kids. One of them, Iris, was chatting away on a phone receiver with a big smile on her face while Otis was holding the disconnected line.

"Yes, you can check it out online if you like," I offered.

"I would if I had a computer," she said.

I hadn't considered she might not have one.

"Oh, I could loan you both of my books. I have two I printed through a self-publishing company on the web." The books were compilations of *Innies and Outties* I sold on *Amazon.com,* through my own website, and comic book conventions such as Comic-Con. With the rise of the Internet in the '90s, self-publishing through the web had become a viable way of getting your work seen by people from all over the world. All you had to do was make a website, post new and original content on a consistent schedule, then promote your work through posting in forums, collaborations with other creators, and distributing via e-mail lists. All you needed to print your own books through start-ups on the web was a few hundred dollars instead of the thousands it cost through traditional methods. With a much lower cost of entry, I was able to sell my own work on a shoestring budget at Comic-Con in San Diego, the largest comic book convention in the country. At Comic-Con, I met comics legends such as Stan Sakai and Scott McCloud in addition to webcomics creators whose work I followed: Shaenon Garrity of *Narbonic,* Dave Simpson of *Ozy and Millie,* and Steve Troop of *Melonpool.* For someone who used to produce and distribute photocopies of their own work on a much smaller scale in school, this was a revelation and dream come true.

"That would be great! I'm always up late and could use some reading between clients."

I had this vision of her reading my work while lying in bed and waiting for her next call, ready to go out at a moment's notice for a fun-filled night on the town with a sharp-dressed man willing to throw money at her.

"You haven't been living in that apartment long. Where are you from?" I asked, switching to standard small talk to dodge a more extensive conversation on the world of porn and escorting.

"Back East. I used to have a beach house on the East Coast until a hurricane came and destroyed it."

"Sorry to hear."

"Yeah, I loved that place," she replied with a twinge of sadness.

"How's your apartment here?" I didn't know much about the apartment building next door other than its apartments were a similar size and shape to the 335 square foot rent-controlled studio I had been living in. The previous tenant was a young woman from Houston whom I knew from the LA swing dancing scene.

"It's a tiny studio like yours, but ours come furnished," she said without coming across as snobby.

"Sounds expensive."

"It's $1,600 a month, but I make more than enough to cover it."

"I bet," I said. Holy cow! That's more than twice what I was paying for the same amount of space.

"Whoa ... I need to get going. I'm late for an appointment," I said, a sudden sense of urgency to finish my morning plans overcoming my desire for conversation.

"That's all right. I should get back to finishing up my laundry. Look, we'll talk later, okay? It was nice meeting you, Leonard," she said with a wink.

"Nice meeting you too, Carrie," I said, blushing from the charming way she carried herself.

Carrie's window had been open every day for two weeks. All she had to do was lean out her window and call my name to get my attention every time I walked down the driveway. The only time we had talked to each other was a brief conversation about what she wanted out of a photo shoot. She needed someone with experience handling models in various states of undress and poses as well as good lighting equipment, of which I had little and none, respectively. I would have jumped at the opportunity to become more involved, but I was skittish over what my friends and family would think about my working with a porn actress, my conservative Filipino upbringing coming to the fore.

Just as I was about to enter my apartment, my cell phone rang. I fumbled around for the phone then answered the call while Carrie leaned out her window to get my attention, her ample breasts nearly bursting out of her tight-fitting shirt and onto the ledge. I told the caller to hang on so I could hear what Carrie had to say. I didn't want to miss the opportunity to get to know her better.

"Hey, babe! I need to go get some wine," she shouted across the driveway.

"You don't mind if I join you, do you?" I said, taking advantage of the opening.

"Yeah, that'd be great. I'll be right over," she replied with enthusiasm.

I went into my apartment, finished my call, and cleaned up the place in case she came in. When she came by, she was dressed in an undersized pink T-shirt showing off her artificially enlarged breasts, skin-tight jeans accentuating her small hips and large rear end, and a pair of low heels. I grabbed my keys and wallet, shut the door, and followed her out the driveway and onto the street. As I walked behind her, a hint of body wash and perfume tickled the air.

We walked the mile to the local Sav-On drugstore, catching up with each other's lives from the past two weeks, our progress slowed by her heels. She had been busy with clients while I had been busy working at my desk job at Festival Graphics.

While at Sav-On, Carrie found some cheap wine; then, we walked back.

When we arrived at her place, her phone rang. She checked the Caller ID, her face turning serious as she did.

"Hang on, babe. I have to take this call."

I took the hint this was a business call and went on an unguided tour of her studio apartment. There was a queen-sized bed in the middle with its headboard against the wall, a four-drawer dresser with photos of a pair of smiling children, a nightstand with a lamp and a couple of books, and a small television stand with a 13-inch TV/DVD/VCR combo next to the window.

"Want some wine, babe?" Carrie asked after hanging up the phone while I took a seat at the foot of her bed.

"Yes," I nodded. She went back to the kitchen and opened the bottle. When she returned, she handed me a glass, took a sip from hers, then sat opposite me on the bed by the headboard.

"Y'know, my skin can get as dark as yours in the summer," she said.

"Really?" Looking at her bronzed skin, I could see she wasn't kidding.

"Yeah, I get it from my dad. He didn't want to have anything to do with my mom since he was already married when they met. Mom was too messed up to take care of me, so my aunt and uncle ended up raising me instead."

"Oh? How'd that go?" I asked.

"I was a real tomboy growing up. I loved karate, but my 'parents' forced me to take up soccer because they wanted me to be more like a girl."

"Wow, you were into karate?"

"Mm-hm, I was mad at my aunt and uncle for not letting me stay with karate, though. They were so strict. I made all A's in high school and graduated a year early so I could get away from them. I was dating the quarterback at the time, but we never had sex because he wasn't Asian, and I only date Asians," she said as our eyes met. I wasn't sure if she was seducing me, but I would be lying if I said I wasn't attracted to the confident way she carried herself.

She continued, "After graduating, I went off to college, got drunk, had sex for the first time, and got pregnant. I then dropped out of school, came home, and got married a few years later. Six months after we married, my husband left me for another woman."

I could hear her disappointment over having to drop out of school, her promising future undone by a single night of bliss. Her story reminded me how fast your life can change, and not always for the better. I looked out her window to see the sky had grown dark. Part of me wanted to retreat to my cocoon of an apartment because of the late hour, but another part of me wanted to know how she ended up working in porn on the other side of the country.

"To support myself, I worked as a stripper. It was an easy way to earn enough money to raise the twins. I went through tens of thousands of dollars trying to retain custody of them, but my husband used my stripping occupation against me in court and I lost custody."

I thought of how expensive it was to rear children under the staggering financial burden of a legal fight and how emotionally wrenching it was for Carrie to have her children taken away from her. I also thought of the irony of having a profession that earned enough to pay hefty legal fees only to have it used against you to take away the very thing you are fighting for.

"A friend of mine in stripping told me the porn industry in LA was easy money, so I moved here to become an actress. I starred in several films before an AIDs scare forced the shut down of production on porn films for several months after a couple of actors contracted HIV. I backed out of my contract and joined an escort agency because I was scared of getting AIDs."

Her idea for reinventing herself may have been unconventional in the eyes of a society that looked down on her chosen industry and profession, but her determination to succeed was a trait to be praised.

"I don't know why I'm telling you all this, but I feel at ease with you."

I responded with a nod, hypnotized by her unflinching gaze and willingness to open up to me. If my listening was helping put her at ease and bring her comfort, then that's what I wanted to do while with her.

"You know, babe, you're not like any guy I have ever met, and I've met quite a few. You're kind and decent. You have this wide-eyed innocence about you that you don't see often in a world-weary 32-year-old. I'm amazed you keep going despite not having any love in your life. Come over here so I can hold you."

I crawled over to her, unsure if getting physically close was such a good idea. At the same time, I wanted to comfort her and tell her how amazing she was to have survived. We embraced each other on her bed for a good long while with nothing keeping us company but the occasional passing car outside, whose sound reminded me of the calm, soothing waves of the ocean.

Feeling tired from the day, she laid herself down on my chest while I held her in my arms as I sat back onto the headboard. Holding her in that quiet room at the end of an evening of intimate conversation, I wanted to protect her from the horrors of her past. After several minutes, we laid down next to each other while looking into each other's eyes and tenderly stroking each other's face until fatigue set in.

Exhausted from the late hour, the unfamiliar bed with the wrong mattress and sheets had me tossing and turning, which kept her awake in turn. "Oh babe, you're so restless," I heard her weakly say before sleep took hold as the sun rose. When I returned to my apartment later that day, all I could think of was Carrie's story and the hard-fought lessons learned from a difficult life.

Over the course of the next several weeks, every time we made contact, either by phone or text, Carrie and I would talk about how much we missed each other like a pair of lovers constantly reminding each other of our existence. Other times, we would exchange a few brief, excited words in the driveway before returning to our respective lives.

Every now and then, I would drive her to the store to pick up any items she needed, like toiletries or pantyhose, since she didn't have a car. And, every now and then, she would come by so I could take pictures of her fully clothed. "You're too good a person to drag into the porn industry," she said. I didn't mind, though. Not having to deal with what other people might think if they found out I was working in porn was a relief.

Constant reminders here and there she was "seeing someone" dashed any hopes I had we would become romantically involved with each other. "Every minute I spend with him is income lost for me," she said in that cold, businesslike manner of hers.

I tried to understand why I was giving her attention since our relationship was a dead-end, but I found her life experience fascinating. Plus, her nonstop chatter whenever we got together helped keep the unsettling quiet of loneliness at bay for a while.

Most of the time, she was either too drunk or high to relieve herself of pain—physical pain from the pins in her back where one wrong touch might send her into paralysis and mental pain from all the trauma she had been through. Since she self-medicated with pot, the best I could do for her pain was listen to her tough it out.

When she talked about her work, she would remind me she was not a call girl or prostitute; she was an escort. "I have never done anything illegal," she said in her defense. I took her at her word. There wasn't any reason for her to lie to me.

"There's no love in what I do, and I have never been in love," she said. "I'm so numb all the time, I wouldn't recognize the feeling if it ever happened."

She could never love me the way I hoped because she only lived for her next call and round of cash to pay her weekly rent. To get more pot. To get more alcohol. To get groceries. To pay her doctor bills. To visit her kids. If it wasn't for her desire to see her kids again, she would have been stuck in an endless loop leading to nowhere.

She would sometimes mention the other guys in her life. The calls she went on. The e-mails she received from placing ads. The agencies for which she worked. I could read how difficult Carrie's life was in her eyes— sometimes it was a tired glance, other times it was a look of sad weariness that lasted for agonizing minutes on end. It was exhausting for me to see her caught in bad habits she didn't want to break out of.

During the weeks after our one night together, Carrie texted me several dozen times a day causing my cell-phone bill to balloon three times the normal amount. When I complained to her about the bill, she quit texting me.

At first, I regretted the drop in contact between us because I enjoyed the attention she was giving me. Carrie may have cared for me, but I wanted more out of the relationship than she was willing and able to give.

Digits

With its infectiously bouncy beat and buoyant singing, Bill Haley and the Comets' "Rock Around the Clock" is silly fun for the lindy hop. As soon as the song came on over the loudspeakers, dancers stepping in time to the beat packed the dark wooden floor of the Masonic temple home to LindyGroove's Thursday-night swing dance.

LindyGroove was the last of the popular LA swing dancing venues to come up during the mid-90s nouveau swing era when The Derby had been ground zero for the scene. Stepping into the classy art deco world of The Derby was like stepping into a world far removed from the quiet suburban community surrounding it. The Derby was distinguished inside by its huge domed ceiling in the main room exposing an intricate wooden lattice high above the bar, small stage, and dance floor with several curtained booths. I went to The Derby on Mondays and Wednesdays to catch live bands and dance, a habit I started after arriving in LA with Angelique, who was teaching creative writing in LA that summer.

The Derby was where I first learned Hollywood style lindy hop in October of that same year through Tip who, with his partner Holly, was one of the top dancers in the region. Christina, one of Tip's other dancing partners, introduced him to me after she found out I was in animation school because Tip used to want to become a background artist for animation. With his stocky build and rugged looks, Tip would have looked more at home in the punk scene than the swing scene if it weren't for his penchant for wearing vintage clothing. Whenever asked how he was doing, he would always respond with "I'm fine, but I'll get over it," followed by a fit of laughter that gave away his jovial nature.

Although my long haired T-shirt and jeans wearing self never got into the vintage clothing many in the scene wore, Tip and his well-dressed circle of friends welcomed me into the swing dancing subculture with its dedication to spreading the gospel of swing everywhere it went. Any time swing music came on over the PA system during late-night excursions to diners and restaurants, we would clear a space on any smooth floor we could find and dance. It amazed me no one ever kicked us out despite the disruption to their normal routine. Both patrons and workers alike would stop whatever they were doing and watch. Some would even join in on the fun.

Through the swing dancing scene, I made friends who shared similar interests and backgrounds. There was Anthony, a comic book artist; Ronny, a pin-up artist who sold posters of her Goth fantasy characters at San Diego Comic-Con; Dale, an aspiring graphic designer and animator; and Heidi, who moved from Detroit to become a fashion designer. Heidi was my first dance partner and we learned how to do smooth style lindy hop together. Over the years, I went out with several women from the scene including Colleen, who worked IT at a local animation studio, Gillian, a political activist with a background in desktop publishing and journalism, and Kendra, a massage therapist with a sensual touch.

Through Tip and company, I was introduced to other venues where the music, including everything from big band and jazz to jump swing and blues, was picked by DJs: Tuesday nights at a dive bar called Paladino's in Reseda, Fridays at the Atomic Ballroom located in a warehouse district in Irvine, and Saturdays at Memories in Anaheim, which took place in an elegant two-story building built in the '30s that served as ground zero for the lively Orange County swing dancing scene. The building's most distinguishing interior feature was its open second floor overlooking the huge dance floor below.

LindyGroove differentiated itself from other swing venues in dress, lax attitude, and integration of jazz and blues style dancing to the lindy form. Many of its attendees could be seen wearing everything from jeans and T-shirts to modern dresses instead of the vintage clothing of the other venues. LindyGroove had a policy of allowing people celebrating their birthdays to bring in 10 friends for free, five of whom had to be first-timers to the club, guaranteeing fresh faces every week.

I circled around the dimly lighted room on the last Thursday before 2005 in search of a woman to dance with me to 'Rock Around the Clock,' but my favorite follows were all taken. I had to find someone fast or run the risk of missing the one time this song I loved would be played for the night. I met eyes from across the room with a long-haired blonde with thick-rimmed glasses and expressive eyes—and made my way over to her. When I reached her seconds later, I hesitated because she was a taller woman than I'm used to dancing with. I asked her to dance anyway, figuring it would be an opportunity to meet someone new.

"I'm sorry. I'm a beginner," she warned.

"Don't worry. It'll be okay," I reassured her as I led her onto the floor, my seven years of dancing experience proving their worth in confidence and bravado.

"Hi, I'm Leonard."

"Becky," she replied as I held her in the closed position.

"Is this your first time?" I asked. Knowing her experience level would help me figure out what dance moves to try on her.

"Yes, but I was here for the lesson," she said as she stepped on my foot.

"Don't worry, I have another one just like it."

She laughed and I found her gentle smile attractive. The first time I spun her I didn't raise my arm high enough because I misjudged how tall she was. "Sorry, low bridge!" She laughed as she ducked. I made a mental note to raise my arm higher the next time I spun her around.

As we danced, she would laugh at her own mistakes, and I made sure to laugh with her to keep her calm. I also tightened my lead up so she could follow my directions better, putting her at ease.

"Are you in school?" I asked. It wasn't unusual for students to come out swing dancing since it was an inexpensive form of entertainment.

"Yes. I'm studying English literature," she said with pride.

"Oh yeah? I studied English lit, too." It was nice to know we had something in common. "I also wrote a column and comic strip for my school paper and self-publish a webcomic."

"I write for my school paper, too! I do science articles for them. What's your webcomic called?" she asked. It was nice to hear her show interest. Most small talk tends to die a quick death when one party stops asking questions.

"Innies and Outties."

"Hm, I think I may have seen it before. What's it about?" Was she serious about seeing my work? There were thousands of webcomics available on the Internet to view and the chances of anyone having seen my little-marketed webcomic were slim to none.

"It's about a couple of kids—a boy who wants to rule the world and the peacenik girl living next door. There's also a mad scientist, an ornery robot dog, and a vegetarian zombie," I said, having refined my sales pitch at comic book conventions.

"Actually, I HAVE seen it before. I remember it being pretty good," she said with a genuine enthusiasm I wasn't expecting. It was nice to know there were people not on my e-mail list or in my circle of friends who had seen my webcomic.

"Oh, cool. Tell me more about these articles of yours."

"Well, I've always been into science, and I want to help people understand and take an interest in science by writing about it," she said.

"That sounds awesome." Anyone who helped explain the mysteries of science to the world was awesome in my book.

"Thanks!" she beamed with pride.

When the song came to its inevitable end, we shook hands.

"It was nice meeting you," she said.

"It was nice meeting you, too. We should dance again later."

"I would like that," she said with a relaxed smile.

"Me, too!" I exclaimed.

I wasn't able to find Becky the rest of the evening in that crowded room, but couldn't stop thinking of her smile and friendly demeanor. When the music and dancing stopped at midnight, I made my rounds and said my goodbyes to all the regulars I knew. I worried Becky might have left without saying goodbye, which wouldn't have been unusual since we only had the one conversation, but would have been disappointing all the same. That's when I caught sight of Becky talking with two guys near the stage at the front of the auditorium. I made my way across the floor toward her, my heart racing faster with each closing step. Would she still be charming and friendly to me after not asking her for another dance? If she was, would she reject me if I asked her out? After she introduced me to her brother and friend, we restarted our conversation.

"You wouldn't mind talking with me while I change out of my dance shoes and into my street shoes, would you?" I asked.

"Yes, definitely!" she exclaimed as she followed me to my chair, talking about her classes at school while I changed my shoes. While I finished tying my shoelaces, I decided to ask for her digits. She was too interesting and interested to pass up. Before I could get the words out of my throat, she blurted out, "Can I give you my number!?!" I did my best to hide my surprise at her enthusiasm while I gave her my business card and phone number. I then put her number in my cell phone. I couldn't wait to talk to her again.

I called Becky up a few days later to schedule a date. Time was running short because I had to leave for Thailand and Becky's busy schedule proved to be a challenge. We were able to negotiate for the following Sunday, days before my flight.

A few hours before we were supposed to go on our first date, Becky called to cancel because she was sick with a cold. I promised to call her when I returned from Thailand to reschedule. If anything, the delay made me want to see her even more.

Discovery

My nose kept dripping like an open faucet the entire 18-hour flight from LA to Thailand. Every time I thought I had blown my nose dry or found the correct head position to maintain an open nasal passage, an onslaught of sneezes would ruin any chance for rest. Allergies, for lack of a better term, suck. At least there were in-flight movies to keep my mind occupied in between sneezing fits.

By the time I arrived in Thailand the morning of January 22nd to shoot pictures at the 2005 Thailand Film Festival, all I wanted to do was get to the hotel, take a shower, and sleep until my first photography assignment of the trip later that evening. It was good to know there was rest built into my schedule and I wouldn't be doing my best zombie imitation while working the first night of an 11-day photo shoot.

When I got up to my room, I dropped my bags, peeled off my clothes, and jumped into the shower. After the warm, powerful streams of water washed away the miserable flight, I went over to the bed, got under the virgin white linens emanating that distinctive hotel-fresh smell, and melted into the soft pillows.

Lying there with my mind wandering around in ecstasy, I reached down and felt something I had never felt before—a tiny hard spot in my right testicle that wasn't supposed to be there. Weird. Where did that come from, and how did it get there? Well, whatever it was, there wasn't anything I could do about it. I went to bed that night and dreamed of being with Becky.

A few days after I returned to LA from the 11-day Thailand Film Festival where I took more than 4,000 photos of celebrities, parties, galas, talks, and events, I drove over to Becky's place to pick her up for our first date. When she opened her door, it wasn't the geeky-looking Becky I had met on the dance floor four weeks earlier. In her place was this stunningly beautiful woman made up like a movie star. She had put in contacts and applied eyeshadow that made her eyes glow in the low light of the entrance. Her lipstick was a bright red that matched her top. We both laughed when I stood on my tippy toes so I could see her eye to eye because she was wearing low black heels that matched her long skirt. I didn't mind, though, I was just happy to see her.

I didn't have much of a plan for us other than going for a walk and finding a spot to eat at an outdoor mall near her place. I thought it would be better if we let the mood decide what kind of food we wanted. We stopped at an Italian bistro where the chairs were so high my feet barely touched the ground.

"So, what are you thinking?" she started while looking over the menu after we asked for a couple of glasses of water. I was glad to see we were both on the same page as far as drinks were concerned.

"That *Empire Strikes Back* is the greatest movie ever," I said with bold conviction, hoping she would respond with similar enthusiasm.

"The food, silly."

"Hm. Chicken Alfredo. You?"

"I'm thinking the same thing."

"The Alfredo?"

"No, that *Empire* is the best *Star Wars* film," she replied with a smile.

Great, a woman after my own heart. This was going to go well.

"What? You don't like the prequels? How can you not like the prequels?" I asked. I wanted to see if she was as unimpressed as I was over George Lucas' stilted attempt to tell the backstory to his own iconic *Star Wars*.

"Ha. Just because I grew up with them, doesn't mean I have to like them. Besides, I love the original trilogy far more, most especially Princess Leia and Han Solo."

"What? How can you not like Jar Jar?"

"How could anyone like Jar Jar?" she said, annoyed at the suggestion.

"Touché. So, I take it you won't be seeing *Revenge of the Sith* then?"

"Well, I do want to see what happens, but I'm not holding out much hope it will be any good."

"I feel the same way. Know what you're getting yet?"

"Spaghetti with meatballs."

After we finished dinner, she reapplied her lipstick, then we got up to leave. I wanted to reach over the table and pull her in for a kiss but decided to hold off until later. Once we left the restaurant, we were walking along the boulevard when a scruffy-looking man approached us. With his eyes fixed on my box of leftovers, he asked, "Do you have any food to spare?" Without a second thought, I gave the entire box to the man, who thanked me and went on his way. I gave a surprised-looking Becky a smile and a shrug to show it wasn't a big deal. She beamed me a smile that made me want to embrace her as she had never been embraced before.

We then walked back to the parking garage with the intention of heading back to her place to put an end to our evening.

"Do you have any pets?" she asked.

"No. Dad never wanted me to have one. Plus, I had pretty bad allergies. How about you?" I asked as we walked up the garage.

"I'm allergic to cats and some dogs, but I had a duck for two years."

"A duck? Huh. What was that like?" I looked around for my car but didn't see it. So we continued walking.

"He was so cute the way he quacked and waddled along. His feathers were soft and oily to the touch."

"Sounds as though you loved it."

"Yeah, I miss that duck."

"And I seem to have missed my car," I said as the concrete ceiling gave way to the night sky. I was pretty sure we were in the correct structure, but we had only gone up the one-way path instead of down. My car must have been on the downhill side. Keeping my cool, I looked up again.

"Oh! We can see all dozen stars tonight!" I said as we walked over to the concrete railing, the bright glow of the city lights obscuring those distant balls of gas.

"Wow. I never thought of it that way," she said with a laugh.

After we enjoyed the glow from the city lights for several minutes, I turned to her and asked, "Do you want to go home, or should we head down to the pier?"

"The pier!" she exclaimed with enthusiasm.

"Okay, let's go."

We walked out of the garage arm-in-arm and made the short walk to the edge of the nearby pier.

"Do you play video games?" she asked after we arrived.

"Just first-person shooters like *Quake III*. I used to play it after hours

85

with my coworkers at my previous job. You?"

"I like playing *Street Fighter*, but I'm a button masher."

"Button masher? What's that?"

"I just keep hitting the buttons frantically until the game is over. My roommate hates it, especially when I win."

"I see. Remind me not to play you at *Street Fighter*."

"Oh, we are definitely playing. You don't have a choice," she said with a playful laugh.

"I see," I said with a smile.

"The waves look really high tonight," I observed. "I wonder what would happen if a huge tsunami came up right now."

"Well, we and everyone else on the beach and pier would die."

"That's a rather morbid thought. Would you be okay if a tsunami hit us right now as in one of those '70s Irwin Allen disaster films?"

"Well, no, but at least the company would be great," she said with a smile.

I reached for her hand, but she was too distracted by the waves to notice. We stood there and watched them roll in until the cold and lateness of the hour prompted us to return to the car.

While waiting to cross an intersection, I sneaked in a kiss on her cheek as we embraced each other to keep warm. She responded by planting her soft lips on my cheek. I was hoping for more, but before we could continue, the light turned green. We crossed the street, holding hands for the first time. I would have flown us to the car if I could have.

We found the car this time, but on the drive down to the exit, I was so nervous I accidentally drove into the curb. Becky grabbed onto the door's armrest while I laughed off my actions, hoping she didn't think less of me after such a stupid, absent-minded move.

The drive over to Becky's was conspicuously silent. Did I ruin the evening when I ran into the curb? Would she say yes to going out again if I asked?

"Do you want to come up?" Becky asked as we closed in on her place.

"Yes, I would like that," I said, surprised by her request.

After we entered, she went to the kitchen to grab us both water while I looked over her DVD collection. There were a couple by animation great Hayao Miyazaki plus several science-fiction and comedy films. I could tell from the DVD collection this woman and her roommates were people I could relate to.

"Do you want to watch something?" she asked as she handed me a cup of water.

"Yes; this," I said as I picked out *Monty Python's Flying Circus* and gave it to her to load into the player. I picked it because I have a soft spot for *Monty Python and the Holy Grail*.

"Good choice," she said.

She took the DVD out of its case and placed it into the player. We then sat ourselves down on the carpet in front of the large TV. While she was fiddling around with the complex remote with its tiny labels and buttons, I leaned in toward her, looked up into those bright eyes of hers, and playfully asked, "What'cha doin'?" She closed her eyes and replied with a soft, sensual kiss that lasted for a good half hour. I was in heaven.

On our second date, I took Becky to Dena's engagement party. Dena, an English lit major from Stanford who worked at an independent film company, was one of the regulars I knew from Game Night with Christa. To start off the evening I gave Becky a rose. "Awww," she said with a warm smile as soon as she saw it. I wanted to give her another so she could keep giving me that warm smile.

We stopped by a Trader Joe's along the way to buy a gift to bring to the party.

"What do you think I should get?" I asked Becky as we stood in the wine section with confused looks on our faces.

"I have no idea. I don't drink alcohol." I was hoping there was a punchline, but she didn't have a clue what to get either.

"Great. Neither do I." While I was happy she didn't drink either, I was dumbfounded as to what I should get. "Great, what should we do?"

"Do you have any friends you could call?"

"Uh… oh, wait. I could call Carlos. I know he drinks."

Carlos was a longtime friend from swing dancing. He was dating Anne, my former dance partner whom I would have competed with at Camp Hollywood the previous summer if she hadn't been late to the competition. Camp Hollywood was an annual four-day swing dancing camp where days are full of lessons and nights are nothing but dancing until you drop. Carlos used to always hang out at the bar when we were at The Derby. After I got ahold of him on my cell phone, he suggested I buy a merlot. I grabbed one and we were on our way to the party. After we got into the car and pulled out of the parking lot, Becky went quiet. I tried not to notice.

"This is just casual, right?" Becky asked with worry and dread.

"Yes," I lied in an attempt to calm her because I didn't want to lose out on the chance to see her again, but couldn't escape the feeling taking her to an engagement party for our second date was a mistake someone with more dating experience wouldn't have made.

When we arrived at the party, I knew all of eight people, including the lucky couple, of the dozens in attendance. It was a good thing too because it gave Becky and me a chance to be in our own conversational world. While we were talking, my friend Andy stumbled into us. Andy was another friend from Game Night. He was an actor from Ohio who looked the part of the so-called Everyman with his average-figured, middle-aged sympathetic look, and soft-spoken voice.

"Hey, Leonard! It's good to see you!" he said as he gave me a light slap on the back.

"Hey, Andy."

"Who's your girlfriend here?"

"This is Becky. Becky, this is Andy."

"Nice meeting you."

"So… when are YOU two getting married?" he asked, looking us both over.

Becky's face went red as she shot me a look that could have killed an elephant.

"Um… " we both said at the same time, unsure of ourselves.

Andy then broke into a laugh. "Just kidding, you two!" he said as he stumbled off.

After several more similarly awkward conversations, Becky and I agreed to head back to my place for quiet time together. There, I shared with her a DVD of Chuck Jones's classic "Duck Dodgers in the 24th and a Half Century," hoping she would like it since it had a duck in it. She had never seen the cartoon before but laughed the whole way through. Like a kid who can't get enough of their favorite movie, I offered to show it again. "Umm, not tonight. We can see it again some other time," she promised. I was bummed she didn't share my enthusiasm for a repeat viewing, but happy she enjoyed it.

Just as I promised at the beginning of the evening, I had her home by midnight. Both of her roommates were up and awake when we arrived. After she introduced me to them, they went into their respective rooms to give us privacy, and we ended the evening with a long makeout session. If this was "just casual," I couldn't wait to see what the next step would be.

For our third date, we went to a formal ballroom dance at a nearby university in a room with a vaulted ceiling, handsome wood interior, and exquisite chandeliers.

"Huh. Not everyone dressed up like they were supposed to," Becky observed of the crowd when we arrived. She looked stunning and elegant in her long black dress, while I was glad I dressed in a suit and tie.

I was expecting Becky and I would spend our evening learning 18th-century social dances together in our own little world, but became anxious when I learned we would be switching partners the entire evening. Despite having to part company, we spent our evening catching each other's eye, both from across the room and in the electrifying moments when we danced together, smiling and laughing the whole time. With her easy-going personality and charming smile, I could see Becky as someone with whom I could have a future.

"I don't know what we're going to do after I graduate," she lamented as a worried expression overcame her face when our fun-filled evening came to a close. Hearing her say that raised my hopes we could turn this into something more long term.

"Don't worry, we'll work things out when the time comes," I promised as we ended the date in another round of kisses.

Carrie was nothing but encouraging of my relationship with Becky, especially when she saw the warm glow on my face after I returned home from each date.

"Feels good, don't it?" Carrie asked with the knowing look of someone who had been in that situation before.

"Yes," I said, unable to contain my giddiness.

My next date with Becky was on Valentine's Day, which proved awkward since we barely knew each other. It was the first time either of us had a date on Valentine's Day. We had considered going out for a night on the town but ended up cuddling in front of her TV and watching Woody Allen's classic ode to New York City *Manhattan*.

For Becky, the movie was a treat because of the Gershwin score. For me, the story's older man, younger woman romance was a mirror of my relationship with Becky, my being 32 and she 21. The relationship in the movie didn't end well, and I worried it was a harbinger of things to come for us. After we finished the film, my worries disappeared with a healthy exchange of playful teasing and kisses before Becky ended the evening so she could work on a French paper.

Upon arriving home, I went to use the restroom, looked down, and discovered my right testicle had swollen to more than 2 1/2 times its normal size. I reached down to feel it, and it was as hard as a rock. That's weird. I had never had that happen before after a date. It couldn't have been a sexually transmitted disease since Becky and I hadn't had sex. Maybe it was a really, really bad case of blue balls? It sure did ache like it, but I had never heard of a testicle acting like that before. Maybe it was something I ate or drank? Whatever was going on, it wasn't normal.

I diagnosed myself online in hopes I might have an infection instead of something serious. I dreaded seeing a doctor because I worried this was something that would cause me to miss work, lose my job, and miss out on being with Becky.

One website said soaking my body in a bathtub full of warm water would relieve the swelling. The next day, I immersed myself in a tub for 20 minutes, hoping my body would return to normal, but all I did was make my skin sting like a bad sunburn. Too stubborn to give up the idea I could cure myself, I went back online to do more research instead of seeking professional help.

Because testicular pain isn't normally associated with a tumor, the dull ache I was experiencing gave me hope it might not be cancer like one site suggested. The rapid growth and hardness of the heavy testicle weighing me down said otherwise. Not knowing what was wrong with my body had me worried I might die of whatever was ailing me. Everything I read, though, said testicular cancer wasn't common among men of Asian descent. Though a favorable gene pool making me invulnerable eased my mind, I couldn't shake this increasingly loud thought it might be cancer.

The Testicular Cancer Resource Center, a website that encouraged those with cancer symptoms to seek professional treatment as soon as possible, contained stories from people who had the disease alongside ones from friends, family, and loved ones. I scoured the site every night after work for hours on end in hopes of finding a story similar to mine to figure out what to do next but was terrified because not all the stories ended well.

One story about a teenager who refused to see a doctor because he was too embarrassed to show himself in front of female medical professionals struck a chord with me. It wasn't so much his embarrassment but the panic and fear he showed when his symptoms moved well past the curable stage. After reading his end days where he prayed to God to make him better, I took to heart the lesson one need not die of embarrassment from this highly treatable form of cancer and summoned the courage to see my general practitioner.

Dr. H had served me well, solving several health issues over the years including allergies, bronchitis, and successful non-surgical treatment of both carpal-tunnel syndrome and tendinitis in my knees. If he could get me through all that, he could get me through this. However, it is one thing to go to your doctor when you have a bad cold; it is quite another to show up, drop your boxers, reveal your newly discovered deformity, and ask, "What's wrong with the family jewels?" I was still hoping this might be an infection instead of 'The Big C' when I saw him on February 23rd at his small one-story clinic, but Dr. H's melancholy eyes and concerned frown said it all when he took a good look at it. Was it as serious as the expression on his face indicated?

"I'm going to prescribe you antibiotics to see if they bring down the swelling. I want to see you again in four days. Contact me immediately if there are any changes," said Dr. H. From the stern expression on his face, I could see this was serious.

As soon as my visit with Dr. H finished, I went straight to the pharmacy, picked up my prescription, popped those pills, and proceeded to check myself every hour to see if the antibiotics were helping. Every time I looked, I kept thinking the magic of modern medicine had brought down the swelling and this nightmare had passed, but nothing had changed.

By the time the four days were done, I checked myself one more time before heading back to Dr. H for my follow-up. I wanted to tell him the antibiotics had done their job and I was cured, but no matter how many different angles I looked at it, no matter how many times I felt it, it was still as large and rock hard as it had been on Valentine's Day. When Dr. H asked if there were any changes, I only said one word while shaking my head: "No."

"I want you to go to the hospital to meet with urologist Dr. K," Dr. H ordered as he handed me a note. Once I got into my car, I placed the note on my passenger seat, closed my eyes, and hoped this was just a bad nightmare I would wake from at any moment. I concentrated as hard as I could, but when I opened my eyes, the note was still there, beckoning me to open it and take in the full impact of its contents. I took a deep breath, then picked up the note with trembling hands. It said, "Swollen testicle. Rock hard." It might as well have said, "Your life, as you know it, is over."

I started the car, pulled out onto the street, and began making the two-mile trek to the hospital. Every car in front of me drove as if they were stuck in tar. I wanted to honk at everyone to get them out of my way. Couldn't they see I had a medical emergency? Every light between the clinic and hospital turned red, stopping me cold for agonizing minutes each time. Were they all doing it on purpose? When I reached the hospital's garage, I circled around. First floor, no open spots. Second floor, no open spots. It was as if the universe was conspiring against me. When I reached the end of the garage, there were a couple of spots open. I thanked the parking gods, then made my way to the walkway connecting the garage to the office building where the doctor's office was located.

The more I walked with that swollen testicle weighing me down, the longer the walkway to the elevator became. When I reached the elevator, there was a small crowd of people waiting. Time stood still as we all waited for the welcoming chime signaling an elevator's arrival. After it rang, the doors to one elevator opened and I made my way in. After the doors closed, I hit the button for the floor I wanted, then the elevator began its ascent. As it did, the walls began collapsing in on me and the other passengers, threatening to crush us like the insignificant beings we were. When the chime indicating my desired floor went off, the walls stopped collapsing, then the door opened and mercifully released me onto my chosen floor.

"I have been expecting you," Dr. K said when I walked into his office, which had a huge window with a stunning mountain view. He was an imposing bespectacled figure of a man with graying hair and balding head. "Go ahead and take off your clothes and put on this gown so I can have a look at what we have here," he ordered after he brought me into an examination room.

After inspecting my testicle to confirm Dr. H's assessment, he put on his doctor's gloves, lubed me up, and checked my prostate. It was far less painful than I was expecting. After giving me an all clear, he sent me to the radiology department in the building next door for an ultrasound. There, I was lubed up again so a plastic wand could glide along my scrotum to see what was going on inside. Compared to the prostate exam, the ultrasound was warm and soothing. I didn't want to leave.

An hour later, I was back in Dr. K's office, taking a seat across from him while he fixed his gaze on me. I wasn't sure what to expect next but suspected the news wasn't good.

"You have a tumor and it's malignant," he said without a trace of emotion.

I wanted to hurl myself through the window behind him so I wouldn't have to hear what was next. I thought of Becky. Would she stay and show support or leave me to deal with this on my own? What were my parents going to think? What about Carrie? And all my friends and coworkers? Would they offer to help me, or would they shun me and leave me to fight this myself? Without anyone to turn to for comfort except the doctor responsible for giving me the worst health diagnosis of my life, I did my best to stay calm by concentrating on my breathing in an attempt to avoid a full-blown panic attack. As long as I kept breathing, I could take comfort I was still alive.

"Without doing a biopsy, I can't be certain what you have is cancerous," he explained. "Depending on the tumor's content, you will have to do either radiation or chemotherapy on top of at least one, if not two, surgeries."

I didn't like the idea of being cut open, but it didn't sound as if I had a choice in the matter.

"First, there will be one outpatient surgery, an inguinal orchiectomy, to remove the affected testicle and do a biopsy to confirm the tumor is cancerous. If it is, then, depending on the type of tumor, it is either straight to radiation or a retroperitoneal lymph node dissection (RPLND) with two or three rounds of chemotherapy," he said. "Unfortunately, I can't do the orchiectomy right away. The earliest I can is two weeks from now," he said.

Two weeks? Considering how fast this tumor had grown since I discovered it, two weeks was like forever and a day. Would my cancer continue spreading during those two weeks? If it did spread, where would it go, and how would my body react? I didn't think I had any option other than wait until the orchiectomy and hope my body didn't spring any other unwanted surprises on me.

Continuing to go out with Becky eased the stress over the impending treatments, but her saying our relationship was "just casual" had me considering breaking it off with her because this might be too much for her to handle. Plus, she had enough to deal with being in her final semester in college. I believed her education was a far more important endeavor than dating and didn't want to be a distraction to her.

"You want to do what?!?" Christa asked after I told her about my cancer and concerns for Becky over the phone.

"I want to end things with her because I don't think she can handle it."

"Look, that girl likes you, and you two should talk things over before you make any decisions you might regret later. Besides, she deserves a chance to prove herself," she said with urgency.

Though I wasn't convinced, I trusted Christa's judgment. She knew me better than anyone from our hanging out and having lengthy discussions on how to live an artist's life after graduating from animation school.

My last date with Becky before the surgery was a birthday party for her roommate at their apartment. It was a fun-filled party where we played board games, ate pizza, and had cake. When her roommates retreated to their rooms and the guests had all left, Becky and I found a quiet moment together on her couch.

"I was wondering if you were free Monday," Becky started. She sounded nervous.

"Maybe." I didn't want to commit myself to anything I might not be able to attend but didn't want to let Becky down either. "Why? What's up?"

"Well, I'm performing in a concert for my vocal performance class, and I want you to be there."

"I would love to," I said. I was honored she had the courage to ask and looked forward to seeing her perform on stage. I found her brave for doing something I would never do.

"Great, I'll see you then!" she said as her face perked up.

"Um ... There's something you should know..." I said. I took a deep breath and summoned every ounce of courage I could muster while she mirrored my worried look with those big, bright eyes of hers. "I'm going into surgery in a couple of days to determine whether I have cancer or not."

She looked me over for an eternity.

"Look, you're not getting rid of me that easily," I told her to relieve the tension in the room.

"Good," she said, putting me at ease with her kisses.

I could have conquered the world after that.

"One thing, though."

"What's that?" I asked, unsure of what to expect from her next.

"I won't be able to make it to the hospital for your surgery since I don't have a car. Plus, I'm knee deep in school work."

"Bummer. It would have been nice to have you there."

"Hm… how about you call me right after your surgery? I'll stay right by the phone," she said with a kiss.

"I would like that. Thanks." I was relieved this relationship was something I wouldn't have to worry about and found her loyalty encouraging. Christa had been right about her after all.

Carrie offered to join me at the hospital and would handle contacting friends and family. She was proving to be the loyal, dedicated, and caring neighbor I didn't know I needed. I couldn't thank her enough. "There is no way I am going to let you go through this alone," she said with determination.

Imelda volunteered to take Carrie and me to the hospital. Imelda was a middle-aged Hispanic woman with a pronounced chin, well-defined cheekbones, and long brown hair. I was thankful Imelda volunteered because it showed me the company was serious about taking care of me in my time of need. My art director Jocelyn, an elegant, older woman with a modern business fashion sense and delightful Dutch accent, volunteered her retired husband Bruce to pick us up after the surgery. He was a soft-spoken man of average height with a round face and sturdy build who, like Carrie, was a cancer survivor.

With transportation and coordination needs taken care of, I needed someone to help me during the recovery at home, which could take several days. Carrie again offered her time, which was ideal since she lived right across from my apartment and worked from home. She cleared out her work schedule so she could watch over me that evening in case I needed any help with food, water, or going to the restroom. I couldn't thank her enough and couldn't imagine what I would have done without her help.

With everything set, it was now a matter of getting through the orchiectomy. I had to keep reminding myself this was minor outpatient surgery and not a big deal. Since I didn't believe in an afterlife, heaven, or hell, the thought of not waking from the cold darkness of drug-induced sleep and leaving this world behind was too much to bear. Would staring up at the doctors be the last thing I ever saw?

March 10, 2005

I was up and alert as soon as the alarm went off at 6 a.m., putting on loose-fitting clothes as requested by the hospital. I then posted my webcomic to the website and mailing list, letting everyone know the gravity of my situation. It was the least I could do to reward my fans for their loyalty through the years. Just as we had planned, I gave Carrie a wake-up call. After her groggy voice answered the phone, I caught a glimpse of her long, dark hair through her window while she stumbled around half-awake looking for all the contact information she needed.

Several minutes later, I heard a knock. When I opened the front door, I found myself staring down at a foot-tall pink teddy bear with "I love you" embroidered across its belly. I gingerly took it, revealing a woman on a mission.

Carrie came over and sat with me on my mattress. We then watched the clock tick well past our appointed pickup time until Imelda showed up at the front door. As we rode to the hospital in silence, the dark of the city passed by us in a blur.

When we arrived at the pre-op room, the nurse took my blood pressure and pulse. While we waited for the anesthesiologist to arrive, I changed out of my civilian clothes and into the vulnerability that comes with wearing a hospital gown.

Sitting at the edge of the bed in that flimsy gown, I tried to fidget away thoughts of descending into forever darkness while at the mercy of Dr. K's scalpel, but it didn't work. I got up and paced back and forth across the room, trying my best not to catch Carrie's eye. I fought the urge to ask her to leave so she wouldn't see me like this.

"Don't you worry, babe. You're going to be all right," she said in her comforting Southern twang that reminded me of home.

I tried relaxing using the idea everything would be okay, but my world was going dark with nothing but the cramped waiting room and its dull lighting as my life's final memory. I longed for a window to view the crisp, blue sky one more time. I focused on my breathing again, but all I could think of was how these breaths could be my last.

Carrie reached out and grabbed my hand, looked me straight in the eyes, and told me, "I want you to concentrate on something positive."

"Like what?" I hadn't grown up with religion and, despite thinking there might be a God, I didn't believe prayer did much of anything other than make you feel good. That's what most people did, right? Pray to God in times of need? There had to be something else I could use as inspiration.

"How about Becky? You could think about Becky," she urged.

I could see Becky's bright eyes and wide smile encouraging me to be strong and brave. All I had to do to be with her again was get through this one outpatient surgery. Just three hours was all that stood between me and bliss with Becky.

The anesthesiologist and several nurses came by the pre-op room around 11 a.m. to administer the IV. A brief burst of pain in my left hand indicated the IV was in. Within minutes, Carrie was treated to a loopy version of me from the combination of sedatives and painkillers.

"Whyyyeee is eeeeverything moooooving arounnnd so much?"

"It's the painkillers, babe," Carrie said with a laugh.

"Stop laaaaaffffing at meeee." I must have had a grin a mile wide.

"I'm sorry, babe. I can't help it. I have never seen you high before. It's cute."

Once the nurse was certain the medication had taken hold, they placed me on the gurney to wheel me away. With escorts clad in green scrubs guiding me, I gleefully floated through the hospital corridors and into the operating room. "Wheeee." Once Dr. K arrived, they put me under. I lasted a whole ten seconds before my world went black.

Nothing but a sea of darkness greeted me when I regained consciousness. I tried lifting the lead weights that were my eyelids but couldn't find the strength. So, I laid there in bed, relaxed, and listened to the soothing sounds of the hospital staff go about their business. It was nice not to worry about deadlines at work, paying the rent, or the latest news headlines for a while. In the darkness, I was relieved by a sense of emptiness from what was once my right testicle. Knowing it was gone gave me the sense everything would be all right.

"Hi, I'm looking for my friend," the distant, familiar voice said with uncertainty. "His name is Leonard."

"I don't know anyone here by that name," the nurse replied in an unsympathetic manner.

Hearing the sound of my name, I wanted to leap from my hospital bed and scream, "I'm over here!" but the darkness was more inviting than the scene playing out across the room.

"I know he's in here because he just had an operation," Carrie said.

"Oh. Do you know his last name?" the nurse said, softening her tone.

"Ah ... umm ... no, I forgot. But he's gotta be around here somewhere. Could you check to be sure?" she pleaded. There was a vulnerability to her voice I had never heard before.

Knowing how forgetful she was, Carrie and I had gone over both mine and my doctor's names so she wouldn't have the problem she was having now. I wanted to curse her for being forgetful, but all that came out my anesthetized body was a faint whisper. Unable to power past the anesthesia, I retreated into the dark recesses of my quiet prison.

Just as I faded into that cold, black comfort, Carrie burst in through the curtains, her tear-filled eyes betraying her thoughts. In one hand was that pink teddy bear with its caring message, while in the other was a bag full of random stuff she picked up while shopping to ease her worry. Judging from her furrowed brow, reddened eyes, and quivering lips, it didn't work. I wanted to cry at the sight of her tears.

Bruce walked in behind her with a concerned look on his face. "How are you doing?" he asked while Carrie gave me a soft, loving embrace, tears flowing down her face. For a moment, Carrie was more than my friend and neighbor, she was the caring mother I needed after I had been drugged, cut open, eviscerated, and given back to reality.

"Your parents said they love you. I'm sorry, babe. You've got cancer," she said, her eyes red from the tears.

Lying there in the hospital bed with Carrie and Bruce by my side, I was glad to be alive and, more importantly, happy that accursed testicle was out and I could move on with my life. Plus, there was Becky to look forward to seeing again, but one thought gave me pause. Would she end our makeout sessions because I had been diagnosed with a major disease? I dismissed the thought because cancer wasn't contagious like the flu.

Dr. K came in and asked for Carrie and Bruce to give us a moment. "It's just as we talked about," Dr. K said as he loomed over me.

I put on my bravest sleepy face and said, "I know." He continued on about waiting for the pathology report, doing a blood test, and getting computed topography (CT) scans of my abdomen and lungs. I made a mental checklist of my next steps in this journey to maintain a sense of much-needed self-control of my emotions about the situation.

"I want to see you again in seven days," he ordered. I wanted to put my right hand up to salute him as he left me with my support group but thought better of it because I didn't think Dr. K would have found it funny. With that, I was discharged and wheeled out to Bruce's car in a wheelchair, painkillers ensuring I didn't feel much of anything other than a strong desire to float away.

Baby steps were all I managed with sharp jabs of pain emanating from the two-inch incision above my right groin. What was a routine four steps to the front door the day before was now a monumental struggle to lift a foot a fraction of an inch. Propping me up with his sturdy frame, Bruce supported my feeble attempts at putting one foot in front of the other as we made our way into my tiny apartment.

After easing me onto the strategically placed pillows on my mattress, Bruce went to check my mail. He handed me a stack of mail on top of which was a *Looney Tunes* Road Runner greeting card. "Good luck and get well soon!" it said in friendly, hand-written cursive. I wanted to throw my arms around Becky and shower her with affection for such a thoughtful gesture, but the closest thing I had to her was that card containing her signature. I started to go blind from the tears welling up in my eyes and tried to wipe them away before Carrie saw them.

"Now you know," Carrie said with reassurance.

I took a deep breath and dialed the familiar number despite the fog in my head.

"Hi," I said, doing my best to put on a brave, confident tone. I didn't want her to think I was weak and unworthy of her affections.

"Hi," she said. She sounded as if she had been crying.

"Well ... the good news is the surgery went well." I tried sounding chipper but didn't succeed. "The bad news is that it's cancer." Listening to her sobs fill the line proved I had failed to ease her mind. I bit down on my lip hard to be strong for both of us.

"Shh ... It's okay," I said in as calm and soothing of a manner as I could muster. "I have a follow-up with the doctor next week, and we'll be able to figure out how best to move forward. Don't worry; everything will be okay."

Tired of bringing us both down with my heavy news, I asked how her day went. She took the cue, and by the end of the conversation, we were talking and laughing as if nothing ever happened. Relieved and comforted by this return to normality with this gift of a woman, a huge crescendo began filling me up like a balloon. I tried to contain it by holding my breath while she continued talking, but it kept growing and growing until a mess of words came bursting out all at once.

"I love you," I declared with drug-induced boldness.

"Aaaaaw," she replied, her voice trailing off before becoming quiet.

Wait. Why wasn't she saying anything? Didn't she love me, too? The only answer I received to my unspoken questions was a long, uncomfortable silence.

"Umm ... I need to get going," I said, trying my best to save face. I wanted out of that conversation before I broke down into a quivering mass of disappointment. I was supposed to be strong, damn it.

"I don't know if I'll be able to come out and see you perform Monday, but I'll do my best," I said as I wavered from the overwhelming desire to end the call.

"I would like that," she said. The uncertainty in her tone struck me cold.

"Me, too," I said, not knowing what else to say.

"Okay ... bye." It sounded like a farewell.

"Bye."

As soon as I hung up, Carrie placed her hand on my shoulder, offering her friendship to fill the un-reciprocated declaration of devotion. I embraced the gesture as if it were my last grasp at sanity. I hoped I had only imagined Becky's silence, but the pain from my incision said otherwise.

"Don't worry, that was the drugs talking. It'll be all right," Carrie said, but I wasn't convinced.

"I don't think she was ready for that," I said. I couldn't believe how stupid I was.

"Quiet, babe, you need rest. Besides, you have more important things to worry about," she said with conviction.

She was right. Where was my head? I had just been diagnosed with a major disease, and I was more worried about romantic problems? What I should have been more worried about was getting rest. It had been a long day and every minute I stayed up meant an even longer night where I would become more and more cranky and unpleasant to be around. The last thing I needed was to drive away the one person who was there to help get me through the night. I then laid down on the bed to get away from the harsh reality of the day while Carrie went back to her apartment.

"I'll keep my window open so I can see you through your screen door. Call if you need anything."

"Thanks for everything, Carrie," I said, disappointment bringing me down.

"You're welcome, babe. Love you!" she said as she closed the door.

Sleep that night kept being interrupted by several attempts by Carrie and me to put everything in its right place. If it wasn't the phones agonizingly out of reach or the constant repositioning of the pillows in a manner yielding the least pain, then it was placing Becky's card where I could see it from where I was lying down without it falling over.

With her card standing there like a makeshift altar, it was as if she was there for me, even if she wasn't ready to declare her love for me yet. Thinking back to the card she sent, I hoped we would see each other again, just as I had done in the minutes before the orchiectomy.

I drifted off for a couple of hours until Carrie came over and roused me from my peaceful slumber, her golden skin glowing in the low light of my apartment.

"Are you an angel?" I asked her with childlike wonder through my drug-blurred eyesight. I found it difficult to fathom anyone who wasn't my parents would ever want to take care of me. Only an angel sent by God could.

"I'm your friend," she replied with assuredness as she handed me a plate of warm green beans and pasta. What had I done to deserve such an exquisite meal? "I want to make sure you eat right. You're gonna need your strength later," she said with the knowing look of a survivor who had beaten cancer herself. I scarfed down the delicious concoction before lying back down.

As the evening wore on, getting to and from the restroom became a more difficult exercise in patience and coordination. Every time I called up Carrie, I had to wait for her groggy self to put down her drink, stumble from her second-floor apartment across the driveway to my first-floor apartment, then use her small frame to support me the agonizing eight feet to the restroom with as little pain as possible.

Carrie's slurred speech and shifty eyes combined with her non-stop chattering made it impossible for me in my weakened state to get a word in edgewise. Whenever pain shot through my entire body like a bolt out of the blue, it would take several excruciating seconds for Carrie to notice. It got to the point where I wasn't sure if she was helping or hurting me whenever she came over. Because she had me drinking water every time, I had to request Carrie come over to help empty myself every hour until sleep mercifully came around 2 a.m.

The next morning, Imelda stopped by, the delicious smell of a bacon, egg, and cheese breakfast burrito filling the room ahead of her.

"Wake up, Leonard! I brought you breakfast!" she said as she pounded on my metal screen door.

"Oh! You shouldn't have!"

I was surprised to see her there. My boss' wife was the last person I expected to see the morning after my surgery.

"Well, I did. This is from everyone at work. We are all pulling for you and miss you," she said in her strong Hispanic accent that hadn't diminished after more than two decades away from her hometown in Mexico.

"You need to get better soon. Edward keeps asking when you'll be back," she said, knowing full well I was enjoying my time away from my boss despite the situation.

My work family may have loved me, but I hated working with Edward because of his lack of understanding of computers. For example, if I were in the middle of implementing one of his designs while he was giving instructions from behind me and a flash of color came up for a split second from the screen that was a result of it updating itself based on my inputs, he would demand that color be used despite the fact I had no way of sampling it for use, then he would throw a tantrum when I couldn't perform. He acted like a child with a short fuse and no patience for pesky facts that got in the way of his creativity.

What frustrated me was I had no independence when working with Edward as I had with Stan and the *Cougar*. Everything I worked on involved Edward sitting behind me overseeing me like Big Brother, giving orders like moving an object a click to the left or right, which was never the case at the *Cougar*. Stan discouraged editors from working the way Edward did because Stan believed we production artists were more than mindless automatons whose sole existence was to be used like puppets on a string. Stan saw us as individuals with pride who did great work with minimal direction. The problem for me was this was Edward's company and he could run it any way he wanted. No matter how much I hated working with Edward, I loved the short two-mile commute because it gave me more time to work on my webcomic in the mornings. It was a luxury in a city famous for the longest commutes in the nation.

Lunches every day at the company were a family affair because we all ate together at the table. It was another reason I stayed with the company. Sometimes, it was only me and my supervisor Danny, a well-built man with a penchant for polo shirts and jeans who also served as the company vice president; other times, it was the full staff. During lunch, we talked about each other's lives, the latest celebrity gossip, the occasional job-related happening, and shared each other's food. It was the closest I had to a family since moving out of my parents' place.

"Don't worry, Leonard. We'll take care of you," Edward and Imelda promised when they found out about my surgery. Their kindness and generosity was a welcome surprise. I couldn't help but think what would happen with my health insurance if I quit Festival Graphics, which I had been considering for some time if just to fantasize about getting out from under Edward's micromanaging ways. Now that I had been diagnosed with cancer, I could no longer entertain that dream. Having health insurance was an essential financial safeguard from going bankrupt over cancer treatments. There was no way I was going to give up insurance no matter how much I disliked working with Edward because I was determined to make sure going broke from cancer was never an option.

After I scarfed down the breakfast Imelda brought, I checked in with my coworkers to thank them for the food. Calling them was like calling home.

"Wow! It's so great to hear your voice!" said our receptionist with a healthy dose of relief and joy.

"Yeah, we weren't expecting to hear from you so quickly," I heard another familiar voice say.

"Get well soon, Lenny!" I heard Edward's daughter say with cheer.

"Is that Leonard? Tell him to get back here quick. This place is falling apart without him!" Edward said with his usual pompousness. I was glad he couldn't hear me rolling my eyes over the phone.

"Did you hear that? Edward wants you back in here ASAP. If I were you, I would stay at home an extra couple of days," Danny joked in that sardonic way of his.

"Don't worry. I'll be back in the office soon enough," I said with confidence. I didn't say I would enjoy it, though.

Happy to be alive and tumor-free, I spent the rest of my day accepting well-wishes and offerings of prayers and support from friends and family from all over the country. A steady barrage of calls on both my landline and cell phone had me managing several conversations at a time. As I handled the calls, visitors streamed into and out of the apartment, bringing me everything from Tootsie Pops to a gift bag of Hershey's chocolate bars. There was so much candy I worried I might die of diabetes before any further cancer treatments started. One major disease per lifetime was plenty enough.

At first, I had no clue how to respond to the prayers because I didn't understand why people were praying for me. After all, it wasn't a prayer that had gotten me through surgery; it was my doctors and a strong desire to see Becky again. After a while, I became heavy and sluggish from all the attention being thrown at me from every direction. I wanted to shut the doors, turn off the phones and computer, get in bed, and hide underneath the covers to get away from it all. Was this experience what celebrities went through on any given day? If so, I didn't want any part of it.

The next morning, I was determined to walk under my own power despite my groin feeling like coarse sandpaper had been used to scrape out my insides. Then again, I should have expected it after having had a huge, rock-hard tumor pulled from my testicle through a two-inch waistline incision. I would have thought going through the scrotum would be the obvious method for removing a testicle, but doing so could have caused cancer to spread through the lymphatic system.

Becky's vocal performance was only two days away, and I wanted to be there to see my inspiration singing up on stage. I wanted her to see I was strong, healthy, and worthy of her love. She may not have been ready to say "I love you," but there was no way I was going to let cancer stop me from enjoying a future with her.

I reached over and grabbed my monopod, which Carrie had placed next to my bed in case I wanted to use it to prop myself up. I then planted its base onto the carpeted floor and eased myself up to a standing position, grinding my teeth to crush the pain away as I did. Using the monopod as a cane, I took a careful step forward, making sure to avoid any sudden, jarring movements, then proceeded around the apartment with great caution.

"Wow, you are STRONG," Carrie remarked with glee when she saw me walking under my own power again.

Being up and active didn't solve everything, though. The simple act of sneezing was a self-inflicted involuntary punch to the gut that knocked the wind out of me and made me want to lie down and curl up into a ball for a few hours. If I could have stopped breathing while remaining alive to avoid those punches, I would have.

Taking care not to push beyond my limits of comfort, I sat down at my computer to answer e-mails before a strong desire to throw up from going dizzy from the painkillers forced me to lay back down. It had been good to have a sense of normality, even if I didn't believe that would ever be possible again.

Concert

"Where is he?" I thought while waiting for Frank to show. I had this mental vision of Becky on stage checking to see if I were there to watch her perform while I wallowed in self-pity at home. Frank was 15 minutes past his pickup time and hadn't called.

I was tempted to make a go at driving my independent-minded self to the concert, but the pain emanating from my groin refused to let me go anywhere. Also, the thought of navigating the large university campus in my handicapped state without help from someone familiar with it, like Frank, was daunting at best.

Carrie suggested I bring a gift for Becky, but I had nothing to offer, having been stranded in my apartment for several days. Carrie handed me the pink teddy bear with its message of love, but I couldn't bring myself to give it to Becky because of its awkward sentiment. The fact it was a pink teddy bear didn't help either.

With time to spare before the concert, Frank pulled his old white Volvo station wagon into my apartment's driveway, parked next to my door, and came in to get me. "Sorry, I'm late," he said.

Rather than admonishing Frank for being late, I focused all that pent-up energy from waiting toward getting into the car as quickly and painlessly as I could.

Traffic was light, and we made it to the university campus in less time than I would have guessed. Frank found parking in a garage a short walk from the theater. When I saw the crowd gathered outside the theater, I relaxed and breathed easy. The show hadn't begun and having Frank drive proved to be the right choice after all.

Limping my way through the sea of unfamiliar faces, I searched for the one I had become attached to these past two months, but Becky was nowhere to be found. Figuring it would be easier to find Becky if I stayed in one place, we took a seat in front of the microphone at stage center. At the very least, I would be able to see her perform.

As we sat down, I caught sight of Becky in a long black dress, walking in with her parents and brother. They looked dressed for a nice night out on the town. Like an over-excited teenage groupie, I waved for her attention. She walked toward me and tenderly grabbed my hand as she passed. Giddy at the sight of Becky and the excitement over her gentle touch, I turned to Frank and said, "That's her!" After seating her family behind us to our left, she patted my head on the way back. I sank into my seat and breathed a sigh of relief. She really did care about me after all.

After she disappeared backstage, the curtains went up and the acts were introduced one by one. My expectations weren't high and the quality of the performances varied from somewhat painful to surprisingly impressive. I had to remind myself these were college students taking a class, even if they did have to try out for it. When Becky took the stage, she started off by seducing the audience with Gershwin's "Somebody Loves Me" one sultry word at a time. Once she had the audience's attention, the drums kicked in and Becky switched to a higher gear with rousing conviction. I found it easy to believe she was singing to me.

Once the show ended, I limped my way outside the theater with Frank trailing. I caught sight of Becky with her family and made my way over to them. I kept my distance since I had only met her brother once and hadn't been introduced to her parents. I thought it rude to intrude on a private family get-together. Growing up, it was common for me and my parents to wait patiently for introductions instead of boldly bounding into a new social situation. Like the disciplined boy I was raised to be, I waited for Becky to acknowledge my presence.

When Becky took notice of me, she paused and gave me a look of uncertainty. Her parents followed her gaze and turned to face me. The pause unnerved me. Did she not want to introduce me to her parents?

"Leonard, this is my dad." He reached out and shook my hand in a friendly manner, which put me at ease.

"And, this is my mom."

I cringed at the wary look her mom was giving me.

"Mom, Dad, this ... is Leonard."

I wanted to slink off into a faraway corner to escape her mom's unflinching gaze of suspicion. Did she not like the way I was dressed in jeans and a T-shirt? My boyish haircut? My dark skin color? The limp I couldn't control? Whatever it was that was bothering her, she didn't say, which made me even more nervous.

Looking at the flowers her parents had given Becky, I thought of Carrie's teddy bear sitting all by its lonesome back at the apartment, waiting for attention it would never receive. As we left the theater, her family forged ahead, leaving us alone, which was a relief because I no longer had to worry about her mother's stare of disapproval.

"Wow! You look great!" she exclaimed, simultaneously giving voice to my thoughts of her while we took refuge under one of the many large trees decorating the campus.

"You were wonderful up there," I said with admiration.

"Thanks! I'm so glad you could make it!" Her enthusiasm over seeing me made my heart skip with joy.

"Me, too," I replied as we descended into caresses and kisses. I had forgotten how convenient it was to date someone who was my height. Since I didn't have to bend down to kiss her, I was saved from killing the mood from doubling over from jabs of pain radiating from the incision point.

"Say, I was wondering ..." I stumbled to find the words.

"Yes?" Becky replied.

"Well ... My parents are coming out to LA this weekend, and I want you to meet them. Would you be interested in joining us for dinner Saturday?"

"Yes. I would like that. I'll be there," she said with a kiss.

I couldn't wait to introduce her to them.

Pathology Report

A week after my surgery, Bruce took me to see Dr. K for my follow-up. My pathology report and pre-surgery blood test results were both ready. I would be lying if I said I wasn't nervous about the report.

"Go ahead and lie down so I can remove those stitches," Dr. K said. I did as he asked.

"Is it going to hurt?" I said after lifting my shirt out of his way.

"They're already out," he replied without hesitation.

I hadn't been lying down for more than a few seconds. How was that possible?

I looked down and, sure enough, the stitches were gone, though the huge scab where he had made the incision was not. It was going to be a nice battle scar to tell stories about later. Dr. K then handed me the pathology report.

"You'll see there was no sign of cancer spreading in the pathology report," Dr. K said. "That doesn't mean cancer hasn't spread. It just means none was detected at the time of the report." I had read about cases where the pathology report had indicated no spread of the disease, but tumors were found later in other parts of the body, requiring immediate treatment. Those cases didn't always end well, especially if the patient ignored the symptoms too long.

I thought of the weeks that had passed after I first noticed that small lump. How much had my cancer spread during that time? I cursed those two extra weeks of waiting for my orchiectomy, and, like a good conspiracy theorist, I couldn't help but think Dr. K waited on purpose. I dismissed the thought as irrational nonsense because there was no basis for thinking that way of him. Besides, I could take heart I was healthy since I had displayed no symptoms other than the enlarged testicle and the dull ache it had been causing.

"The best way to check for more tumors is a CT scan and blood tests," Dr. K said. "Testicular cancer starts in the testicle then moves through the lymph nodes, up to the lungs, then the liver, and beyond. If there are detectable signs of cancer in any of these areas, they will show up on a CT scan."

I didn't like the idea of more CT scans because radiation exposure increases the chances of getting another cancer.

"Based on the type of testicular cancer you have, several rounds of concentrated radiation are no longer on the table as a treatment option," Dr. K said. "You can either have the RPLND performed now or wait and see if your test results continue to show signs of cancer. If they do, then we will have to perform an RPLND in addition to two rounds of chemo. If they don't, then we will continue monitoring you through tests."

Through my research on the RPLND on *TC-cancer.com*, the all-day surgery didn't sound appealing because it required a 10-inch long vertical incision in my abdominal area followed by moving many internal organs to remove the retroperitoneal lymph nodes. The possible complications from bowel obstruction, possible infection from the large incision, possible damage to internal organs, a physical recovery time between two and three months, and collection of lymphatic fluid resulting in bloating didn't sound much better.

Also, one wrong nerve cut while removing the lymph nodes could lead to impotence. I had never wanted to have kids, but the possibility of no longer having the option to choose if I had to do the RPLND spooked me into banking sperm as a precautionary measure. Although Becky and I hadn't talked about having kids, it didn't hurt to plan ahead.

"I know a doctor who can do the RPLND. He's very good," Dr. K said.

I had been warned by websites I was reading my doctor might recommend someone he knew to perform the RPLND and to turn him down. You didn't want to become someone's practice run for a procedure as complex as RPLND.

"How many has he done?"

"Two dozen, I believe."

The two places with the most experience with RPLND in the United States was the University of Indiana, where world-famous cyclist Lance Armstrong was treated during his bout with testicular cancer, and Sloan-Kettering in New York. They had performed the surgery hundreds of times and had far more experience with complications and recovery. From what I had read about the RPLND, I wanted an experienced hand, much more than

108

the one Dr. K was proposing.

"I need to think it over," I said, not wanting to insult him for helping out.

My research said I had a six-week window from the time of my orchiectomy to when I needed to have the RPLND done. After that, the increased chances of cancer spreading beyond my lymph nodes would render the operation moot. At that point, if more tumors were found, my only option would be chemotherapy.

"Do you have time to do a CT scan tomorrow?" Dr. K asked.

"Can I do it today? I would rather do it now since I'm here." Plus, I needed to make sure to give myself time to spend with my parents, who were arriving the next day for a weekend stay.

"Yes, you can do it now. I'll call radiology and let them know you're coming."

"Thanks."

Bruce and I then took the 10-minute walk to the radiology department. They impressed me with their efficiency by having my paperwork ready for me when we arrived. After finishing my paperwork, they handed me a thermos-sized plastic canister and had me sit in the waiting room. "Go ahead and drink half of this now and the other half in 30 minutes."

After Bruce and I took our seats, I looked over the canister. There was a small illustration of a fruit on the label of the barium solution, which would be used to help my abdominal area show up better on the CT scan. That drawing on the label had me wondering, though. How many patients did it take to complain about the taste before someone came up with the brilliant idea of engineering the barium to taste like berries? I lifted the canister and placed the straw between my lips, mentally preparing myself for the worst. I took a deep breath, held it, then sucked the solution through the large straw as fast as I could to taste as little as possible. It went down like cold, liquid candy and tasted like a fruit smoothie mixed with a heavy dose of chalk. Part of me wanted to spit it back out, but I downed it as if it was the most satisfying milkshake I had ever been given. Bleaugh.

An hour and a half later, I was brought through a door with a picture of a cat on it. Upon entering, there was a small office full of computer equipment to my left with a huge window displaying the CT scanner in the room I was heading toward. Inside the bright room was the CT scanner itself, a six-foot-high, freestanding slab with a donut hole in the middle of it. Placed in that hole was a moving platform that slid back and forth.

"Go ahead and lie down. You can prop your feet up with this pillow."

After I laid myself down on the platform, the radiologist stuck the IV needle into my right arm. A steady, sure hand makes it go in easy. Once it is in, it is like having a large foreign invader under your skin you want to claw out with your bare hands.

After inserting the IV, the radiologist left the room, leaving me alone with the machine, the IV, and my thoughts. I wanted to reach over, yank the IV out, and run right out after him. After all, if he didn't want to be exposed to all that radiation, why would I? Knowing this was part of my journey to a cure, I opted to lie there and wait for further instructions.

"Take a deep breath and hold it," a scratchy-sounding recording told me over a loudspeaker attached to the CT scanner. Loud whirring from the machine indicated it was on, and moments later, I was automatically wheeled through the CT scanner. While looking up at the scanner's ceiling, I caught sight of a sign adjacent to the scanner's lenses stating, "Don't look at this light." I found it charming someone thought to include the warning so patients wouldn't go blind during testing. In less than thirty seconds, the scan was over.

"You may breathe."

The radiologist returned and had me raise my arms above my head. With a press of a button, he released iodine into my bloodstream so my blood vessels would show up nice and clear on the scanner. Within seconds, a warm, gushy feeling enveloped my entire body. I had been told it would feel as if I wanted to go pee, but it felt more as if I wanted to go take a dump. I fought that feeling with every fiber of my being. The last thing I needed was to become gossip fodder for the day.

"Take a deep breath and hold it."

Less than thirty seconds later, the scan was complete. I went out and met up with Bruce, who agreed to join me for comfort food at the nearby IHOP.

I was tempted to go ahead and do the RPLND and chemo instead of continuing with all these tests to determine whether or not I still had cancer. Doing so would have made certain I was cured sooner rather than later. If anything, I was glad I had a choice. Not everyone who goes through a major disease like cancer is so fortunate.

Parental Visit

It had been eight days since my surgery, and my parents were arriving in California to see me. They were in the middle of moving from Texas to Hawaii, where Dad was building a house for his retirement. "I'm sorry we can't be there, anak ko," Mom told me after she found out they couldn't make it to my surgery. It was the first time in my seven years of living in California I regretted moving the 1,600 miles. I wanted to chastise them for abandoning me when I needed them most, but throwing a tantrum over the phone would have been a useless exercise.

"It's okay, Mom. Everything will be fine. It's just a little outpatient surgery," I said, unconvinced of the truth I was telling her. Surgery, even a minor one, carries risks.

"Be strong, boy. I love you," Dad said with his usual gruffness.

Asserting my independence by getting behind the wheel of my own car for the first time in days, I approached the airport terminal at LAX. I drove at a snail's pace so I wouldn't miss my parents among the crowd of people milling about. I caught sight of Mom by the curb, wiping tears from her face with a crumpled-up napkin that desperately needed replacing.

Seeing my fair-skinned mother and dark-skinned father curbside with their luggage, they were dwarves among large, fair-skinned giants, serving as a physical reminder they were different. Mom looked pretty standing there with her shoulder-length permed hair dyed black. Dad's expressionless countenance from his youthful-looking face told me he was thankfully sober.

Mom and I exchanged waves as I pulled over to the curb and parked. As soon as I got out, Mom rushed over and embraced me. "I'm so sorry we couldn't make it here sooner, anak. We should have been here," she said as she lost her composure. With her arms wrapped lovingly around me while her tears fell, I was an eight-year-old child again, smothered by her motherly attention.

"Honey, we need to go," Dad urged after airport police told us to clear the white zone.

We loaded their bags into my car and headed over to Festival Graphics; it was Friday, and I still had work to do pushing pixels for Edward.

Upon our arrival at Festival Graphics, my coworkers were all smiles and greetings when my parents arrived with me.

"Thank you all so much for taking care of him," Mom said with a warm smile.

"You're welcome. He's very important to us here," my supervisor Danny said, hinting at Edward's need to have me around. I wanted to roll my eyes at Danny but thought better of it. I didn't need to make a scene with my parents there.

For lunch, my parents and I, plus several of my coworkers, went over to the restaurant next door. I frequented the restaurant with its black ceiling, black walls, black curtains, black tables, and black chairs because their burgers reminded me of Dad's wonderful cooking after tennis tournaments, but with a side of greens instead of fries.

"Leonard, how are you doing?" Imelda started.

"So far, so good. Just waiting for the test results from yesterday's CT scan."

"I'm so glad you went to see the doctor, Leonard. It sounds like you caught it early. Did your parents teach you to go to the doctors?"

"I don't know where he learned that," Dad said of my seeing the doctors on my own. "It definitely wasn't from me." Mom just smiled.

We briefly went over my treatment options, but Dad noticed the waitress, a young, attractive white Latina wearing a white dress shirt and black slacks, her hair tied back.

"Hey, you're very pretty. Are you single?"

I shrunk into my chair as she laughed. "No, I have a boyfriend."

Thank goodness.

"That's too bad," Dad said. "My boy here, he's single."

"Leonard is already seeing someone, aren't you?" Imelda said as she turned to me.

"Yes, her name is Becky and she's meeting us for dinner tomorrow," I said to my parents.

"Oh, that's great," Mom said, looking hopeful.

After we finished lunch, I drove my parents back to my apartment, then returned to work.

Just before leaving work, I made a follow-up phone call to Dr. K for the results of my CT scan. With my phone in hand, I froze. What if it were bad news? Then what? I took several deep breaths, pictured a beautiful sunny day with a gentle breeze, and called.

"You're all clear," Dr. K said after I got him on the line.

With a sigh of relief, I went downstairs to my car. As soon as I took a seat inside, I thought of my mother crying the whole flight from Houston to LA. Long-repressed memories of her sobbing after fights with my inebriated dad in a language I never learned came spilling forth like a cascading waterfall, choking the life out of me as they did.

I tried to find a comforting memory in my childhood to clear my watery eyes and loosen my throat's stranglehold, but I saw nothing but misery in my father's temper tantrums and Kevin's death. I thought of how much I disliked Edward's over-inflated ego over his graphic design skills, especially his preference for putting bright colors like cyan and magenta side by side in his work. Everyone in the office but him winced with revulsion at the sight of them together.

I thought of my carefree dates with Becky, but her silent reply to my emotional declaration came echoing back, overwhelming the joy I had those precious few times we had spent together.

Then it hit me. All those worries about the past could be left behind for a better future where I would be working at a great job, coming home to a loving family, and being free of cancer. Once my eyes dried after several minutes, I took a few deep breaths, started the car, and made my way home.

When I arrived home, Dad was drunk with two double shots of gin while at lunch and who knows how much vodka since. My tiny apartment, with my bookshelves, drawing table, computer, broken futon, and home entertainment system coupled with a lack of seating options, looked packed with both my parents, Dad's sister Auntie A, and her husband there. Auntie A was a small sturdy woman with short, dark hair who treated me to leftover Filipino food whenever I visited her and my uncle. From the expectant looks on their faces and their nice shoes that matched their business casual clothes, I could see they were ready for a night on the town together.

"Hey, boy! Come here! Have a drink!"

"Umm ... no thanks, Dad."

Having never been much of a drinker, contracting a major disease like cancer wasn't enough to get me started. Plus, the last thing I wanted was to be a surly, angry mess like Dad.

"You should come with us, Leonard. It'll just be a couple of hours. It'll be fun," my uncle said in a casual tone.

"Actually, I just want to go to sleep," I said as I eased myself onto the mattress. I didn't want any part of their evening plans because I resented them for encouraging Dad's drinking. Staying in was my way of getting back at them.

Mom took care of me by preparing dinner, much as she had always done for me. I was glad she took the time and made the effort.

The next morning, the plan was to go shopping with my parents then meet Becky for dinner followed by swing dancing at Pasadena Ballroom Dance Association. It probably wasn't the best idea to go dancing so soon after my surgery, but I thought I was well enough to give it a shot despite Mom's fear I might split open the incision and spill my guts out. I promised to limit myself to a couple of dances, hopefully with Becky. It would be the first time we went swing dancing since we met on the dance floor. Seeing her again would make this whole experience worth it.

As we went from store to store, I kept checking my cell phone every few minutes, hoping for a phone call from Becky.

When we arrived back home, there was a knock on my door. For a moment, I thought it might be Becky, but when I opened the door, it was Carrie, dressed in a striped tank top and jeans. If it wasn't for the platform shoes with their transparent plastic straps, she could have passed off for a normal person.

"Hey, babe. I saw you come home so I decided to come over and meet your parents," she said with a big smile on her face. She must have been waiting all day to meet them.

"Mom, Dad, this is Carrie. She was the one who's been taking care of me. Carrie, these are my parents."

"Thank you so much for watching over our Leonard. He's our only one," Mom said, full of grace and polite as ever.

"Aww, shucks, it was nothing. He's great. I'm very proud of him. He's so strong."

I couldn't help but smile at Carrie at that moment. She could be so humble and caring at times. A real catch.

"Leonard says you work from home," Mom said.

"Yes, I am self-employed and work in the entertainment industry," she said with great pride. She didn't mention it was the adult part of the industry, and I was glad my parents didn't press with more questions. The last thing I wanted was a scene between them. "Fortunately, I get to work from home, which made it easy to take care of him."

"We can't thank you enough."

"Your thanks are plenty enough," Carrie said with confidence.

Listening to Carrie's exchange with my parents reminded me how much

I missed good old Southern hospitality.

As the minutes ticked down toward dinner, there was still no phone call from Becky. I tried calling again, but it went straight to voice-mail. Taking one more look at the clock, I took a deep breath and left that dream behind.

Since I had no idea what type of food I wanted, I hadn't bothered with reservations anywhere near PBDA. When we arrived in Pasadena, a hearty, Italian family-style dinner at a popular restaurant in the area sounded appetizing. Upon entering, we were greeted by the delicious smell of freshly cooked Italian food and a two-hour wait. I could tell by the angry growl from my empty stomach, there was no way I was going to last the two hours to get in.

As Mom and I turned to leave, she looked around the sea of people, confused.

"Where's your dad?"

I looked to my left, right, and out the door, but there was no sign of him. Where could he have gone? We had only been there a few minutes, and I could have sworn he was right behind me.

Mom turned to the hostess.

"Do you have a ba ...?"

Before she finished her question, I was carving my way through the crowded restaurant with ease. When I reached the bar, Dad was standing there, wallet in hand, a wide grin spread across his face, and an empty margarita glass in front of him. I wanted to hit him.

"C'mon, Dad, let's go. The wait's too long here and we need to find somewhere to eat."

We ended up stopping at another Italian restaurant down the street. It had a much darker ambiance and the hosts were better dressed. Inexperience with restaurants colored Dad's voice while he took a peek inside. "Are you sure you want to eat here? I don't think we're dressed for this."

Dad was right. We weren't dressed for dinner at a nice restaurant. As a family, we rarely went out to dinner and only dressed up for special occasions, but I was too hungry to care how we were dressed, whether or not Dad was drunk, or that Becky hadn't bothered calling me back. I just wanted food.

"We'll be fine," I told him with assurance. We got in. No questions asked.

After dinner, I took my parents to PBDA's Saturday-night dance. I no longer cared about Mom's concern I might aggravate the incision point, I just wanted to cut loose and dance. Getting back into the familiarity of the swing dancing world would help me get away from thinking about cancer for an hour or two, do something fun with my parents, and get over the fact Becky, the woman whom I had used as my inspiration to conquer my first battle with The Big C, had stood me up.

The room where the dance was held was both gym and auditorium, where a live band played on the small stage. My first dance was with a friend whom I had known for years. I chose her because our dance styles meshed well, and more importantly, she would do her best not to hurt me if I asked. It was good to be back out on the floor, dancing those familiar steps in time to the music I had grown to love in the years since I started, even if it was only for a few minutes.

"Oh! We thought you were Becky," my parents said when I introduced my friend to them. I corrected them with a small voice, trying my best to hide my disappointment it wasn't Becky. She should have been there.

"Wow! You two dance well with each other. Did Leonard tell you we dance, too?" My parents had picked up ballroom dancing after I moved out. Mom and I had danced together on previous visits, but I found it difficult because of her death grip on my hands. Crushed knuckles made doing a simple turn more of an adventure than it needed to be.

Dancing was one of the many positive things they had done together since they became empty nesters. It was fun watching them on the dance floor during one long break between dances. They looked more in love than in all the time I had spent with them growing up. I couldn't have been more proud or happier for them. Fighting the soreness from my incision, I danced with a couple friends I trusted who didn't push me too hard. It was great not to worry about anything other than the dancing. I called it a night after an hour because I was winded from having been out shopping all day with my parents coupled with the effort it took not to split my wound open and bleed to death.

The next day I took Dad digital camera shopping at his request so he could take pictures of his new life as a retiree in Hawaii. In search of a camera that was "powerful and easy to use," we stopped by a huge electronics store in Burbank considered a mecca for tech-savvy people. With childlike curiosity, Dad eyed the *Invaders from Mars*-themed set pieces decorating the store, something I had done my first trip there many years before.

We went straight to the camera section in the back of the store, where the alarm system was overwhelming the store with its presence for some unknown reason. After listening to our needs, the sales rep brought out an open-box Canon digital point-and-shoot. It was a nicer camera than I would have bought, and I worried Dad might balk at the high price tag.

I took note this particular camera had only a couple of controls on it and was designed for ease-of-use. "We'll take it. C'mon, let's go," he said to me. Dad never did have the patience for shopping. His attitude had always been to find what you need and get out as soon as possible. Was he always anxious to get back to his drinking when he did that?

We arrived back at my place to find Mom had packed their belongings. I winced in pain at the sight because it meant their three-day stay was finished. She had to return to Hawaii to interview for a registered nurse position, and Dad had to work with contractors to finish their house. Watching them pack was a sad reminder I didn't visit them often enough.

I took my time getting to the airport so I could enjoy having them around longer, but we arrived early despite my dawdling. I didn't want them to go knowing how much happier they were now, but I couldn't have them stay either. I would have lost my mind with all three of us in my 335-square-foot studio apartment for anything longer than a couple of days. I popped open my car's hatchback then unloaded the luggage at the curbside drop-off. After the luggage was gathered on the sidewalk, Mom burst into tears as we embraced each other.

"You take care of yourself, anak," she said with worry.

"I will, Mom," I told her in an attempt at calming both of us.

I will never forget the sight of her in tears, watching me leave, her hand clutching her purse closely while standing with her toes pointed slightly inward. I went over and embraced her one more time, unable to contain my sadness. I wanted to show them I was healthy and strong but was failing miserably. I kept expecting Dad to mock my misery, but it never happened.

"It's time to go," Dad said. With that, the moment ended and they disappeared into the crowded airport.

I left not knowing where to go or what to do. I wandered in and out of various electronics stores to get my mind off cancer by finding comfort in the soulless gadgets contained within them. Failing that, I went home.

When my parents were there, the place was alive with their presence. Now, there was just an empty stillness, but it wasn't as if they hadn't left their mark. Mom had taken the time to make my bed. It was a loving, caring gesture I appreciated all the more now that they were gone.

Oncologist

With the orchiectomy and initial tests behind me, I was transferred over to Dr. C, an oncologist who worked in the same building as Dr. K. He was listed on the Testicular Cancer Resource Center as an expert because of his close ties with the University of Indiana. This knowledge gave me the confidence I needed to conquer The Big C.

However, what I was conquering was rather nebulous. There wasn't much to do other than visit doctors and be scanned, poked, operated on for a couple of hours, and asked a bunch of questions. Most of my so-called battles involved nothing more than waiting. Waiting in traffic. Waiting in the waiting room. Waiting in the examination room. Waiting for the X-Ray. Waiting for the CT scan. Waiting for the results. Waiting for the next appointment. Instead of an all-out war with skirmishes and battles, this fight against cancer was nothing more than a lengthy exercise in patience.

I called up Dr. C's office to set up an appointment for blood work and to see him about my case.

"Unfortunately, I'm not available to see you because I'm going out of the country for a couple of weeks," he said as my heart leaped into my throat. "The earliest any of my colleagues can see you is next Friday," he continued. Time was of the essence because my six-week window for having an RPLND done was closing. Thinking about the deadline made me go light in the head. This was a disaster.

Trying to remain positive, I told him, "I would like to go ahead and schedule for next week, then." After I gave his assistant my contact information and hung up the phone, I slumped into my chair. I wanted to know what was going on with my body now, not two weeks from now.

Not 10 minutes after I hung up the phone, it rang. I was surprised to see the Caller ID indicate the call was from Dr. C's office. Curious, I picked it up.

"Hi, Leonard? This is Dr. C again. I have changed my mind. I want to meet with you tomorrow before I go on my trip."

Hearing him speak those words with the enthusiasm of someone who loved helping those in need restored my confidence in having approached him. We scheduled a morning meeting since I already had an afternoon appointment at the sperm bank.

"I pretty much follow the University of Indiana template when it comes to testicular cancer. You know, the place where Lance Armstrong was treated," said Dr. C, a middle-aged man with a round face, big smile, and friendly eyes.

Everyone used Lance Armstrong as a point of comparison with me since he had conquered Stage 4 testicular cancer, won the Tour de France several times over, and created the cancer-fighting Livestrong Foundation. He was a hero to all and an amazing success story that inspired many. After all, if he could survive cancer and thrive afterward, so could I. To be in close touch with the same center responsible for Armstrong's fight against cancer gave me confidence in Dr. C.

It didn't matter Armstrong later confessed he cheated to win those titles because his story had served its purpose in helping frame cancer as an enemy to be conquered instead of feared. Plus, I could see why many people believed in an afterlife. It gave them hope for a brighter future in the hereafter where they might not have had any hope otherwise.

"According to the pathology report, your particular tumor had a high amount of yolk sac content. This makes it easy for us to track your cancer via tumor markers," he said. Dr. C's confidence in his ability to track my cancer brought me a tingling sense of growing confidence and relief. He made it all sound so easy.

"If your tumor markers remain unchanged and elevated, you go straight to chemotherapy. If they fall to a normal level, then it is either an RPLND or surveillance," he said. "You'll have to come in for weekly blood tests to have your tumor markers checked."

That meant a lot of trips back and forth from my apartment to the hospital, which took anywhere between 25 minutes to an hour each way depending on which day of the week and time of day, not to mention all the waiting around for results.

The time away from work was a major inconvenience I had to work around. Festival Graphics's word they would help me get through this made accepting these terms easier to swallow. Another positive was if I wanted to have an RPLND done by the experienced hands at the University of Indiana or Sloan-Kettering, Dr. C just had to make a phone call to schedule it. Dr. C's reassuring words gave me a chance to take a few deep breaths and relax.

"Although I'll be out of the country, my colleagues and I all work in conjunction with one another, so it doesn't matter whom you work with while I'm gone," he said with a confident smile, putting me at ease with his experienced charm.

Dr. C did say one thing that surprised me since he was an oncologist whose specialty was working with cancer-fighting chemicals.

"If I were in your shoes, I would have gone ahead and done the RPLND."

His decisiveness was almost enough to sway my decision to having the RPLND right then and there, but the idea of subjecting my body to additional stress sounded unnecessary. So, on to more tests, then.

Later that afternoon, Bruce took me over to the sperm bank, which was discretely located in an unmarked brick building near the hospital. You wouldn't know what it was unless you were looking specifically for it because there were no exterior signs indicating its true nature. Security in the foyer was observed by a camera and closed off with an electronic door. Beyond the exterior glass door was a rather plain lobby with a smoked-out receptionist slide window. Standing in the foyer waiting to be let in, I had this desire to put on a big hat, sunglasses, and trench coat to hide my identity while whistling the theme to *Mission: Impossible*.

Once inside, I experienced the joy of filling out the multitude of forms typical of any first visit to a medical facility. I met up with the manager who disappointingly didn't look or sound anything like a spy. He spent an hour informing me about fertility tests, sperm storage, in vitro fertilization, artificial insemination, and how many vials of sperm I would need for those. I hadn't known how complicated it all was until I spoke with him. To be honest, I wanted to know how much sperm I needed to put in the bank, when to make a deposit, and how much it would cost. Get in, find out what you need to do, do it, and get out. Like father, like son.

After the meeting was a short wait before I went off to give urine, semen, and blood samples. I found it tough to do the semen sample since I hadn't thought to bring any of my own inspirational material. None of the videotapes set next to the large TV were ones I would have picked myself. Thinking about how many other guys had made deposits in that cramped room through the years didn't help either.

I was determined to stay until I left a sample because it was essential I get one done that day to maximize the number of my deposits since I would be required to wait several days between visits in order to maximize my sperm count. If the tests showed I needed the RPLND, then my time was fast running out for making deposits. I closed my eyes and let my thoughts drift to my own fantasies. Once my deposit was made, I was more than happy to get out of there.

For my tests over the next couple of weeks, waits for Dr. C took as long as three hours because he was busy working with worse cases than mine. To pass the time away, I began editing my third *Innies and Outties* compilation. I was supposed to complete it for the 2005 San Diego Comic-Con so I could go down and sell them in the Small Press section with Becky as my helper, but my cancer check-ups derailed my plan. So, I decided to shoot for the 2006 Comic-Con as a completion date instead.

To edit the book, I printed out every single strip to be organized as I saw fit. I took this stack of strips with me to every doctor's appointment, reading it over and over again until I found an over-arching story out of the numerous daily comics I had completed over the course of two years. Hours of waiting passed in the blink of an eye.

For the webcomic itself, which I was still producing every morning to start my day before heading off to Festival Graphics, I had shifted the stories in *Innies and Outties* from Otis and Iris trying to conquer the world to covering my cancer experience as it happened. Instead of giving cancer to one of the kids, I opted to use Harold, a vegetarian zombie, since I could put him through all sorts of medical tortures without fear of reprisal from readers, injecting him with a dose of humor and wisdom as a victim of circumstance. The opportunity to relate my experience to an audience on a daily basis was the closest thing I had to a spiritual ritual during this period.

Alpha

"If I had to choose a religion, I would choose Buddhism," I told Matthew over lunch one day. Matthew was a business consultant brought in to help with the Thailand Film Festival. He was an all-American boy-next-door type with a handsome smile and nerdy glasses. I found the father of two easy to talk to because he sympathized with my frustrations of dealing with Edward's difficult personality.

"Why?" he asked. Matthew had a genuine curiosity about him that made me want to open up to him.

"I like its peaceful introspectiveness," I told him. With encouragement from Wynn, I had read the *Dhammapada*, a collection of Buddhist aphorisms. Sayings such as "Our life is the creation of our mind" made a lot of sense to me. I believed we make our own stories through our actions and interactions with others, so I lived by the guidelines set forth within that book.

"You should read Thich Nhat Hanh's *Going Home: Jesus and Buddha as Brothers*. You'll find Christianity and Buddhism are more alike than different and Christianity isn't as much a threat to your beliefs as you think it is," he told me, his passion piquing my curiosity. "If you're interested in learning more, you can join us for Alpha."

"What's Alpha?"

"It's time spent with friends chatting about Jesus."

"I don't know. Sounds weird to me." Everything I knew about Christianity came from watching movies where characters would go to a confessional to speak to a priest, from observing people and groups who gathered in meeting rooms to pray and listen to sermons about the Bible, from my parents teaching me the Lord's Prayer, and from the few times my parents made me go to church, where I would try my best to stay awake.

"Look, it's only for one night and you'll be getting a free dinner out of the deal," he said with a laugh. "Plus, it might help you deal with your cancer experience."

Not one to turn down a free chance to add weight to my slender frame, I accepted his invitation to participate in an Alpha Course at an Episcopal church located a short drive from my apartment. In addition to possibly helping me with cancer, I liked it would give me a chance to learn more about this religion so many people followed and defended. Most Christians I met were friendly enough, so there wasn't anything to fear or worry about.

According to *Alphausa.org*, the Alpha Course is "an opportunity to explore the Christian faith in a relaxed setting over 10 thought-provoking weekly sessions." For the course, groups of six to seven people are seated at each of the nine round tables covered with crisp, white tablecloths. At each table is a group head who is there as both participant and discussion moderator. Up front is a podium where the presiding priest sets the topic to discuss while dinner is served. Once dinner is finished, your group talks about anything that comes to mind related to the topic.

My table had a mix of people ranging from their 20s to retirement age. Matthew headed the discussion at our table. Since I was familiar with him, I found it easy to open up and speak freely.

The sermon was about author Leo Tolstoy and his journey to find meaning. Tolstoy's *Anna Karenina* was my book of choice during my trip to Europe, so I took an interest in learning more about this author whose work I admired. Tolstoy had gone from youthful exuberance to famous author to family man without finding fulfillment. It wasn't until he discovered Christianity and how to live a life of service through Christ that Tolstoy found what he was looking for.

Tolstoy's story was interesting because it was a side of the author I had never known. If he, who had never been affiliated with a religion before, could find fulfillment in a Christian life, then it was possible for me as well. During the discussion, everyone came across as intelligent and full of life, asking questions about Tolstoy's fascination with Christ's offer of salvation for our sins. By the end of the evening, I was intrigued by this Christian idea of being in the service of others, like feeding the homeless, giving donations, and sheltering the poor. It was a much different and more meaningful discussion than ones I typically engaged in about books and movies and, if these were the types of discussions Christians engaged in on a regular basis, then I wanted to be part of those talks.

Between my job at Festival Graphics, working on my webcomic, going out swing dancing regularly, waiting for and taking surveillance tests, and trying to maintain a semblance of a social life, I was too busy to think about attending more Alpha classes. The simple act of getting through the day was more than enough to keep me occupied. Thus, the concept of becoming more connected to God through Christianity had to wait for another time.

Decision

Two weeks after my initial meeting with Dr. C, my post-orchiectomy blood tests showed all my cancer markers were moving in the right direction. Learning Dr. C had been correct in his assessment this cancer would be easy to track put me at ease.

I was so high off the thrill of having the markers normalize, I wanted to give Becky the most affectionate kiss the world had ever seen, but she was nowhere to be found. Awkward as it may have looked to an invisible audience while in my apartment, I gave myself a hug and pat on the back after I received the good news over the phone from Dr. C. If no one else was going to do it, I might as well do it myself.

With my tumor markers returning to normal, priority shifted to anything that showed up on my CT scan. Dr. C also ordered a Positron Emission Topography (PET) scan, which is like a CT scan on steroids. It does a good job of detecting anything unusual in the body that is metabolically active, like a tumor.

"This isn't a common test for testicular cancer, and I'm concerned your insurance won't approve it, but I would like to at least try," Dr. C said. It was comforting knowing Dr. C was willing to take risks based on the latest cancer-fighting data available. Dr. C's insurance concerns proved unfounded when the request was approved without incident. With everything going so smoothly, I could have dodged bullets if I wanted.

Unlike the CT scan, the PET scan was definitely not good for claustrophobes with its half-hour scan time through a machine the size of a large living room. While going through the plain, beige interior of the machine, I found myself wishing for paintings to look at, like the frescoes on the ceiling of the Sistine Chapel. Some music would have been nice, too, but I can see how dancing in place to your favorite tunes would have made for blurry body scan images. After the PET scan was completed, it was time for my CT scan, which took all of five minutes.

I had fun talking to the tech guy afterward because he was geeking out over the machinery. "We're getting a new machine with better accuracy to replace the one you just went through," he said. I was tempted to ask how inaccurate the current one was but thought better of it. I didn't need to put myself through that kind of stress.

Later that same day, Dr. C contacted me with the results.

"All clear," he said with a congratulatory cheer in his voice.

"You now have two options," he continued. "You can either go through the RPLND now to remove the lymph nodes—thus ensuring no tumors will ever grow there, or you can opt for surveillance. Either way, the cure rate is 98 percent." Surveillance may sound covert and mysterious, but it's nothing more than continuous testing with a combination of blood tests, chest X-rays, and CT scans by doctors at set time intervals for, well, the rest of my life. If a tumor was found during surveillance, chemotherapy would follow if it proved malignant. If no tumor was found, then life would continue for me as 'normal.'

After I outlined the surveillance protocol to Matthew, he told me, "You're going to be lit up like a Christmas tree," referring to all the X-Rays and CT-scans. "There is an increased chance you can get cancer from the radiation. Not a big chance, mind you, but a chance nonetheless."

It was a calculated gamble because the benefits of finding possible tumors early with relatively painless detection tools were worth the risk. Also, while under surveillance I had to be the responsible type who had the discipline to make it to every single appointment and test asked of me. Any lapse could let a previously missed tumor metastasize unchecked, which could lead to severe complications or death. So, no pressure.

"Just do what the doctors tell you," Dad said in response to my decision-making process. "If it were me, I would have done the surgery and chemotherapy already. I don't like watching and waiting because they might not catch new tumors before they spread." While I understood Dad's fears, the message I took away from him was that he trusted the doctors enough to do the treatments but didn't trust himself enough to go to the doctor for checkups. With several weeks of experience under my belt, surveillance sounded like it would be more of the same. At least, that's what I was hoping for, considering I had been receiving nothing but good news so far.

I called Wynn to see if he had any advice for me. He had been studying to be a nurse and following my cancer experience on my e-mail list.

"Going through the RPLND and chemotherapy guarantee you will have complications no matter how smoothly the procedures go. While you would be comforted with the idea of a 98 percent cure rate, you will also have 100 percent complications in the short term with possible long-term effects as well," Wynn said. Neither idea sat well with me. After all, the recovery from the orchiectomy was an awful experience, even if it was short-lived. Did I want to gamble I was in the 70 percent of men who were already cured with the orchiectomy alone?

"You can talk percentages all you want, but your personal cancer percentage is 50 percent. Either you have cancer or you don't. According to the test results, there is no evidence of there having been any spread of the disease in you. Remember, either way, surgery or surveillance, the cure rate is the same at 98 percent," Wynn said.

I thought Wynn's logic was sound even if the math wasn't. After all, in terms of statistics, the chances you may or may not have more tumors had little to do with whether you have cancer or not. The tests may say you don't have cancer, but they aren't 100 percent reliable. Thus, there is a chance they might have missed a tiny tumor. Let it go undetected for a few weeks, and it might kill you.

With all the tests so far indicating zero presence of more cancerous tumors, it was becoming increasingly likely I was already cured and this side trip through The Big C would be a much easier experience than I, or any of my friends and family, hoped or expected. There was only one choice and it was an easy one to make.

So, I opted for surveillance.

Dr. C then proceeded to tell me stories of patients who had undergone the surveillance protocol. I almost told him not to because I was worried he might make me regret my decision, thus undermining all the confidence I had built up from my conversations with Wynn and Matthew. Call me stubborn, but I had made my decision, and I wasn't going to back away from it no matter what Dr. C said.

"I had one patient have a one-centimeter tumor show up in the PET/CT scan and went through three rounds of chemo and was cured. Another patient lapsed on his surveillance plan and came back with metastases all over his body and died later."

He wasn't telling me these stories to shake my confidence; he was telling them so I was aware of the consequences of not following protocol. One thing was for sure, he had my complete attention.

"It's important you call the doctor to follow up on the results. Sometimes patients don't call, thinking everything is fine. What then happens is the doctor forgets he's supposed to look at results or never receives them. Later, the patient returns with a cancer diagnosis that could have been caught early but wasn't."

Yikes. I had read the stories before, but hearing them from the voice of experience—one that had spent years dealing with cancer patients—had me take notice. This was serious stuff, and one lapse could mean the end of me.

"I'm not worried about your reliability and intelligence, Leonard. I want to make sure you have no qualms about following up," he said, looking me straight in the eyes to make sure I heard every word.

"Don't worry. You can count on me."

With that, he sent me on my way, and for the first time in two months, I no longer had a weekly doctor visit planned.

Falling Out

"Is that what you think of me?" Carrie asked, offended I had refused to give her the Percocet she had requested.

"You think I only want your drugs?" she said with rising anger.

"No," I said with a steady, sure voice. "It's obvious you care for me, but I don't like this idea of yours." I didn't like she was self-medicating without a doctor's approval, even if it was to alleviate the physical pain she suffered from serious injuries sustained years before.

Seventh-grade health class taught me prescription drugs were meant for the patient they were prescribed to and no one else. I had no way of telling what kind of effect the doses I had remaining would have on her and refused to give them to her out of care for her health and well-being. Plus, I didn't want the legal liability if anything happened to her from taking my drugs.

For weeks, I had been more concerned with my frequent visits to the hospital for lab work than the leftover painkillers from the orchiectomy. I had been so consumed by the test results, I had pretty much forgotten the drugs when Carrie asked for them.

"You aren't going to give them to me, are you?" she asked, softening her disbelief over my refusal to her casual but stern request.

"No, I'm not," I said. Though the drugs may have been mine to give, I didn't like the idea I was contributing to someone's drug habit, a concept beaten into my head by the "Just Say No" marketing campaign of the '80s. I could tell by the pained sound in her voice she was hurt by my rejection. "That's all right. Don't worry about it," she said in an attempt to save face. With that, she went back to her apartment.

Over the next few weeks, I stopped looking up at Carrie's window every time I passed to avoid another confrontation with her. One day, tired of me ignoring her, she leaned out her window and stopped me cold in my tracks to ask how I was doing. We began talking again like two old friends, but weeks would pass between conversations after Carrie hired a photographer to help with her escort business.

Every now and then, she would come over and we would catch up, our conflict over the Percocet having been consigned to the distant past, but it was nothing like the closeness we experienced our first few months of knowing each other. When she moved away several months later, I re-learned how much simpler my life was without that familiar Southern twang of hers.

Stubbornly refusing to give up in the face of a no-win situation, I went out with Becky a couple more times over the next two months in hopes of rekindling our romance. The reason she stood me up was her father had a medical emergency and she had turned off her phone. I accepted her explanation, but getting back together proved difficult. Our formerly fun-filled banter was now punctuated by long periods of silence. Kissing was no longer an expression of attraction, but our way of hanging onto a more carefree time.

I kept hoping we would get back together after she graduated, the stress of school behind her and my cancer treatment behind me. After her graduation ceremony in May, I left a message on Becky's voice-mail. When her name came up on my Caller ID later that day, the emotionless voice on the other end of the line was a bitter reminder of how far we had grown apart after such a great beginning.

"I don't think we should get together and talk about us in person," she said with lifeless formality as if this was an obligation she had to slog through to graduate.

I tried negotiating for one more date "for fun" hoping I could win her over again by holding her close and whispering sweet nothings into her ear. She refused to budge, though.

"I thought about it for a while and realized I don't want to date anyone."

I wasn't sure if I should take that as a compliment or an insult—a compliment because she thought enough of me not to consider someone else, or an insult because she didn't think enough of me to remain together. I wanted to tell her to stay and be mine forever but it was painfully obvious that whatever magic I thought we had between us was gone, and any attempt to revive it was futile. I wanted to lash out and hit something hard to beat away the heartache.

"You're great, and I want to keep you as a friend. You're the first person I have ever been able to talk to. I enjoy that and don't want to lose it."

With a click, she was gone. I never heard from her again.

"AAARRRGGGH," I yelled in frustration while throwing a lot of soft things around my apartment so I wouldn't have to clean up afterward. Once I tired myself out, I laid myself down in bed with the disappointing realization my inspiration for getting through cancer was nothing more than a self-made delusion.

Since it was our slow season at work, the Festival Graphics office was at its most bare. The lunches I used to look forward to every day because of the wonderful sense of camaraderie had fallen into a routine of ordering in and talking about which Hollywood celebrities were closeted homosexuals, the significant others with whom they were or weren't sleeping, and so on and so forth. I found the occasional puffy cloud visible through the office's many windows far more interesting than their catty gossip. I saw myself wasting away the hours at the office in isolation, working for a man whom I didn't like at a place I was increasingly unsure about so I wouldn't go broke from taking care of a disease I might not have anymore.

During this time, Edward was away from the office looking for business opportunities. Without Edward there to help him work on design projects, there wasn't much for me to do at work other than browsing the Internet for hours at a time. It takes a surprising amount of energy to fill your day when your only task is to babysit an idle computer. I spent most of my time mentally replaying my relationship with Becky over and over again, but the more I reflected on our relationship, the more I realized there wasn't much I could have done to change the outcome.

With Becky gone, I was at a loss over what to do with my life. Without someone to love, cherish, and care for after having survived a brush with The Big C, I was back to being a loner but with the added burden of cancer surveillance. I initially regretted allowing Carrie to link my thoughts to Becky when I needed it most, but couldn't blame her for wanting me to be positive and happy during a difficult period like any good friend would. Looking back, Carrie was the rock I needed, not Becky.

Was there something else I could have used for inspiration instead of Becky while in that waiting room with Carrie in those moments before the orchiectomy? Something with infinite patience, love, and understanding that would bring me peace in times of need? Something greater than life itself?

Without a framework to explore the answers to those questions, I set them aside for a later time. That time arrived sooner than I expected.

Dad

Phone Call

With every muscle and joint crying mercy after five non-stop hours of dancing at the annual swing dance convention known as Camp Hollywood, I wanted to drag my weary self into bed and sleep the entire next week.

Stepping into the darkness of my studio apartment at 3 a.m., I was about to drop into the familiar comforts of home when I caught sight of the tiny, blinking red light across the room proclaiming I had a waiting phone message. I usually don't bother checking messages on my home phone since most of the calls on that line are from places trying to get their grubby virtual hands on my money, but took a peek just in case. When I read the name and time on the Caller ID, a single thought overcame the fatigue of the evening.

My parents never call me that late.

"Leonard, it's your mom. You need to fly to Hawaii immediately. It's urgent. Your dad. He's in intensive care and not going to make it. Please look up and print out information on vasculitis when you get this," the shaky voice on the phone message pleaded. Dread and urgency overcame physical exhaustion as the thought of my mother frightened and alone drove me to book the first flight out to Hawaii.

As soon as I caught sight of Mom's long face and tear-soaked eyes in the Intensive Care waiting room, I rose above the fatigue of having been up all night and through the five-hour airplane ride and gave her something to hold onto as we embraced. Beyond her was a closed door, and through its window, there were several machines looming over a hospital bed with all

132

manner of cables and hoses hooked into the unconscious figure of somebody who sort of looked like my father. For a moment, I refused to believe it was him. My father was full of anger and fight, ready to go a few rounds of tennis at a moment's notice, not this bed-ridden mess before me. Mom's tight grip on my hand said otherwise.

"We've done all we can to stabilize him," one doctor told me. I watched through the window as a nurse prepped Dad for a dialysis to clean the toxins from his body and help alleviate the pain he had been complaining about for months. Knowing his pain was abating brought me relief but was it going to be enough to restore him?

"We've pumped him full of every antibiotic we've got to give his body a fighting chance. His overall prognosis is bad because the vasculitis ... well, it's everywhere. We've done everything we can, but we fear he's slipping away," the doctor said.

Looking at the incapacitated figure on the bed, I kept hoping Dad would open his eyes, yank out the hoses and needles, push those machines aside, and boldly walk out of that room with an invisible orchestra triumphantly blaring in the background, but he didn't. He couldn't. The weight of inevitability wouldn't let him.

After the doctor briefed us on the medical horror show that was my dad, my cousin Elmer took us to the tiny, sparsely furnished two-bedroom apartment where Dad, Mom, and her sister, my Auntie C, had been staying since they arrived in Hawaii. Auntie C was on a trip to the mainland and wouldn't be returning for a few days. Wishing I was back at Camp Hollywood dancing the rest of my weekend away, I did a few playful slides across the wood floor to take my mind off Dad's failing health.

We then visited the house Dad was building for his retirement. Though unspectacular on the outside, once we entered it was apparent Dad's two-story design was an efficient use of the lot. Walking onto the second-story backyard balcony revealed a breathtaking view of the island. The unfinished kitchen and bathroom counters revealed there were only a few decisions left to make as the house was almost ready for my parents to move in.

"He was healthy on Friday," family members solemnly remarked as hopes for a quick recovery faded. In only 48 hours, Dad's health had deteriorated rapidly. He had lost a lot of weight, was suffering inflammation all over—most visibly in his swollen, discolored hands and fingers—and his lungs and kidneys had failed.

"Dad's going to be all right, right?" I asked Mom. I was hoping she would have words of comfort even if they were nothing more than white lies.

"No, he's not going to make it, anak," Mom said. In front of me was no longer my loving, caring mother, but a registered nurse who had faced the cold reality of dying patients for decades. Based on what Mom and the doctors had said, any notions of his surviving were nothing more than wishful thinking. Losing him was like losing half my world. Even if it was the half I didn't always like.

Death

The next morning, I organized all of Dad's papers and bills in dozens of stacks spread out over every inch of my bedroom floor. I found putting everything in order helped get my mind off Dad and the machines for a while. Plus, it gave me a sense of responsibility as the temporary head of the household.

"What are you doing, anak?" Mom asked when she walked into the room to see if I was awake for breakfast.

"Putting all the bills in order," I replied while crouched in front of all the papers.

"Oh, you didn't have to. I already know what's due when."

There was a casual confidence to Mom I had never seen before. It was refreshing to know she was on top of things even if it did take the wind out of my sails to find out I wasn't needed. After Mom briefed me on the family finances, we bought groceries, went to the bank, and had lunch before heading back to the hospital.

When we arrived back at the ICU, Mom let out a bloodcurdling scream. Dad's blood pressure had dropped by half from the day before. We thought he was doing okay since his vital signs were stable when we left him in that freezing cold room with its unyielding lights and machines pumping like there was no tomorrow. We were wrong.

We rushed over to his side, each of us taking one of those cold, swollen hands we once feared when he lost his temper. When Dad's breathing started wavering, I requested Mom talk about the good times we had all spent together. If these were his final moments, I wanted him to know we treasured his time with us. I may not have always liked him, but he deserved it as much as anyone else who ever lived.

I talked about his beloved Ford Thunderbird and Mercedes Benz 380SL. Dad took great pride in keeping those cars looking their best to show them off to friends and family, teaching me cars were more than mere transportation to get from Point A to Point B. They were personal rewards we could enjoy for many years as long as we took care of them.

We talked about vacations we had spent together, including our cruise to Cozumel—our last vacation as a family. The portrait of him and Mom beaming smiles in front of the leaderboard for a blackjack tournament stood out as one of the few pictures I remember of him smiling while sober.

We talked about the time my parents returned all the money they had been collecting from me as rent so I would quit wasting it on junk, like CDs and VHS tapes, and have travel money for my trip to Europe. It was a decision that changed my perception of my parents from difficult overlords to loving caregivers who wanted nothing but the best for me.

I talked about Dad's collection of dozens of tennis trophies he had won over the course of three decades at local tournaments in and around Houston, each containing its own triumphant memory. I may not have shared his love of playing tennis, but I did understand the excitement of competition and the satisfaction of a job well done after many dedicated hours of practice.

Mom talked about his 50th birthday party, his retirement party, and all the good times they had spent together. Tears rolled out of Dad's barely open eyes as they stared up into the bright, unforgiving lights. Could he hear our love for him? I liked to think so.

"Honey! Don't go!" Mom pleaded.

Standing there looking at Mom with Dad, I reached into my bag, pulled out my camera, and took pictures of Mom tenderly holding Dad's hands as his labored breathing became even more erratic and his already low blood pressure fell further into the abyss. It was the first time I had ever seen her so loving toward him and I wanted to capture the moment before it was forever lost. When his pulse began its fade to nothing, I put the camera down and held Dad's hand with Mom until Dad's eyes went dim, the three of us united for one fleeting moment.

A nun came by minutes later to pray over and bless Dad's inert body with holy water. I respectfully kept my camera down and watched her say a prayer from the opposite end of the room. After the nun left, Mom clung to Dad's body tightly.

"You're not supposed to die! You promised you'd be with me forever! Why did you leave? Why?" she pleaded at the top her lungs while pounding her grief into that bed with all her strength. Listening to her piercing screams of sadness, I wondered if anyone would ever love me as much as Mom loved Dad at that moment. I wanted to reach out and tell her everything would be all right, but it wasn't. Her partner of more than three decades was gone, and there was nothing I could do other than let her wallow in her loss—for both of us. When she calmed down, I reached over and took her hand.

"Let him go, Mom. Let him go so he can be at peace."

She pulled away from him, then held my hand as we walked out of the room, neither of us turning back for one last glance. Mom and I still had each other, though I wasn't sure what that meant for our immediate future.

Later that evening, Auntie B, a quiet, diminutive woman who looked as if she were always smiling no matter her mood, organized a prayer circle asking God's mercy for Dad's soul at her home, a sprawling rectangular two-story house big enough for three families. "We will be doing this every night from the time of Nardo's passing until he's buried," she declared. "This is required so Nardo's soul goes to heaven."

In a small, well-furnished room that could pass as an altar for Jesus because of all the religious paintings and icons that were neatly strewn about, I, Mom, and other members of the family sat down on an intricate rug in a prayer circle while Auntie B took a seat in front of everyone. Once seated, she closed her eyes and put her hands together in prayer. Kneeling in front of her in their regular street clothes, everyone else including my mother closed their eyes and joined their hands in prayer, mirroring Auntie B's motion. Once everyone had settled into their respective prayer positions, Auntie B began by reciting the Lord's Prayer in her heavily accented voice with everyone joining in unison. Sitting there, I cracked opened my eyes and looked around at family members with their eyes closed and hands clasped. They all looked so obedient and humble. I felt as if I were a stranger intruding on a private ritual and had no business being there since I hadn't grown up Catholic.

"Our father, who art in heaven, hallowed be thy name. Thy kingdom come, thy will be done, on earth as it is in heaven. Give us this day our daily bread and forgive us our trespasses. And lead us not into temptation, but deliver us from evil."

Once everyone finished reciting the Lord's prayer, Auntie B continued.

"Heavenly Father, we are asking for your mercy and forgiveness for our dear Nardo." I closed my eyes and listened for a sign from God, but all I could think of was this: Why would an all-powerful supreme being with an infinite universe to play with pay any attention to our localized concerns? The only response I received to my unspoken question was a great, big nothing.

Looking around the room, I watched the others' serious countenances and listened to their soothing words spoken in unison and thought I might have been going about this prayer thing all wrong. Did God speak to them and not me? Had God abandoned me because I hadn't been a good, church-going Catholic all my life like most others in my family? Maybe he didn't speak to me through prayer because I didn't believe in heaven or hell. Was he using my cancer experience and Dad's death to send me a message to shape up or else?

I left the prayer circle and headed over to the next room, where my cousin Marie and several other family members were. Having never seen Dad pray, I suspected he would have spent the time drinking with friends and family rather than praying.

"No praying for you either?" I asked Marie, whom I had known since childhood. She was short and plump, had big, dark eyes with long, dark hair and was dressed in slacks and a dress shirt.

"No, I'm not into it. It doesn't do anything for me."

"Funny, I was thinking the same thing."

After the prayer circle finished, my mother and Auntie B made preliminary funeral and burial arrangements with a funeral planner who was present. I took a step outdoors, closed my eyes, spread my arms, and took in the warm, gentle breeze. It was a soothing contrast to the hospital room hours before. Following more prayers, Mom and I returned to the apartment to recover from the open wound that was our family.

Wake

Days later, Dad's wake was held at a medium-sized Catholic church near Auntie B's home. When the pallbearers brought Dad's casket to the front of the church, I took out my camera and started taking pictures, not out of any sense of posterity, but because I wanted to express my grief by capturing everyone else's. Moments I captured included Mom screaming in agony as she buried her head in her hands while the pallbearers brought Dad's body past her, Dad in his coffin with the portrait of his younger self overlooking him like a guardian angel sent to protect him, and family members wailing in mourning while hovering over him.

Throughout the wake, there was an endless sea of people streaming in to pay their respects to my father. Many had the same last name as ours, but none of my family recognized them. I found it odd to have so many mourners present whose only connection was the name, but I didn't kick any of them out. In fact, there were so many people there we ran out of thank you cards and programs.

Other pictures I took included everything from the floral wreaths to grieving family members. It was the only way I could keep from falling to the floor and screaming with frustration at the top of my lungs to a god whose will I didn't understand.

During a moment of rest, I felt a slight nudge at my ribcage. "Your mom ..." one of my cousins started to say.

Before he finished his sentence, I was right at her side looking down at Dad. "Come on, honey, wake up and open your eyes one more time," Mom pleaded to my still father. I don't know about Mom, but the sight of Dad opening his eyes would have had me running for the door. Mom's continued pleas jolted me back to reality.

"Look at all the beautiful flowers. I'm sorry we couldn't get the carnations and gardenias like you would have wanted." I both held Mom and gave her something to hold onto while her piercing screams split the chapel air with her grief, that endless sea of people joining in with painful wails of their own as if on cue.

After Mom's hysteria died down, we gathered with the rest of the family in front of the casket for group photos, like tourists at a historical monument, only much better dressed and with more somber faces.

"Cousin, do you think it would be appropriate for me to smile?" Auntie C's son Jarick asked under his breath when it came time for Mom's side of the family to have their photos taken. Though I didn't answer him, it took every ounce of my being not to laugh at his innocent question while the picture was taken. The last thing I needed was my being disrespectful of Dad's memory captured forever in a still for all the world to see.

After the photos were done, the family disbanded, and we went our separate ways for the evening. I wanted to pull my favorite cousins together so we could talk about what happened, but their weary countenances only wanted the comfort of their beds. On the way back to the apartment, Mom said, "I want this to be over so I can move on." The stress of the last few days was getting to her, but I didn't believe she was ready to leave Dad behind yet.

If someone had asked me, I would have said I wanted to move on with my life ... the sooner, the better.

Funeral

"Who's going to call me stupid now?" I asked the cold, still body that was my father as bugs crawled over his face with impunity during the final viewing of his body at the church while a statue of Jesus Christ loomed tall behind him. I stood there and stared into Dad's lifeless eyes, ignoring the pesky mosquitoes I had been swatting futilely at for the past hour. This would be the last time any of my family would see Dad before his body was taken to the gravesite for burial. Behind me, sad wails reverberated throughout the church from the dozens of mourners in the pews dressed in their well-groomed mourning clothes, a marked contrast with the sunny, breezy Hawaiian paradise beyond the front doors.

While my tears flowed unrestricted, I whispered my final goodbye. As I did, the room and everything in it dissolved into a warm, loving glow enveloping both me and Dad. Within that glow, all the pent-up anger and bitterness I had built up over having to deal with Dad's numerous tantrums through the years dropped away like the tears from my eyes, revealing a calm, gentle presence that embraced both of us, like a mother with her newborn baby. From that presence, there was a soft, soothing whisper that only said one thing: "Everything will be all right." I nodded in agreement, then looked into that presence and, for the first time in my life, I understood what Annie meant when she told me her brother Kevin had gone to a better place—a place full of light and love that was overseen by a loving, caring God, the creator of all things.

God was no longer some nebulous, all-encompassing universe, but a loving entity overseeing us all who cared about my concerns and well-being. I wasn't just surrounded by his creation as I had believed. I WAS his creation. I could see both heaven and hell were real places where our souls went after our time on earth ended. Also, Auntie B's prayers were no longer silly superstitions, but a plea to a merciful God to be reunited with our loved ones in heaven. I wanted to stay within that presence and bask in its glory forever and ever, but then the light faded to reveal I was back in the church, standing over my father's still body. I looked up at the large cross on the wall looming over the chancel and made a promise to dedicate myself to learning about and following God's plan. I didn't know or care what that plan was. All I knew was I had to follow it.

The rest of the final viewing and funeral went by in a blur, though some memories stood out.

There was the woman who passed out in church while Mom pleaded for everyone to tell their loved ones how much they cared in case the unexpected happened. There was the long, quiet ride from the church to the burial site where members of the family all stared out the windows, lost in thought while the clouds clung to the nearby Hawaiian mountaintops.

There were the placement and removal of the US flag from Dad's coffin while 'Taps' was played. There was the smiling soldier who, despite having performed this ritual many times before, was straining to hold back tears while he handed the veteran's flag to Mom. There was Mom clutching the flag and cross in Dad's honor during the burial as if she were still holding his hand while I watched my cousin Jojo shoot pictures with my camera, wishing he would pick a better angle. There was that huge feast after the burial, where we all stuffed ourselves silly in Dad's memory.

After the funeral, several relatives and friends of the family suggested I move to Hawaii to take care of Mom as if she were debilitated or dying. She and I both argued this wasn't the case at all. Because of my cancer surveillance schedule and insurance needs, I would not be moving from LA or leaving Festival Graphics for Hawaii anytime soon. Also, I couldn't see myself stranded on an island, any island, no matter how pretty, because I needed the space and variety LA offered.

That night, I went to bed and dreamed of the day I would be reunited in heaven with Dad so we could play a few sets of tennis while God watched from the stands.

Christianity

Alpha

With this new-found desire to do God's bidding in the wake of Dad's death, I wanted to know what Christianity had to offer. Did it have the answers to the meaning of life? Did heaven and hell exist? Would I see both Kevin and my father in heaven when I died? How could there be a heaven and hell if the earth was round with a molten core and the sky gave way to space? What was God's plan I had heard so much about? Was my getting cancer, Kevin's death, and Dad dying part of that plan? What does the Bible say about God and his nature? Could a book containing stories written thousands of years ago have relevance in today's world? Who was Jesus Christ?

What I discovered during my first Alpha session at the Episcopal church after my orchiectomy was there were adults like me who had similar questions and issues with Christianity. What I found fascinating was how exploration of these issues served to reinforce the notion following the teachings of Jesus Christ was the correct path to heaven. With a new series of Alpha classes being offered at the same church in September of 2005, I thought it would be a good, solid introduction to my new life as a Christian and give me an opportunity to honor the memory of my father and serve God's will.

"The reason I decided to go to church was because the girls were hot," said Jimmy, the presiding priest of my new Alpha course, which took place in the main meeting hall on the church campus. As before, the roundtables were covered with white tablecloths and there were six to seven chairs per table. At my table was a mix of young and old with different ethnicities and backgrounds, including a well-groomed Chinese man and a couple of young women in their late 20s. They all looked like middle-class professionals who had just gotten off work and, instead of hitting happy hour, had come to Alpha in search of meaning in their lives.

Listening to Jimmy confess why he started attending church marked the first time I had ever heard a priest talk that way, shattering any notions all priests were boring. Also, in the room of 50 people, many were women. Jimmy wasn't kidding about them being hot and there was a good possibility I could find a mate who could help me fulfill God's plan. It was a matter of setting priorities and putting forth the time and effort needed to meet someone. As much as I wanted to find a mate, learning more about Christianity took precedence. After all, if I wanted to meet a Christian woman, becoming a Christian man was the first priority not the second.

During our next Alpha session, our table head, a 30-something woman with a lot of enthusiasm for Jesus, declared "Jesus is a pretty cool guy, even after you strip him of the Messiah title, thanks to his message of love and peace."

Thinking of Christ as a wise mortal teacher made him less intimidating and more relatable than seeing him as humanity's savior. I could see how accepting Christ as a good teacher opened up the possibility of accepting Christ as the Son of God. Of course, making the mental leap from believing Christ was an ordinary mortal to divine being would require a tremendous amount of suspension of disbelief on my part. It was a leap I wasn't ready to make because I was too grounded in a world defined by science to believe in such an incredible statement, even with my recent epiphany.

At another session, one of the guys in my group made an announcement. "I'm leaving the love of my life after 10 years, and this church is the biggest reason," he said. Many congratulations flowed from the group as he basked in the glow of the attention.

I found this both fascinating and disturbing at the same time. Fascinating because he was so open and loving toward the church, and disturbing because it was such a sudden change.

Curious as to how his partner reacted to the news of this transformation and departure, I would have been perplexed as to how someone I had been with for 10 years could make such drastic changes in their life after a few church services and religious education classes. Maybe if this was someone who had invested their entire life in a belief system and needed to push someone away who didn't believe the same way, it would have made more sense. But his decision was based more on spur-of-the-moment emotion rather than intellect and logic. To be fair, I couldn't say for certain because I didn't know the full story of their relationship. I had a tough time putting my full support behind his decision because of his flimsy reasoning, though I kept those thoughts silent out of respect for him.

At another session, our presiding priest read aloud a humorous paper describing the Bible in only 50 words. After receiving a one-hour summary of both the Old and New Testaments, they gave us a handout noting the differences among major translations of the Bible currently available. I found the nuanced differences between translations a reflection of the times during which they were completed. For me, this showed the Bible was continually being repackaged for each successive generation of worshipers.

I also learned the Bible had fascinating stories in it, several of which I had been exposed to through pop culture, like director Cecil B. DeMille's *The Ten Commandments*. I had never associated that movie with religion because I thought it was just another special-effects-laden story like any other science-fiction work I enjoyed growing up due to its spectacular rendition of Moses's parting of the Red Sea.

Jimmy's confession of joining the church to chase women piqued my interest because I could see he was someone with whom I could have a round of beers while watching a football game at a sports bar. I learned that, in addition to speaking at Alpha on Wednesdays, he ran the Saturday-evening service at the Episcopal church. I decided to attend his services because I wanted to hear more of what he had to say.

Unspectacular on the outside, the chapel interior was warm and inviting with a mix of soft incandescent lighting and candles. Upon entering the nave for the first time, I sat in a wooden pew as far from the chancel as possible despite the inviting interior with its well-lit pulpit backed by a lavishly decorated golden fence beckoning you in through the darkness of the church entrance.

"All of you sitting in the back, come forward. We won't bite," Jimmy said before the service.

With Jimmy's soft-spoken request beckoning us forward, I got up and made the short journey with several others. When we reached the front, we were greeted with smiles and hellos by the circle of a dozen congregants, who ranged in age from mid-20s to retirement, male and female, mostly white, but with a couple of minorities there. No one was dressed in their Sunday best, though many were dressed in relaxed business casual attire.

Jimmy led the service dressed in casual jeans and dress shirt. His down-to-earth demeanor, charming smile, and charismatic way of carrying himself gave the service an intimate, informal feel. It was much different from the rigid formality of a Catholic service with all its pomp and circumstance. Concerned I might say the wrong thing at the wrong time and offend someone, I was relieved to see printed programs to guide me through the service.

Much of the service was conducted with us gathered around Jimmy while he spoke, like kids around a campfire for story time. For communion, we passed the bread and wine around like desserts at a small party. It was like being in a small bar where everyone knows your name. A home away from home.

Afterward, we were invited to stick around for good, healthy snacks. I stayed so I wouldn't have to worry about scrambling for dinner later. I found this sense of community appealing and relaxing in addition to friendly and welcoming. I decided to keep coming back because it was better than staying home alone in my apartment with nothing more than my computer, books, and movies to keep me company.

During one of his Saturday-night sermons, Jimmy said, "The church will always be there for you when you need it."

I was glad the church was an institution that had stood the test of time and would continue to do so long after I died. The permanence of it was appealing because it gave me a shelter to fall back on in case I needed it. I wished I had known this earlier in life. It would have given me a place to go to when things got bad with Dad and might have made my experience with The Big C easier to handle because it would have reduced my dependence on Becky for inspiration.

Later, Jimmy said, "You should read the Bible first, then study it. Then again, you don't have to read the Bible at all, but it's there if you want to."

I somehow accepted these contradictory statements without question. It was Jimmy's attempt at making the Bible less intimidating to read since it looked like an awfully large book for 10 measly commandments. However, this non-committal approach made the scripture less relevant to believing in God, attending church, or following a religion. It was easier for me not to read the Bible and avoid all that messy thinking when I could take the priest's interpretation as Gospel instead.

Another Saturday-night sermon on work talked about how having a job is God's will because God would like you to provide for yourself and others, no matter the job. This message hit home because I was struggling with my work at Festival Graphics. While Edward was away drumming up business, Danny encouraged me to do my own design work for the firm. When Edward returned and found out Danny was letting me be more creative with my work, he stormed into my office area with angry eyes, flared nostrils, and upset jowls.

"Your graphic designs are awful, Leonard. Stop being a creative. You are not a creative. You are a production artist and must do exactly what you are told!" he screamed in frustration, scattering the rest of our coworkers to their offices as he did. "You have no sense of color and couldn't design your way out of a paper bag."

I resented working with Edward's mocking nature because it was similar to playing tennis with my father and being forced to listen to him call me stupid whenever I made a mistake. Jimmy's sermon gave me a ray of hope while working with Edward because this idea I was performing God's will meant I was doing good for a power greater than me. The reward was God's love. That a higher power loved me for all my flaws was comforting, especially for someone who had rarely experienced love other than from my own parents. It made Edward easier to deal with by diminishing his importance. After all, who was more important than God? Definitely not this man.

"Did other people's prayers help you get through cancer?" the Alpha group asked during a discussion on prayer. We had been talking for several weeks and I had become comfortable enough with the group to mention that my cancer experience played a part in my being in Alpha, so it wasn't a surprise to have them ask about my experience.

Thinking about the question gave me a chance to isolate what prayer meant. Based on my experience with prayer after Dad's death, it had little to do with an external being granting wishes.

"It helped show me I was loved by people whom I cared about," I replied.

Saying those words out loud made me wish I had been praying to God rather than relying on my wish to see Becky again, something I didn't mention at Alpha. I didn't want to give the impression I was a lovesick fool who made questionable decisions. I was there to make friends and be a part of a community, not push them away with my emotional neediness.

After one of Jimmy's Saturday-night sermons at the Episcopal church encouraged us to follow that voice in our head telling us how to be happy, I followed it through to its logical conclusion by buying a new car. If that voice was God's way of telling us how to be happy, then that was the voice I wanted to use as my guide. "God will provide," Jimmy had said in his sermon.

I started shopping that summer for a new car to replace my eight-year-old Acura, which needed a couple of thousand dollars' worth of work on it. I figured the money would be better spent on a down payment for a new car. Dale, my friend from swing dancing whom I used to carpool with to dances, had been shopping around for a replacement for his Mercury Cougar and had me look over his shopping list. What caught my eye on his list was the Mazda Miata. After having owned a pair of fun-to-drive, front-wheel-drive Japanese cars, I decided I wanted a fun, lightweight, sporty car with good handling and rear-wheel drive to easily get the car sideways in a corner. Fitting the description perfectly was Mazda's two-seat roadster, which I had long forgotten existed.

My first experience in a Miata was back in 1993 with Mike, who was friends with my old college friend Shannon. Mike was a blue-eyed blonde with the body of a junior linebacker. He was from a well-off family and loved America, God, apple pie, and science. He loved driving his Miata with the top down at up to triple-digit speeds on the highway. Through local streets, he would whoop and holler while taking corners with wild abandon. I never knew how much I wanted one until I took Mazda's just-released 2006 redesign for a test drive, which met my expectations of what a Miata should be: fun.

"You're buying a Miata because God told you to?!?" an incredulous Christa said when I told her over the phone the next day why I was buying a new car.

Christa offered to buy my old car when I hinted at putting it up for sale because she liked how well I took care of it. Plus, I was willing to sell it to her for cheap to raise money for the down payment for a brand-new Miata.

"It was God's will, who was I to question it?" I reasoned, five years of auto loan debt be damned. Less than a week after that test drive, I bought the Miata just as God wanted.

Beta

At the end of our last Alpha session, there were love and hugs all around. Of the seven people in our group, only three of us would be returning for the next step in becoming Christians: the Beta course. The other four weren't wholly convinced Christianity was for them and that was the last I saw of them. As for me, I wanted to know more of what Christianity had to offer based on the positive vibe I had during Jimmy's sermons. Sad as I was that my time with friends at Alpha was ending, it was time to move on in my journey to become closer to God and fulfill his will.

While Alpha had been centered on discussions of our doubts and issues with Christianity, Beta concentrated more on us fulfilling our "calling" to becoming Christians. It proved to be a more serious commitment, which in this case meant homework, something I never had in Alpha.

During the first Beta session in November of 2005, we were asked to suspend our disbelief Jesus Christ existed and was resurrected. Although they were trying to be helpful, the request set off an alarm bell. If Christ was real, why ask us to do this? I had always been under the impression Jesus Christ had been a real historical figure. After all, if so many people believed in Christ, he had to have existed, right? It was a question that had never occurred to me before because I never thought to ask.

One of our homework assignments asked us to talk about what our lives would be in the Kingdom of Heaven. I had seen many cartoons, television shows, and movies depicting heaven as a place up in the clouds where angels with wings played harps, people were reunited with loved ones, and everything was quiet and peaceful. Try as I might, all I could come up with was a big, fat nothing.

If Christ didn't exist, why would heaven exist? Or hell? Without salvation through Christ to reach heaven, the idea I would play tennis with my father in front of God was far-fetched and silly. Also, I couldn't accept the idea of angels who lived out their lives on clouds above us because clouds appear and disappear out of thin air all the time. How could anyone live in a place so impermanent? No wonder there was so much talk of angels on earth protecting us. They were down here because they kept losing their homes to evaporation.

Another assignment had us write God an acceptance letter into heaven. I had a problem with this because I couldn't write an acceptance letter to join a place high off the ground because I was scared of heights. Why would I want to subject myself to an eternity living in fear of looking down? Hell's underground dwelling was much more appealing to this acrophobe, though there was that whole nasty bit about eternal torture to consider. Once again, I ended up with a big, blank sheet of paper.

Was Dad correct about my being stupid? Was I too stupid to believe?

I set aside my problems with Beta and kept attending Saturday services because I found hope and inspiration in Jimmy's sermons. Learning more about God and his will may have been nothing like what I was hoping for based on my experience in Alpha, but I found church was an easy way to meet people with whom I had one thing in common: Christianity.

In April of 2006, a new priest, a musician, took over the Saturday services, but they weren't the same. This priest was an older, heavy bald man who spoke softly, but with a thick British accent. I found myself tuning out the sermons because I was spending more time trying to decipher his accent than absorbing the points he was trying to make. He would start off with a lengthy, rambling anecdote about some happening in his life, usually revolving around music, then he would go on and on until reaching some semblance of a point. If anything, I was only getting an incomplete word of God from this particular priest.

I found the deceptively soothing songs he sang to be too repetitious, pounding me softly into submission with their dull, derivative messages of love and hope—a far cry from Jimmy's uplifting sermons. Also, his multimedia backdrop of Christian art, with its pre-Renaissance ideas of Jesus and religion as the central subject, was hopelessly out of place in early 21st-century LA. Was this priest's idea of a service how I wanted to worship the all-powerful Creator of all that is seen and unseen?

Still, this priest was a man of God and, thus, had the word of God and if he had the word, then I should continue listening to what he had to say. So, I kept attending this house of worship to show my appreciation of God and all he had done for me, most especially for sparing me from further cancer treatments. Plus, being in that sacred space reminded me of being around Jimmy and the charismatic way he carried himself, even though he was long gone. If this new priest was God's new messenger for me, then I would honor and respect his wishes and keep attending to hear more of God's word because it was God's will.

Easter

Everyone I knew was either out of town or spending the holiday weekend with family instead of attending the Easter Service at the Episcopal church. When I mentioned to them I was interested in attending the service, they encouraged me to go because it was a beautiful experience for them.

When I arrived, I was greeted at the door with a smile, a candle, and a program, then guided through the dark of the nave to an empty seat in one of the pews to my left. The only light was from the sun shining through the stained-glass windows and the entrances to the church. I could see in the dim lighting the church was packed with shadowy figures filling the pews. As the service began, we lit the candles as a representation of Christ's victory of light and life over darkness and death. Those warm, glowing lights in the darkness looked like beacons guiding us into a safe haven.

Once all the candles were lit, the service continued with the words "May the light of Christ gloriously rising dispel the darkness of our hearts and minds." A chill ran up my spine as my hairs stood on end at the thought of Christ as a symbol of hope for this cancer survivor.

Listening carefully to the words, I found myself questioning the idea of darkness being "vanquished by our eternal King." If darkness were vanquished, why does an evil like cancer still exist? And, if darkness still exists, how can we as followers of Christ claim victory? If our King was so mighty, why were there so many problems with the world? Maybe we were supposed to understand Christ intended for us to defeat the darkness, but that means darkness hasn't been vanquished and Christ's coming was for naught. Plus, why did God need lowly mortals to do his work? Couldn't this all-powerful being simply do it himself? I silenced those thoughts as the service kept going.

The next idea to set me off was hearing Christ's sacrifice was to pay for "the debt of Adam's sin." This made no sense to me. The idea a supreme being would make a pair of flawed creatures in Adam and Eve who disobeyed his orders because of a talking reptile sounded far-fetched. Punishing all their future descendants was excessive and cruel. Adding a story about how this supreme being sent a part of himself, a son, to redeem this one action from thousands of years before so future generations could be saved, but only if they believed the son of this supreme being was the one, true path to heaven, didn't help much on the credibility scale either. It all seemed as if it were made up, even if it was the word of God.

The opening prayers finished, it was on to the first lesson from Genesis 1:1–2:4a. Its opening concept of God creating a separate heaven and earth reminded me of the thousands of years human beings believed we lived on a flat earth. Was this false notion of a pancake planet really the word of God? Also, the mere mention of heaven had me thinking back to Beta class. More specifically, how I had come to the conclusion I didn't believe in the existence of heaven, which meant I didn't believe in the existence of hell, which nullified this idea of saving your eternal soul through Christ to ascend to heaven and enjoy the glory of God, which made me ask why I was even sitting through this Easter service in the first place.

Flipping through the program, I could see the story of Easter and the coming Christ as savior wasn't going to get any better. Out of politeness for the others in the pews, I remained glued to that seat and listened to the rest of the service, but my attending had been a huge mistake. There had to be another way to honor and worship the creator of everything we know and don't know other than these silly stories.

I kept looking around, hoping there were others who were as flabbergasted but found nothing but contented faces. By the time the lights went up to signal the resurrection of Christ to whoops and hollers from the congregation, I wanted to get out of that church and return to a reality free of myths born from the minds of men claiming they had the word of God.

Autocross

On the way home from swing dancing at Atomic Ballroom in Irvine one rainy March evening at 3 a.m. in 2006, I decided to give the car a little more throttle than usual on a rain-soaked boulevard. I was hoping to instigate a controlled slide across the slick tarmac as I did with my Nissan in the rain. Instead of an easy slide as I was expecting, the car's rear end pitched violently right. I panicked and yanked the steering wheel, but failed to catch the rear end as it swung violently the other way. I snapped the steering wheel the opposite direction in a desperate attempt to gain control, but the car's rear end came around and pulled me into the opposing lanes. As the car spun like a top on the wet pavement, my world became a blur. I held my breath and closed my eyes tight while hanging onto the steering wheel for dear life, hoping for the car to come to a merciful halt, fully expecting a disheartening crunch accompanied by the caving in of metal, glass, and plastic all around me. This was it, I thought. This was how I was going to die.

When the world stopped spinning, I took a few deep breaths, opened my eyes, and saw the car had ended up perpendicular to the curb on the side of the street I started from. I was thankful I didn't damage my car by hitting the curb or, worse, another vehicle. I wouldn't have been able to live with myself if I had hurt someone else. I looked to the left and saw the coast was clear. To my right, there were headlights in the distance. Hoping it wasn't a cop, I drove away from the scene, doing my best to avoid another incident with nothing hurt but my pride.

After doing that unexpected maneuver in the rain, I followed the problem to its logical conclusion and decided to learn how to become a better driver in a controlled setting. I looked at various safety and performance driving schools in the area, but couldn't find anything affordable. Several weeks after that spin-out, it was on *Miata.net*, an Internet discussion forum popular among Miata enthusiasts, where I found what I was looking for in autocross, a motorsports competition where drivers use their vehicles to navigate a series of elements marked by orange pylons on a closed course. It was the kind of controlled environment where I could learn car control through hands-on experience because I wanted to make sure I would never make the same mistake again, especially with a passenger.

I found out CalClub, the local chapter of the Sports Car Club of America, a national club and sanctioning body for professional and amateur motorsports, was hosting an autocross school in the area and signed up in May for the July school, which cost far less than the other alternatives I had looked at.

The two-day school took place on the airport runways at El Toro, a former Marine Corps Air Station in Irvine. The wide runway we would be driving on was surrounded by tall grass with hills to the north and east providing a beautiful backdrop to the soundtrack of the occasional singing bird. If it wasn't for the fact it was an Environmental Protection Agency Superfund site, it would have been a nice place to have a picnic. The only structures nearby were abandoned aircraft hangars and a large RV park on one of the other runways.

After I parked my car and got out, it was like my inner Hot Wheels child had died and gone to sports car heaven. Everything from Miatas, Corvettes, and Porsches to BMWs, Minis, and Subarus were driven by men and women of different sizes and ethnicities aged 16 up through retirement age, many of whom were dressed in T-shirts and jeans. In other words, they weren't that different from any regular Joe you met at a local watering hole.

Day one started off with a chalk talk for the students by Lisa, the head instructor, a stout older woman with long graying hair. She explained what apexes were, how a car reacts to a driver's inputs, and why that all matters when driving through a course as fast as possible. After the talk, I was introduced to my instructor for the day, Mike, a soft-spoken older Filipino gentleman with a big smile and easy-going laugh who had been doing autocross for years.

The first drill was the slalom, an autocross element consisting of a line of cones several feet apart that you zigzag a car through. For the second drill, we did the skidpad, where you drive around a large circle to the limits of tire adhesion and learn how to control the amount the car slides using the accelerator. Once we were done with drills, we walked the course in preparation for driving laps in the afternoon. During the walk, we were taught how to navigate the mile-long course with its mixture of slaloms, sweeping curves, and 180-degree turns.

After lunch, I was given the opportunity to unleash my inner hooligan on the course with Mike as a passenger for a lap. It was an adrenaline-fueled dance between me and my car as I wove through the course at the car's limit. Well, I liked to think I was cornering at the car's limit. I learned how slow I was through the 70-second course when Mike bested my time by eight seconds in my car, an eternity in a sport where the difference between winning and losing is measured in thousandths of a second.

Knowing what was possible, I spent the rest of the day getting the car to go faster by being more aggressive, changing my driving line to carry more speed, driving smooth and controlled, and getting closer to the cones, but couldn't catch Mike's lap time. The second day was more of the same as my time kept getting closer to Mike's.

On my final lap, I entered the fastest part of the course, a long sweeper, faster than the tires could grip. After I lifted off the throttle and turned the steering wheel, the front end found some grip and the rear end kicked out. I turned in to the slide and drove sideways through the corner at 50-mph like I had been driving that way my whole life. "Wheee!," I yelled as the tires squealed while I giggled like a kid at play the whole way through. It was like nailing a dance move so well that you and your partner perform as one, completely in tune with each other's movements. It was a divine experience

I couldn't wait to replicate, and was something I could never do in normal, everyday driving without losing my license. It was enough to convince me to begin participating in autocross competitions held on Sundays.

It was Sunday, October 15, 2006, when I woke up at 5 a.m. and made the hour-long drive to my first CalClub region autocross competition at the California Speedway parking lot in Fontana, some 50 miles east of my apartment.

When I arrived, I emptied my belongings out of the trunk and taped printouts of my numbers and class letters to my car doors. I then walked over and checked in at the registration table. Once registered, I drove my car to tech, where volunteers check that your battery is secure, the throttle won't stick, loose items have been removed from the trunk, the seatbelts and brakes work, the wheels aren't loose, and you have an approved helmet. Since my car was relatively new, I thought there would be no issues, but my left front tire had an air leak in it from a nail I picked up on the drive over to the event. They refused to pass me at tech until I got it fixed.

A gentleman of average build and short, light-brown hair wearing a T-shirt and jeans calling himself Patch, who was behind me in line for tech, offered to fix the tire in the paddock, which is the marked off area where you park your car before and after a competition. Patch jacked up my car and removed the tire, then used a pair of pliers to remove the two-inch nail. It was nice to see people in the autocross community were friendly and helpful, even to someone they didn't know. After the tire was patched and put back on the car, I inflated the tire with my car's air compressor, then drove back to tech, where I was given a sticker to apply to the windshield indicating my car had passed the safety inspection. The same sticker would be used to keep track of my three runs on the course during my run group.

With a half hour left before the first car was sent out, I walked the orange cone marked course once before attending the novice walk. A young woman named Christine, a member of a well-known racing family in the region who had been competing for years, conducted the walk. She led us through the course, giving us basic instructions so we wouldn't get lost. Once the novice walk was over at 8:30 a.m., the course was closed for walking. Both novices and veterans alike then attended the driver's meeting led by the event master and safety steward. At the meeting, the pair gave us a lecture containing general rules and safety information so none of us would get hurt.

Once the 9 a.m. starting time for my group came around, I was in the grid with my helmet on ready to compete in my three runs. My first run was an adrenaline filled rush as the car pitched and rolled like a ship at sea while I navigated the course. I came in with a time nine seconds behind the open class leader, but good enough to open with a lead in the novice class. Once I got back in the grid, I was shaking like a leaf from the adrenaline rush.

The other novice in my class, an engineering student named Joey, had scored a DNF on his first lap because he Did Not Finish the course as designed. A DNF meant he either missed or was on the wrong side of a course element while driving. He was driving a stock Pontiac Solstice, GM's two-seat convertible that was a direct competitor to my 2006 MX-5.

For my second lap, I drove faster but hit a cone in the slalom, which counted as a two-second penalty against my time. Although I improved my raw time, the penalty meant no improvement on my first-run time. After the run, I was again shaking like a leaf from the adrenaline.

For my third and final run, I managed to drop my time enough to put me in the novice class lead by a scant .061ths of a second over Kenneth, a novice driving a Mazda RX-8, who was running at the same time Joey and I were. Joey ended up with a time seven seconds slower than mine.

There were three other novices who competed the rest of the day, but none of their times beat mine, which gave me the win in novice class. It was my first trophy since my days of playing tennis. Yay me!

Winning novice class on my first try wasn't without its drawbacks since the rules stated anyone who wins novice class must participate in the regular, open class against experienced drivers with better-prepared cars. I decided to keep competing, hoping the competition would force me to become a better, faster driver sooner.

Without church to hold me back, I began competing in the two to three autocross events a month held near both LA and San Diego. Like my father with tennis, I had found my Sunday activity of choice and it had nothing to do with church.

In March of 2007, I received a phone call in my office at Festival Graphics from the accountant. "Leonard, can you come into my office so we can talk?" Sharon asked. Since I had never been called into her office before other than for paperwork, I assumed I was going to be fired, not for insubordination or poor work, but because the company couldn't pay the bills after losing its main client due to a situation beyond its control. Without any work coming in, I sat there at my computer every day pondering what my next career move would be. The reason I stayed was to keep my health insurance, which

I needed to help me financially with my cancer surveillance checkups, the results of which were still all-clear. That said, losing my job meant I wouldn't be able to pay my rent, my car, go dancing, or compete in an autocross. My life, as I knew it, would be over. When I walked in, I saw both Sharon and Imelda already seated.

"Leonard, have a seat."

I went ahead and sat down.

"As you know, we don't have any work coming in. So, we have to let you go."

It was the second time I had been let go from a full-time job in four years. My parents had instilled in me landing a full-time job was a goal to aspire to because it meant long-term stability, but I now knew that was not the case. The first time had been my fault because I couldn't keep up with the long hours, but this time was beyond mine or the company's control. Either way, it was a disappointing end.

"Okay. I understand," I replied with little emotion. It was all happening so fast that it didn't seem real at all.

After I signed paperwork marking the end of my time there, I made the long walk back to my desk and packed my belongings. As I did, tears streamed forth as I looked back on my time there with new insight. No longer were Edward's micromanaging design sessions showing little self-awareness of his own shortcomings a career liability; they were valuable lessons on how to approach a graphic design project from scratch. Also, the lunches I had grown weary of became fond memories of familiar faces finding distractions in absurd Hollywood gossip.

The tears didn't fall for long, though. Sharon got me in touch with the recruitment agency that helped me land the job at Festival Graphics. They had me start a temp job the next week at a large advertising company 15 miles south of my apartment. Within a month, I was hired full-time with health insurance benefits that included a plan with all of my doctors. Since I didn't have to take the time and effort to find a new team of doctors, it was a huge load off my mind to know my cancer surveillance would continue without any changes.

During my first year and a half of participating in Saturday autocross practices, I rode along as a passenger with drivers of various skill levels. I took what I learned from experienced drivers and imparted my newfound wisdom to those new to the sport. The most gratifying part was when the newbies showed immediate improvement based on my instructions. Their smiles and thanks were what inspired me to volunteer to become the novice coordinator when the previous one stepped down in February of 2008.

As novice coordinator, I was responsible for welcoming novices to our events. I would begin my day by arriving early to walk the course two or three times. Doing so gave me an idea of what to say on both the morning and lunchtime novice course walks, which consisted of me leading a group of novices around the course and providing them the mental tools they needed to succeed. Other duties included driving instruction—where I would drive a student's car for a run, and coaching from the sidelines—which was necessary when I was unavailable to do driving instruction because of a rule on competition days where you can't instruct unless you have already finished competing.

Novices ranged in age from 16 on up to retirement and included men and women, mothers and daughters, fathers and sons, boyfriends and girlfriends, husbands and wives, and everyone in between. Some had previous racing or track experience while others had only played video games or came in with no experience at all. Regardless of their background, they were all looking to have fun with their vehicles. Cars they brought included everything from a rental Mustang to the family VW wagon to the latest Aston Martin sports car. Watching my students improve over the course of a season from trophy fodder to trophy contenders for Sunday competitions made me a proud and happy teacher.

The best part of being novice coordinator was it gave me the opportunity to be in service of others as God intended while doing something I was passionate about, taking to heart the sermon Jimmy gave about finding our God-given passions to better serve him. A win-win situation, if you ask me.

The Christian Feminist

"That shirt is not going to get you any chicks," Teveya told me with a look of disdain. A petite woman with a snickering laugh and a wiseguy demeanor, she was a longtime friend from swing dancing who always encouraged me to meet new women. She didn't like I was still single in my mid-30s and had taken it upon herself to coach me on my approach.

"You need to learn how to peacock," she told me.

"What?"

"You know. Peacock. Show yourself off," she said with a friendly nudge.

It was May of 2008 and we were at our Thursday-night hangout, LindyGroove. I was wearing my "Book Club" T-shirt, a parody of Chuck Palahniuk's *Fight Club* rules. I had obtained it a few years back at San Diego Comic-Con from the creators of the library-centric webcomic *Unshelved* to declare my interest in reading books to the world. Teveya rolled her eyes in disapproval at first sight of its huge pink letters declaring my nerd status.

One woman did show an interest: Emma, a cellist in her early 30s with sky-blue eyes and long blonde hair complementing her fair skin. She caught my attention while we were dancing with other partners on the packed dance floor. She looked light on her feet with her long limbs and slender body. I walked over and asked her to dance after the song ended.

"I like your shirt," she said with a laugh.

"Hi, I'm Leonard."

"Hi, I'm Emma. I just moved to LA."

"What brings you here?" I asked.

"I'm going to be in an independent Christian rock band."

Interesting. Hadn't heard that one before while out dancing. "What do you play?"

"Cello."

"A cellist in a rock band?"

"Mm-hm."

"So, you moved to the big, bad city to join a rock band, hm? That's pretty cool."

"Yes, I'm very excited," she said with a smile.

"You should be."

She lamented there weren't many female artists in rock whom she could model her career after. I didn't buy her argument and named several female artists on my iPod, including '80s rocker Joan Jett, riot grrrl Kathleen Hanna of Bikini Kill and Le Tigre fame, and Sleater-Kinney, a female trio hailing from the Pacific Northwest.

"If you give me your e-mail address, I'll tell you more," I told her with confidence.

"Okay!" she said with the excitement of learning something new.

Over the next few days, Emma and I exchanged several e-mails. I found her charming and engaging enough to get her phone number. During our first phone conversation, which went much longer than I had planned, she came across as confident and level-headed while being the type of person who liked to throw themselves into a new interest with the intent of mastering it.

When I arrived at Emma's apartment for our first outing, I rang her doorbell, but nobody answered. I took a walk around her neighborhood to kill time in the intense late Spring heat wave with temperatures in the 100s, figuring she had been delayed by traffic. Just as I was about to wilt from the effort of walking, Emma called my cell phone.

"Sorry, I'm running late. I've been church shopping all day and just got out of a picnic at a Presbyterian church not too far away," she said.

"How was it?"

"I like it a lot and think I have found a new home. I can't wait for the next service." I could hear her satisfied smile over the phone.

I knew Presbyterian was an offshoot of Christianity, but that was the extent of my knowledge. When she arrived, Emma was dressed in a bright colored, short-sleeved shirt and jeans. She looked every bit the nerd she claimed to be during our first dance with her small, rectangular-shaped eyeglasses that complemented her slender bone structure.

"Do you go to church?" she asked.

"I used to go to an Episcopal church, but I didn't like the direction the services were heading after they brought in a new priest. The multimedia presentations weren't doing it for me."

"I understand. It's difficult to find a good church."

I wasn't sure if she liked my answer to her church question. Showing skepticism over church never goes well when speaking with someone who attends church regularly. I suspected this elephant in the room was going to rear its ugly head sooner or later and we weren't going to last past two or three outings. I didn't care, though; she was charming enough so far and a few enjoyable dates would be a nice break from my everyday.

We continued our conversation in the air-conditioned cool of the Norton Simon Museum. As a cello teacher, she enjoyed watching her students grow but knew they were doomed by what she called "the dead end of classical music performance" because they would have to play the same boring standards over and over again. She wondered how they would fare after they moved on from her teaching.

"I quit the classical music scene because I found it creatively stifling and didn't like female musicians were sometimes chosen to be in an orchestra more for their looks than their skill. I found refuge from the classical music scene when an opportunity to join a Christian rock band in LA came up. I'm going through a loosening up stage in my life in an attempt at reinventing myself," she said during one our breaks from looking at the artwork. We finished up our visit with a walk through the modern art section featuring sculptures of ballerinas by Rodin, though there was still plenty to see.

"That was a good museum. I would like to go back sometime, but we should also do some other activities together," Emma said with a smile as we were leaving the Norton Simon.

"I would like that," I replied. How could I turn her down after a pleasant afternoon together looking at art?

"Good. I'm glad," she said.

My main concern with Emma was I didn't want to get involved with another woman in a transitional phase, even if I did like she was in her 30s, which was a nice change of pace from all the 20-somethings who showed up swing dancing at LindyGroove every week. Every woman I had ever dated had been in a transitional phase, transitioning right past me and on to the next guy. I squelched my doubts and accepted her invitation to do more activities since we were getting along well. I liked her frank, honest stories of the classical music world because they gave me insight into something I knew little about, and decided she would be good practice for my next relationship if it didn't work out.

A few days later, I sent her an e-mail telling her how much I liked her smooth voice. "You're so sweet," she replied. It was nice to know she could take a compliment.

It hadn't been looking good for when I would see her again after Emma canceled a couple of outings, but she surprised me with a phone invitation to see *The Chronicles of Narnia: The Lion, the Witch, and the Wardrobe* with her. I hadn't read the books but was curious about Disney's attempt to cash in on the success of both the *Harry Potter* and *The Lord of the Rings* film series. I convinced her to meet me at Disney's El Capitan in Hollywood, a wonderful spectacle of a theater to behold with its lavish interior reminiscent of European colonial architecture evoking '20s Hollywood. Upon entering, Emma marveled at the intricate decorations on the ceiling and walls. She also enjoyed the pre-movie show, a live performance featuring actors in costume that served as a brief introduction to the movie.

I was less enthused by the movie itself because I found the climax of the overtly Christian film frustrating. The kids are told they have a purpose never made clear to the viewer in a similar vein to the way Christians talk about God's unknowable plan and how inspiring that plan is. Plus, while

I understood it was meant to represent Christ's sacrifice for our sins, the resurrection of Aslan the lion to inspire the kids came across as a contrived plot point thrown in on a whim. It was not a movie I would recommend to my non-believing friends. Emma, who was familiar with the Narnia books and hadn't seen many movies, liked it.

The next weekend, Emma and I met up for lunch at a French-inspired restaurant with family-style picnic table seating located in a shopping district restored to the look and feel of a small Western town circa late 19th– early 20th century.

"I have a problem fulfilling the role of follow as a feminist, but I understand it's part of the dance," she said.

"Huh, I hadn't thought about it before," I said. "I do know there are females who lead and males who follow since instructors have to know both. Plus, it helps to know both when practicing. What about it bothers you?"

"It puts women in a subservient role. They must follow whatever the male lead does without any creativity of their own." I found Emma's conflict fascinating because it was a perspective on swing dancing I hadn't heard before. Plus, I appreciated her ability to work past her articulate misgivings and enjoy the dance.

"That's not true. Follows can and do improvise, plus they have their own moves, like the swivel, that men don't do."

"Yes, that's true. Despite having to follow, I do love to dance, especially with you since you're such a good lead."

"Thanks," I said while glowing with pride built up from years of dancing experience.

On our next date, we returned to the Norton Simon Museum to catch exhibits we missed the first time. We stopped to take a break at a seating area located within a painting gallery in the museum. I took note of Emma's blouse, which matched her brilliant blue eyes, and her knee-length white skirt, showing off her slender legs. I wanted to run my fingers along them to see how she would react.

"I like that you're the type of guy who opens doors for me," she said with a blush. "I like the idea of chivalry."

"Doesn't that run counter with you being a feminist?" I said with surprise.

"Although I'm a feminist, I'm still a woman," she said while turning red.

"Wow. You're blushing."

She blushed even more.

I leaned in toward her and took in her scent. "You smell good."

She blushed again.

After we finished admiring more of the Norton Simon collection, we walked around a nearby outdoor shopping center for a while, stopping at stores that piqued our interest. Inside a home furnishings store, I waited until we found ourselves alone then surprised her with a brief hug to break the ice, causing her to blush again.

Once we finished our walk, she invited me over to her place for ice cream and chocolate. We sat outside on a wooden bench swing in the shade and watched the afternoon go by while we cooled ourselves off with those delectable treats. I wanted to give her a gentle kiss to show how much I enjoyed her company but held off because I didn't want to get ice cream and chocolate all over us.

With the day coming to a close, I got up to leave and she rose to give me a goodbye hug with the fading sun's light poking through the trees. As she embraced me, I gave her a kiss on the cheek, then caressed her soft, shoulder-length hair. She gave me two more hugs before running off with "I have to go!"

I wasn't sure what to make of her.

It didn't take long to find out.

"I'm rather freaking out because it was so much easier when we were in the flirty stage. Now I have all kinds of other emotions and hang-ups, which I don't know how to reconcile!" she said in a panicked e-mail. I waited a couple of days to respond so she could calm down, then sent her an e-mail. "Wanted to tell you I'm looking forward to holding hands and being near you ..." then hit the return key several times to force her to scroll down and added, "for dancing."

"You're such a tease!" she replied.

I couldn't wait to see her again.

After we met up dancing at LindyGroove a few days later, I walked Emma to her car across the street from the club in the garage so she could drive me to mine, which was on one of the upper floors. We got in and I directed her to my car.

She parked next to my car, looked at me with her deep blue eyes, smiled, and asked, "When can I see you again?"

I reached over and held her hand, which caused me to go flush with excitement and anticipation.

"That's really distracting," she said as she blushed. I wanted to lean over and kiss her. "I'm free a couple of nights next week if you want to get together."

"We'll have to play it by ear," I told her since my work schedule changed from day to day. I made a move to kiss her, but she pulled away.

"Not yet," she said as she raised her hand to block me.

"Okay," I said, trying my best to hide my disappointment.

She leaned over, gave me a hug, and we said our goodbyes.

The next time we saw each other, Emma and I took a walk around her neighborhood late one chilly evening, holding hands while we compared the many Craftsmen homes lining the tree-covered streets, like a couple out house shopping. She pointed out the various aspects of the neighborhood she had grown to admire the past few months, like the occasional tire swing begging for attention and the way the trees sheltered the entire street from the bright moon above. Embracing each other to keep warm in the evening chill, it was good to have her close, not because I didn't have a sweater, but because I enjoyed her company and found her attention to detail charming.

When we crossed the street to return to her small, one bedroom apartment, we held hands with our long, slender fingers interlocked. It was once explained to me by a woman I dated holding hands that way indicated we were romantically involved with each other.

I tested Emma by changing to a more friendship-like simple handhold. Would she retain that hold, showing she was more friend than a potential lover? Would she let go showing she wasn't interested? My doubts fell away when she changed it back to having our fingers interlocked. We went inside and had tea to warm up then sat on her couch and alternated between embracing and cuddling before lying down.

"I have to admit, I don't feel comfortable talking about my faith with you," she said.

Uh-oh. Lacking confidence in holding an intimate conversation was not a good sign. "Why not?"

"I'm afraid you'll make fun of me."

I shook my head. I didn't want to mock her faith because it meant a lot to her. Also, I didn't want to drive her away because I enjoyed the way she articulated her thoughts and couldn't help but admire her good looks, most especially her slender lines and those captivating blue eyes of hers.

"If our relationship is to move forward, then you have to be a part of that faith," she said, snapping me back to the reality before me.

If her faith was the primary reason for her charm, grace, and intelligence, then I wanted to know why to see if I wanted to be in this promising relationship. However, the skeptic in me wanted to know something. "What does that mean exactly?"

"You have to attend church and read the Bible with me."

I had been anticipating this conversation ever since she talked about her church-shopping experience. It had been two years since I had been to church when I met Emma. In those two years, my Sundays were filled with movies, books, creating art, working overtime, and participating in autocross events.

Being in service of others as our autocross club's novice coordinator meant more to me than participating in competitions because I was fulfilling God's will. I reasoned if God told me to do this, then he would be cool with my missing church once or twice a month, right?

I doubted I could convince Emma to allow me to continue with autocross on Sundays because she wanted a much deeper commitment from me than three or four Sundays out of a month. For me, autocross had become a religion, much like any fan or participant who develops a passion for their sport of choice, like Dad with tennis. The prospect of losing it to be with this woman gave me pause. And yet, I found Emma's desire for me to be faithful to her and God appealing, knowing she would be loving and devoted to me if I accepted her terms.

"Okay, I'll do it. I'll attend church and study the Bible with you," I said.

"Really?"

"Really," I said as she showered me with kisses. It wasn't the response I was expecting, but I wasn't complaining.

"However ..."

"Yes?" Uh-oh. Now what?

"I am adamantly against pre-marital sex. I do admit, though, not having sex is torture for me," she said with a disconcerting frown.

It was good I didn't have a problem with being chaste. I hadn't been with anyone in years because I only wanted to be with someone who cared for me as much as I cared for them. Emma's wish to marry me as a God-fearing Christian made remaining chaste with her until marriage a no-brainer in my book. Still, two 30-somethings not having sex in a city known for its loose morals sounded like a recipe for a bad comedy.

"I reject five guys a week, but I prefer being with you," she confessed.

"Aw," I replied in a deliberate attempt to avoid revealing how attracted

I was to her.

"Do you realize we haven't been on a real date yet?" she asked.

"What do you mean?"

"You know, the kind where I dress up cute and we go somewhere."

"How cute?" I asked, excited by the thought of Emma dressing up for me.

"As cute as you want," she growled as she leaned in for a kiss.

Needless to say, it took me a few hours to get out of her place that night.

On our next night together, an evening of driving around town to find secluded spots to watch the evening sky as we chatted about whatever came to mind, Emma stopped me from kissing her goodnight after I parked in front of her apartment.

"Wait. I want to know you better before we move forward with this."

"Oh?" I said, both surprised and disappointed at not having the opportunity to enjoy her soft, moist lips.

"I have been torn between our recent physical intimacy and my desire for more verbal interaction."

"Okaaaaay." So, all those hours of us talking with each other these past few weeks didn't matter? I was confused.

To appease her worry, I spent the rest of the evening asking her questions about her family, what she was like growing up, and what she enjoyed about music and LA, all of which she answered.

"Thank you for tonight. This meant a lot to me," she said.

Breathing a sigh of relief, I hoped as long as we kept our lines of communication open, we could work all our conflicts out.

It was a couple of weeks before we saw each other again because I was either tired from work or Emma was sick with a cold. While looking for a spot to watch the sunset, we were drawn in like moths to a flame by the sound of big band music floating through the air. We ended up at a free outdoor community jazz concert not too far from where she lived, and for the next hour, we danced in our seats to the upbeat tempos of compositions by Benny Goodman, Duke Ellington, and Artie Shaw.

After the concert, we returned to the intimacy of my two-seat roadster instead of going back to her place. We sat there enveloped in darkness and gazed up in awe at the night sky.

"Amazing, huh?" I said with wonder.

"Yes, God did an amazing job creating all this."

"But what are we supposed to do with it?"

"Whatever he wants. Being in the service of God is the greatest gift we can give him for giving us the gift of life."

"But what does that mean exactly?"

"It means all you have to do is listen and he will tell you what he wants when the time comes. You just have to be ready for it."

She made it sound so simple, but thinking back to the prayer room at Auntie B's left me doubting I would hear what Emma could hear.

"What do you think of porn?" Emma asked as we were lying together on her couch the next time we saw each other. "Any guy who marries me has to give up porn because I want it totally abolished, and there is no way I'll have it in my house."

Thinking back to my experience at the sperm bank and my friend Carrie, I could see porn has its place in the world. Despite its problems—prostitution, human trafficking, sex slavery, and addiction—it is still a product of human nature and desires. Porn may be objectionable, but it exists because there is demand for it and to destroy it is to deny something primal to our very being. At least that's what I thought about saying. What came out of my mouth was a tentative "okay," which Emma didn't like at all.

Though Emma's anti-porn stance was admirable, I found her idealism suffocating. I didn't like she didn't trust adults to make their own decisions on how to express themselves sexually, instead wanting to impose her own narrow beliefs and controls on them by eliminating porn altogether.

At the end of the evening, Emma shot me a look of disdain when I went in for a kiss, putting her hand up to stop me. "I'm worried you only think of me physically."

I found it an odd thing to say considering the lengthy conversations we had been having.

"I want you to tell me why you like me beyond the physical part."

"I like that you're a woman of faith. I like that you're a musician. I like that you're passionate about church. I like that you're modest. I like that you throw yourself into your interests. I like that you're dedicated and determined. I like that you took the risk of moving here. I like YOU and being physically attracted to you is icing on the cake."

"Thank you, I needed that," she said as she gave me a goodnight kiss, clearing my head of all doubt and worry over Emma's line of questioning.

Emma invited me over to her church one Sunday in an attempt at incorporating me more into her life. Emma had said nothing but good things about her church, and I wanted to experience this goodness myself. After all, if this was a person I was considering spending the rest of my life and having kids with, then I should see firsthand what I was getting myself into.

As usual, Emma was running late and I had arrived early. Her church was a small congregation where everyone knew each other, so I immediately stood out when I approached the entrance of the small A-frame building.

"How did you find us?" the well-dressed greeters asked.

I wasn't sure how to answer, so I made up something. "Oh, I'm here meeting my girlfriend." It wasn't far from the truth, and I didn't see any harm in calling Emma my girlfriend. After all, we had been going out for a couple of months and talking about getting married.

"Hm. Who is it? There aren't many single girls here we know of."

Thinking it was none of their business, I walked back to my car without answering, then cursed myself for not waiting for Emma before going in. When Emma arrived, we went in together, holding hands as we did. As we sat down in a back pew, I recounted my experience with the greeters, but she was too absorbed in getting mentally ready for the service to pay much attention. I took it as a sign things were still going well between us. Our holding hands through the service was another good sign.

After the service, we went out for coffee and met up with a couple members of the congregation Emma knew.

"What did you think, Leonard?" Emma asked.

"Your church is very different. Much more serious than the Episcopal church I attended."

"Fascinating. Serious how?"

"Well, our sermons are more down-to-earth and the priests try to relate Bible passages with what's going on in today's world. This was a more strict interpretation of the Bible as the word of God."

"I guess we are a serious congregation. Many of the attendees are in seminary."

I didn't know what that meant, but smiled and nodded in agreement, though I couldn't escape the idea I was in way over my head.

The following day, Emma's name popped up on my Caller ID just as I arrived home from work. Instead of the sweet-sounding Emma I had been going out with the past couple of months, I heard something else.

"I am freaking out right now," she said, her voice shaky and distraught. "I can't believe you called me your girlfriend, especially to my friends at church. I want to just be friends. No kissing. No cuddling. No more physical closeness. Nothing."

I couldn't believe what I was hearing. Two days before, she wanted me to move with her to her hometown. Now, she wanted space. Lots of it. And because I had called her my girlfriend? I couldn't believe a single wrong word was enough to derail our relationship.

I didn't contact her for 10 days in hopes she would come to her senses. When I reached out to her, Emma and I agreed to meet up at a busy shopping center whose architecture looked as if it was taken from a movie set in a small Midwestern town. I wasn't sure what to expect from her. Was she going to yell and scream at me or were we going to kiss and make up? Expecting the worst, I steeled myself just in case. I didn't want this meeting to turn into a scene in a public space.

When I found her among the shoppers milling about the central plaza, we gave each other a long, loving embrace, then both apologized before descending into gentle caresses and affectionate petting. Holding her in my arms again, I got the sense we were back on track.

"I want to have kids with you, but I'm not ready for a serious relationship," Emma told me five weeks of dating later while lying on the hillside grass near the old LA Zoo as the afternoon light gave way to twilight. She was in a summer dress and I was dressed in a T-shirt and jeans. Emma would make a good mother because of her thoughtfulness, but I didn't know what to make of her not being ready for getting serious. Like Jimmy telling us we should read the Bible though we didn't have to, I wasn't sure how to reconcile the two contradictory thoughts. I considered this while watching the nearby carousel close its gates for the day.

As the sun faded away from view, we drove over to Griffith Observatory where we walked over to the observation telescopes and embraced each other while gazing across the city lights to the horizon. I was enjoying holding her in my arms when she inexplicably pulled away from our embrace after a billboard caught her eye.

"I want to end all objectification of women," she said with resolve.

I looked over at the billboard she was looking at featuring a scantily clad woman holding a wine glass but wasn't as affected by it as Emma was. Was it because sex sells had been ingrained in me for as long as I could remember or that I didn't see anything wrong because I was the target audience? I couldn't tell either way.

"The sooner we end this type of exploitation, the better."

I felt stupid for not comprehending what she was talking about because I lacked her perspective.

"It bothers you that much, huh?" I said after a long silence.

"Yes, it does. It's like I'm being called to this fight."

Whatever it was that was calling to her, wasn't calling me.

Over the next couple of weeks, instead of spending time with me, Emma attended dinners with friends in addition to seminars on human trafficking and how it related to prostitution and sex slavery. She wanted this idea of helping women overcome unequal treatment in a male-dominated world to become her lifelong passion, her objections to being thought of as a sex object bubbling over into crusade territory. For the next several days, she pushed me out of her life even though I expressed support for her decision to pursue this passion.

The next time I saw her was in the warmth of her apartment.

We were cuddling on her couch watching television when Emma pulled away from me without averting her gaze.

"I have always felt Jesus's presence right at my side my entire life," she confessed in a serious manner.

I was tempted to make light of the situation by looking around the room for Jesus but thought better of it as she observed me with those penetrating blue eyes of hers. I could see by her serious countenance this was a big deal for her. I thought about telling her I could sense his presence too, but I was too dumbfounded to say much of anything. It worried me she was referring to Jesus as if he were an imaginary childhood friend she never grew out of.

Judging from the disappointment on her face, I didn't hide those thoughts well.

On the way home, several questions came to mind. Did I want to be with someone who was in a hurry to get married, yet offended over being called my girlfriend? Did I want to be with a feminist who held such narrow views on sex? Did I want to be with someone who wanted me to give up autocross Sundays for attending church and reading the Bible? Did I want to be with someone who believed an invisible being walked beside her, guiding her at all times? The answer to all of my questions was a no-brainer.

The next time I saw Emma at her place, I walked up to her and, instead of giving her a loving embrace, then coming inside with her, as she was expecting, I kept my distance.

"I care deeply for you, but I think it would be better if we don't get together anymore," I told her as we stood outdoors in the dark.

"I like you very much, too, but we can never be together," she replied.

With that, I turned and walked back to my car and made the long drive home. There was no way I was going to leave behind my skepticism for Christianity, even for someone I liked as much as Emma.

A few days later, Emma sent me an e-mail. "I don't know how to move our relationship forward anymore," she said. I wasn't sure if she meant a friendship or romance. Part of me was hoping we could work out our differences and begin moving forward again because our relationship had so much promise in the beginning. I didn't see her again until she showed up dancing the following week.

After LindyGroove closed for the evening, we went over to her place for a talk. When we arrived, she chose to remain in the claustrophobic confines of my two-seat roadster. It was nice to get a chance to talk with her again, but I wasn't sure what we hoped to accomplish without her seeing how important it was for me to hold my own beliefs and her being willing to compromise. Sitting there, I watched her in the darkness, her eyes staring off into the distance.

"I want my future mate to be a hardcore Christian missionary and won't accept anything less than that," she declared to the windshield.

I sat there unable to respond as the weight of her words sunk in. Though the idea of helping others was appealing, I couldn't see myself spreading the word of Christ when I wasn't sold on the concept of Christianity. Emma's hard line on her mate being a Christian ensured there would be no negotiations, compromise, or reconciliation between us.

Return to Church

Needing something to fall back on for emotional support after the end of my romantic relationship with Emma, the longevity and stability of church was the obvious choice, just as Jimmy said. I decided my mental approach to church had been wrong and to give it a second chance. After all, there must be something to this obedience to the Great Unknowable. If someone I respected like Matthew could follow God's will through religious worship, then so could I. Knowing my return to the Episcopal church would help me continue on my path to eternal salvation and the road to a better afterlife in heaven with God gave me confidence.

While I was rediscovering church, my mother was becoming involved with a Catholic church near her home in Hawaii. She spent every day praying the rosary, singing in the choir, and developing friendships she would not have otherwise. I was happy she had discovered a community she could call her own. We had talked of her moving to LA several times, but stopped after her simple, quiet demeanor and desire to be with me kept clashing with my need for independence.

When I went to visit Mom in late 2009, she took me to attend a service at her church, which took place in a plain-looking brick structure that could have easily been mistaken for a business office. We entered the building and seated ourselves in a pair of folding chairs in the back of the large auditorium. I observed most of the parishioners in attendance were of Asian or Hawaiian descent with many dressed in their Sunday best.

Without a handout to follow, I was struck by how everyone knew the hour-long service by rote. I found the service distancing and mechanical because everyone stood up, sang, recited prayers, sat down, and knelt on cue. I kept worrying I was doing everything at the wrong moments, embarrassing my mother in front of all her friends. Then came the communion, where those who have accepted Christ as their savior become one with him by eating his body and blood.

"You can't go up for communion. You're not Catholic anymore," Mom whispered with gentle outrage.

"What are you talking about? That's crazy. Even though I don't attend a Catholic church, I'm still a baptized Catholic."

With that, she relented and I went up and had my body and blood of Christ, not knowing I was being disrespectful of the Church.

My experience at Mom's church forced me to reflect on how much my time at the Episcopal church was spent listening to the same service over and over again with the only differences being the sermons, readings, and hymns. In total, maybe a fourth of the service was different from week to week. The rest was a reinforcement of our covenant with God. The only thing I found inspiring at the services was the sermon. Yet the message was always the same—be nice and obey God's commandments, and you will help both you and those you know attain everything you desire and go to heaven. I was glad I had autocross on Sundays two to three times a month to break the monotony of it all.

Every now and then during the Episcopal church service, I would stop, look around, and watch the congregation go through the motions of standing, sitting, kneeling, standing, the exchange of handshakes and peaceful greetings with our neighbors, and taking communion followed by more standing and sitting. It was an odd ritual to perform every week as followers of a god who demanded our love and attention because we were his creation. I didn't like how I would go back to my regular life after each service and forget what was said.

After services, I had a routine as well. Go outside and hang out for a bit, complain or compliment the weather then thank God either way, say my hellos to people I saw for five minutes out of a week, then catch up on everyone's latest gossip before returning to my apartment. Occasionally, the 20s/30s group who made it to church, and there weren't many who did, would go out for lunch afterward. I enjoyed the lunches because it was time spent with friends.

As the months wore on, I couldn't escape the nagging thought I had made a terrible decision by settling for the Episcopal church because I was never challenged to do much other than say I believed in a higher power for the chance at an afterlife in heaven. I found myself wanting more thoughtful discussions on religion and spirituality, like the ones I had in Alpha, but I was too content with the status quo of hanging out with my church friends to do much about it.

The Great Pumpkin

Art Show

"Sorry, I couldn't make it last Saturday. How did it go?" I asked Caleb. He was a tall, lanky pale young man in his late 20s who strived to make the world a happier place through fun-filled public improv performances. We were having lunch one day in early 2010 at the Subway near the satellite television company where we were working. I found freelance work there as a production artist through a former coworker after losing my job in advertising because of The Great Recession of 2008. This job allowed me to pay the bills and continue my cancer surveillance uninterrupted. With nothing but all clear results, monthly checkups had given way to semi-annual checkups.

"It went well, man. Everyone was laughing and had a good time." Caleb had invited me to a public improv performance he was doing based on a famous board game. "How was your Sunday?"

"Good. Relaxing. I didn't do much."

"Do you go to church?"

"No."

"Why not?"

"I'm not sure I should say."

"Go on, you're in a safe place. I won't judge you."

I hadn't talked about my issues with church with anyone since dating Emma, but Caleb's request didn't raise any mental alarm bells.

"I used to attend an Episcopal church but didn't like the direction the services were going after a new priest came in. I do believe in a higher power, but not the way it's presented in the Bible. I thought about going into Catholicism, but I don't like how Mary is worshiped as if she were a god herself."

"I understand. Yeah, that can be difficult."

I listened for judgment in his voice and facial expression but found none.

"Listen, you're pretty open-minded and sound like a good person. Have you considered Mormonism? I think you would be a good fit with the community." There was an earnestness to his voice I found appealing.

"I don't know much about it, but if you think so, I don't see why not." I only had a vague familiarity with Mormonism from a couple of female friends who identified themselves as Mormon. My other exposure to Mormonism was a neglected copy of the *Book of Mormon* given to me by missionaries at my apartment door years ago. It was sitting on my bookshelf next to copies of the King James and New Revised Standard Versions of the Bible.

"Well, we're having a mid-singles conference in April. It's a big matchmaking event for eligible men and women from the ages of 27 to 40. It would be great if you could come."

It sounded like a good opportunity to meet single women close to my age who were marriage minded.

"When in April?"

"The weekend of the 23rd."

"I can't. That's my birthday weekend." I didn't like the idea of spending it with strangers, even if it was an opportunity to meet single women.

"It's okay. Don't worry about it. There will be other opportunities. I'll let you know."

"Okay, thanks."

Several months later, Caleb invited me to display work for an underground art show for those who do art as a hobby. I brought the third compilation of my webcomic because it was the project that helped me pass the time away while waiting for doctors during my first weeks of cancer surveillance.

The presentation space for the show was a long, narrow pedestrian tunnel that ran underneath a boulevard east of the 405. Above ground, the only way you knew the tunnel existed was from the green iron railings marking the stairwell on either side of the eight-lane street. Spanning the entire length of the concrete tunnel was a colorful abstract mural, which was painted on both sides. The tunnel was lit with overhead fluorescent lights that gave off a pale bluish color, hardly the best way to show off artwork.

Before the show started, I browsed the many pieces on display while the artists put them up on the walls. Most of the art consisted of paintings and photographs. Caleb accommodated my work by bringing over a small, round table. We placed a couple books on it so several people could view them at once.

"Did you bring any books to sell?" he asked with an equal dose of concern and curiosity.

"Um, no. Should I have?" I hadn't given it much thought.

"Yes, this would have been the perfect spot for it."

I shrugged. It was too late to go home and pick up more copies. Besides, I was more excited to have people look at my work again than making money from it as I had done at San Diego Comic-Con years ago. To be honest, I hadn't expected much other than the experience of being in a show. Plus, it would be a good opportunity to practice my social skills and maybe get an e-mail address or two.

I suspected most of the artists and attendees were Mormon, though I didn't know what the difference was between Mormons and Christians. Everyone was friendly enough, but finding anyone with whom I could engage beyond small talk about the artwork proved difficult. Just as I worried I wasn't trying hard enough to meet someone, I caught sight of a petite blue-eyed redhead who greeted her posse with a combination of high fives and a bewildering array of fist bumps and secret handshakes. When her friend who had been reading my book introduced us, Zoe was surprisingly accessible in the friendly way she extended her hand to greet me with her shoulders cutely bunched up and head adorably tilted when she smiled.

An hour later, I caught sight of Zoe standing against the wall looking small and frail, almost lost, much different from the confident young woman who happily bounded in earlier. I could tell she had been crying because her eyeshadow had run a little, but I thought it better not to ask why because I didn't want to upset her more.

"Hi, Zoe," I said as I cautiously approached her, making sure to call her by her name.

"Hi. Leonard, right?"

"Yes. Good memory."

"Are you LDS?" she asked, narrowing her eyes in a stand-offish manner. Luckily, I knew LDS was short for the Church of Jesus Christ of Latter-day Saints, the official name for the Mormon church.

"No," I said, shaking my head. I knew enough not to fake it.

"Do you have any passions?" she asked. "I like to learn about people's passions because it says a lot about them."

Hm. This was more direct than the usual small talk I encountered.

"I race cars."

It may not have been completely true, but it was an easy way to describe autocross without overwhelming her with detail.

"Sounds dangerous," she said with a raised eyebrow.

"Well, it's not wheel-to-wheel racing with other cars on a track, it's one car at a time on a closed course. Speeds are no faster than on a typical highway." I wasn't sure if I had her convinced.

"That sounds safer, but I don't want to have to worry about you, Leonard," she replied with a look of concern.

"Aw, that's sweet," I said. "It's nice to know you care."

She blushed.

"Any other dangerous passions I should know about?" she asked, again raising an eyebrow.

"No, but I go swing dancing once or twice a week."

"Ooo … I love ballroom dancing! Foxtrot and tango are my favorites, though I like swing too. I wish I had the time to do them now," she said. It was good to see her light up after looking so maudlin moments before.

"Tango is a beautiful dance. I took two years of Argentine tango lessons," I replied. Like Zoe, I didn't have the time.

"I agree, it's very pretty. I would love to do it again someday."

The sadness in her voice had me wondering if she had fallen for someone who could dance at some point.

"What about you? Any passions I should know about?" I asked.

"I used to be a standup comedian."

I was impressed she had the guts to get up on stage and put her humor out there for a live audience.

"Why did you quit? Too difficult?"

"Too lonely. It's a lot of long hours of traveling by yourself," she said with a big sigh.

"I hadn't thought of that." I could see her traveling from gig to gig, at first excited and thrilled at performing before a live audience, then the long hours on the road away from friends and family taking their toll.

"What comics do you read?" she asked. "You must read some since you do your own."

I rattled off names of online and newspaper comics I liked, both new and old: *Bloom County*, *Calvin and Hobbes*, *Peanuts*, *Narbonic*, and *Pearls Before Swine*. "You?"

"I read a lot of manga and watch anime. I used to be a big *Sailor Moon* fan when I was young. Do you watch any anime?"

"I used to back in college, but not anymore. I love Hayao Miyazaki's work, but I know some don't consider his work traditional anime." It may not have been an exact match in interests between us, but it was close enough. "Do you have a favorite movie?"

"I LOVE *The Lord of the Rings* trilogy. My family spends every Thanksgiving watching the entire trilogy from start to finish," she said, fond memories widening her grin.

"The regular theatrical or special extended editions?"

"The extended editions, of course," she replied, coming across like the true nerd I hoped she was. "We go all out and dress up, too."

I gasped at the thought of her whole family excited to be dressing in costume. It sounded so much fun. "Wait, you've been watching the entire LOTR trilogy as a Thanksgiving tradition for years and didn't invite me? What's wrong with you?"

"I didn't know you," she said with a laugh and look of disbelief.

"Well, you do now. So, no excuses."

She blushed, then leaned in and whispered into my ear. "Can you keep a secret? I only tell people I like this."

"Yes, of course," I whispered back. How could I not keep a secret for this charming young woman?

"I do modeling and perform in costume for an acting troupe to entertain guys."

I didn't find either secret scandalous and wasn't sure why they were secrets in the first place, but was glad she shared a secret with me. For the acting troupe, she would dress in frilly outfits and perform on stage for a male audience, then sit and chat with the guys while playing board games. From the way she described it, it sounded like an innocent version of Carrie's escort experience.

The more we talked, the more I kept her off balance in our conversation, causing her to blush and laugh several more times, a good thing in my book. I knew she was out of college, but she looked young. I pegged her for being 25, which was younger than my preferred dating age of at least 30 and just below the unwritten dating rule of half my age plus seven.

"Can I have your e-mail address? I'd like to talk to you more." There was no way I was going to leave without staying in touch with Zoe. I hadn't had a first conversation go that well in years and understood how rare they were.

"Yes, I'd like that." She looked as if she meant it.

She then left with her friends to see a movie with an hour left in the show, giving me an opportunity to look for her piece. When I discovered it on the other end of the tunnel, I found myself staring at an anime-styled body profile she painted of herself in a faceplant pose. The untitled piece could have easily been titled "Failure."

First Date

It took two days for Zoe to add me as a friend on Facebook. I accepted her friend request and found through her Facebook page that, yes, she was 25 as I had thought, and yes, she was single. Part of me didn't want to ask her out based on my previous dating experiences with younger women. I waited a day to give myself a chance to come to my senses before sending a reply, telling her she didn't give me a chance to forget her e-mail address and asked if she wanted to go out. She said yes.

I was a couple of minutes late arriving for our first date at a mall food court near her apartment, and just as I started texting her, she came up to me talking in a blur. Lucky for me, it was dark and she couldn't see how clueless I looked over not being able to keep up with what she was saying. After I acclimated to her fast-talking style, we picked up food at a Ramen noodle place. Once we finished dinner, we wandered through various stores at the mall.

"When I was a kid, my family would eat together and recite Shakespeare at the dinner table," she said. "What were your dinners like growing up?"

"Wow, we just ate in silence with the TV on in the background." Her upbringing sounded much more intelligent and thought out than mine.

"That sounds more normal. Do you like Shakespeare?"

"You're probably going to laugh, but it was my worst subject when I was majoring in English lit."

"I understand. Shakespeare can be difficult for a lot of people."

"What's your favorite book?" I asked.

"Jane Austen's *Pride and Prejudice*. Have you ever read it?"

"I was able to get a third of the way through but found Austen's writing tedious. Have you read *Pride and Prejudice and Zombies*?"

"Oo, I want to read that. Is it any good?"

"I like it because every time the book got boring, which was a lot of times, a zombie would liven up the story. I'll let you borrow it next time I see you." Throwing that out there gave me a reason to see her again.

"That would be great, I'd love to read it!" she said with enthusiasm.

"Do you think you'd ever be able to date a zombie?" I asked, following a train of thought.

"I don't know, I never met one."

"How about vampires?"

"Again, never met one, but they do sound intriguing," she said playfully.

"Ever watch any horror films?" I asked.

"I try to avoid them. Especially R-rated ones."

"Why?" I sensed a strong willingness to stay innocent despite her playful attitude.

"I don't like them because I get emotionally attached to the characters. Too emotional, really. Do you like R-rated films?"

"I do. The first one I ever saw was *Halloween,* a slasher flick from the late '70s. I was six years old."

"You were six?!?"

"Yes, my neighbor took me and her kids to see it. I spent the entire movie scared to death hiding behind her. It took me 10 years to get over the trauma and watch it again."

"That's horrible."

"It's not so bad now."

"Well, I'm glad you got over it, but I could never watch a movie like that." Hearing her say that bummed me out because it meant we would never sit down and watch my favorite R-rated films, like Martin Scorcese's epic gangster drama *Goodfellas* or the virtual science-fiction adventure of *The Matrix.*

"What's your favorite book?" she asked.

"*100 Years of Solitude* by Gabriel García Márquez. I love it for its scope, sweep, and language."

"What are you reading now?"

"Anthony Burgess' *A Clockwork Orange.*"

"What's it about?" Having just gotten out of a conversation on how she couldn't watch R-rated films had me wondering if I should talk about the violent adventures of gangster Alex and his droogies that included everything from breaking and entering to rape and murder but also Alex's redemption through rehabilitation.

"I don't know if I should talk about it. You might think less of me."

"Try me." There was an earnest curiosity to her I found attractive. How could I not tell her? So, I obliged her request. She listened intently without saying a word.

"Do you like this book?"

"Yes, I like it so far. I find its use of language interesting because it's a combination of several different languages all at once."

"That does sound interesting."

Her comment surprised me because it lacked any sort of judgment to it. There was a long pause in our conversation as we walked in and out of several stores. What could she be thinking?

"I know how old you are," she said after several minutes of silence.

"Oh?" I said as I cringed from what sounded like an accusation. Was she going to dismiss me because of my age after such a solid beginning?

"Yeah, I figured it out myself after seeing the photos you posted of your 20-year high school reunion on your Facebook page. I'm smart that way," she said with a wink. She was such a flirt. "You're older than I normally date, but I wanted to go out with you because I was so impressed with the manly way you asked me out."

Manly? That was a new one. Nobody had ever called me manly before. Regardless, I was glad the age difference didn't bother her. The more we talked, the more I found her attractive, fun, and witty, but there were downsides.

"I want to die of Type 2 diabetes," she declared with pride at one point.

"Why on earth would you want that?" I asked. I was incredulous anyone would wish anything so horrible on themselves. I was hoping she was kidding. After all, she did say she was a stand-up comedian.

"Because it means I would die happy from eating desserts."

I knew she was trying to be funny, but I wasn't thrilled to hear such a morbid thought. After my bout with cancer, I didn't consider major diseases to be fun or happy times.

Another trait I didn't care for was her self-deprecation. She didn't like her own artwork despite her drawing skills, which were better developed than mine at her age. I would have been proud to have her skill at 25.

"By the way, I keep a dating blog," she said.

"Um ..." I replied, unsure how to respond. I didn't know whether she was telling me this because she wanted me to see it or warning me not to do anything stupid. Knowing she wrote about her dating experiences in a public forum made me nervous because it meant my actions were put under the microscope without my having a chance to respond to any compliments or criticisms.

"Don't worry. I have written nothing but positive things about you," she said in an attempt to put me at ease.

She continued on with tales of horrible dating experiences with unenlightened suitors, including one who wanted to get married after their first date. From what she was telling me, she had this way of attracting clueless bad boys that had me question why she was out with me since I wasn't the type of guy she normally dated.

She said she was busy on weekends, which made me cautious because she may have been already seeing someone else on those nights. Not that years in the dating scene had made me paranoid or anything.

"You're doing very well, by the way," she said with a smile, tilting her head as she did.

"What do you mean?"

"Dating. Us. Together. Tonight."

I was relieved to hear her say that though it was more forward than I was expecting.

I escorted her back to her car, unsure if I wanted to get involved with her. She was so ... different. Different in the refreshing, confident way she exuded charm and grace while at the same time innocent with a hint of naughtiness. When we arrived at her car, she used her car door as a physical barrier between us, preventing me from touching her. I wasn't sure if she did that on purpose, but I was okay with no kissing on the first date. If anything, it gave me the incentive to ask her for a second date. When she finished her stories for the night, she closed the door and gave me a goodbye hug as we promised to see each other again.

Toast

On our second date, Zoe and I had dinner at the Farmer's Market, then took a walk through various shops at The Grove before stopping at the small park located on the east side of the complex. We found a park bench and sat next to each other, admiring the Christmas lights hanging overhead.

"I found your YouTube channel," I said after we took a seat. The channel contained fan videos of cartoons she enjoyed growing up.

"Please don't look at those again," she said as she blushed. "I was young when I made them."

I found it funny she made five years sound like ancient history.

She bombarded me with questions about my interests in books and movies through the night, much as we did on our first date, and not wanting to reveal too much too soon, I held back on answering them all to save some conversation for possible future dates.

"I like that you have good diction," she said. "It's charming the way you stumble when you speak. You come across as introverted but confident."

Someone who likes the way I speak, finds me charming, and doesn't mind I'm an introvert? What lottery had I won to deserve the presence of someone who could deliver such a sharply observant compliment without a trace of cynicism? I put my arm around her to show I liked her. She pulled in close then laid her head on my shoulder. That tender gesture was enough to clear my thoughts of all my troubles.

"You smell good to me," I said as I took in her scent.

"And you to me," she replied.

After a while, we shifted to cuddling with each other and tenderly put our hands together to compare them. "I like your hands. They have an elegant shape to them," she said while intertwining our fingers together so we could hold hands. It was nice to be physically close with someone again. It was nicer because we were getting along so well. I kept expecting her to push me away and tell me how boring or stupid I was, but it didn't happen.

"I don't like going to clubs," she said. "I prefer the company of books, video games, movies, and TV shows."

There was a sad loneliness in her echoing my own that made me like her even more. I was going to give her a kiss at the end of the night, but she bolted out of my car as soon as I came to a stop at her place. I couldn't tell if she was playing hard to get or not interested.

"She really impressed me," I told Christa over the phone the next day.

"Is she cute?" Christa asked.

I sighed.

"You're toast," Christa said with a mischievous laugh.

Weeks passed as Zoe canceled out a couple of times and we kept moving our next date back. At one point on her Facebook status, she hinted at another guy she had been with, and I found myself pulling back emotionally to avoid getting hurt, though we did have a good Facebook chat a couple of days later. My curiosity over her religion had me do a Google search on Mormons dating non-Mormons, which led me into more reading up on Mormonism in general. I didn't like what I found.

Mormonism

A couple of months after Caleb left the satellite television company, Caleb's friend Calvin was brought in as an art director temp to take Caleb's place. A former tattoo artist, Calvin cast an imposing shadow with his great height and build, though he spoke softly with a lighthearted laugh that hinted a painful past. He had several tattoos left over from his days as a tattoo artist, which could be seen when he wore the occasional T-shirt. We got to know each other while shooting pool on our lunch breaks in the company's downstairs game room.

Calvin had an alcoholic father, like me, and became addicted to drugs, unlike me. His former career choice as a tattoo artist then brought him into a questionable lifestyle and crowd. When he dropped out of the tattoo artist's life, all his friends associated with it abandoned him. After that, he converted to Mormonism and married a Mormon. He was now a clean, sober, and happy family man. I was intrigued by how much of a positive influence the religion had on him and decided it warranted further study.

My first investigations into Mormonism were innocent enough because I was learning how to date a Mormon woman without scaring her away. The rules were no different from dating any nice, conservative religious woman you wouldn't mind bringing home to Mom, date, marry, and have a family with. My experience with dating Emma was going to be a lot of help here. At the very least, it would be a nice time with a pretty, intelligent woman.

So, I did more digging into Mormonism to see if Caleb was right about my being a good fit. As an English literature scholar, I was always more fascinated by negative criticism first and worked from there when researching papers. My initial exposure into the inner workings of the religion Joseph Smith founded in the early 1800s was *Exmormon.org*, which contained stories of those who had left the Church of Jesus Christ of Latter-day Saints and who were recovering from their former lives as keepers of the faith. It probably wasn't the best place to start, especially when you're trying to date a true-believing Mormon.

Reading up on marriage and kids, I learned Mormons aspired to get married in the temple where they are sealed to their Mormon spouses for eternity. Kids were seen as and taught to be children of God, sent down from heaven to live as human beings. Women were viewed as holy vessels for these holy children. Any knowledge gathered in our world transferred with Mormons to the afterlife. Therefore, the more talents, skills, and knowledge acquired, the better prepared a person would be for their second life. I found all this appealing because it gave meaning and purpose to marriage, having kids, and getting a good education.

Mormons also believe in the baptism of the dead, where you can have someone baptized after they have died so they can join the rest of their friends and family in Mormon heaven. Though the concept of family togetherness both here on earth and in the afterlife was a positive aspect, I didn't like how the living could be so selfish as to presume the dead would want to be baptized Mormon in the first place. I can only imagine the surprise and shock of a Mormon family's favorite atheist great-grandfather when suddenly appearing in Mormon heaven after being baptized.

Reading more on Mormon ceremonies, I found the wedding ceremonies were full of secrets, like handshakes and passwords, which have been purposefully hidden from temple-unworthy Mormons and potential converts. I found this to be in direct conflict with the *Book of Mormon* itself because there are several references to how secrets are the devil's handiwork. Contradictions like these made me cringe. Perhaps details of the Mormon faith could have used a good editor before going to print.

From my reading, the main objective for Mormons was to earn your way into the celestial kingdom, the highest of their three heavens. Mormon men earn their way into the celestial kingdom by being married and sealed in the temple, paying their full tithe, performing the good works assigned by revelation from God, and obeying all of God's commandments. The rewards for men achieving the celestial kingdom included being close to God and becoming like a god of their own planet while being sealed with their family forever and allowed plural wives. The oddest part was Doctrine 137 of their own *Doctrine and Covenants*, one of the sacred texts in LDS theology, states you don't need knowledge of the celestial kingdom to reach it, negating all the rules previously stated, even the need to be a Mormon first.

The whole idea of becoming a god of my own world wasn't much of an incentive for me. The experience of playing LucasArts' *Afterlife*, a computer simulation game made from the *SimCity 2000* game engine, was too close to being a near-god. My problem was I got tired of having to micromanage an entire world praying to me all the time. Answering all those prayers, dealing with souls, and controlling the fates of every living being was a tiring business. Who needs that? Definitely not I.

"Nobody likes being fooled. Nobody," Calvin said after he told me how he didn't dwell on the details in Mormonism because they brought doubts. In fact, he didn't want to think about the contradictions at all. He believed the revelations he received from the Holy Ghost were proof enough Mormonism was true. He told me, "We don't know what's beyond death except what is revealed by divine revelation."

In my opinion, divine revelation as a means of obtaining answers for this life or an afterlife can be dangerous because it isn't based on anything other than a feeling. Any Mormon could have a revelation the LDS Church had strayed from the *Book of Mormon* and gone off and started their own fundamentalist offshoot. Smith must have seen this problem early on because in *Doctrine & Covenants* he declared only the president of the Church has the right to receive revelations directly from God. Not everyone got the message, hence all the Mormon fundamentalist groups in existence, including many that, unlike the mainstream LDS church, still practice polygamy, which allows men to have more than one wife.

Jon Krakauer's *Under the Banner of Heaven* told the case of one such fundamentalist LDS group where two brothers murdered their younger brother's wife and child because the brothers had a revelation from God saying to do it. I couldn't think of any instance where a mainstream Mormon would approve of the brothers' interpretation of the revelations they received, but it did show how revelation could be twisted to an individual's desires. After all, who would go against God's will if they believed they were speaking directly to God?

Also mentioned in Krakauer's book was the Mark Hoffman case. As recently as the early '80s, Hoffman sold many forged documents to the LDS Church relating to the history of Mormonism. Though these documents were later found to be forgeries by third parties, why wasn't the Church warned of the true nature of these documents by a revelation from God? Did God turn a blind eye to the one, true church and allow them to spend millions of dollars on fake documents? For an organization that marketed itself as having all the answers to God's plan, this must have been an embarrassment for them.

After talking about how much I liked Zoe, Calvin joked I was going to convert to Mormonism. "You could learn a lot from a good woman like her," he said with a huge grin on his face.

"I'm not converting."

"Why not?" he asked, narrowing his eyes and deepening his voice as his grin disappeared.

We ended up getting into an argument over the differences between Mormonism and Christianity in interpreting biblical scripture. While Mormons believe in Jesus Christ, it is not the Jesus Christ of the Bible I was used to in the Episcopal and Catholic churches because the ideas and stories presented by Mormonism ran counter to the biblical concepts I had learned.

Calvin defended his faith by telling me the name of the church was The Church of Jesus Christ of Latter-day Saints and that alone was indicative enough of its adherence to the teachings of the one, true Jesus Christ. By that logic, Calvin could change his name to Jesus Christ and the church would be all about the one, true him.

He then gave me the standard Mormon line of how they study the Bible as it is "translated correctly," which I found odd because the LDS Church has never done its own official translation of the Bible from the original Hebrew, Aramaic, and Greek. It still relies on the antiquated King James Version, considered by modern scholars the least accurate of the popular translations. During the course of our discussion, he didn't like my aggressive, critical tone and believed I was attacking his religion when I was only trying to satisfy my curiosity and have my questions answered.

"You'd better figure out what you want out of this girl and quick," he warned. I was none too happy with his uncompromising words of warning.

As someone with a personal history of not believing in heaven, hell, original sin, and Jesus Christ as savior, I found myself having major difficulties swallowing the pill that was Mormonism. Not only was it completely different from any depictions of Christ I had encountered previously, but it also ran counter to any sort of science-based reality I knew. Although odd to outsiders, Mormonism had worth because of the healthy relationships it fostered between family and friends with similar beliefs. Mormonism, like all religions, was true for its believers because of the benefit of being around a community of like-minded people.

The Shadow

On our third date, I took Zoe to a restaurant I had never been to before that Christa's husband Frank recommended. He liked finding nice restaurants for him and Christa to dine at and I wanted to take Zoe somewhere nice because our first two dates had gone so well.

Zoe was wearing a new pair of eyeglasses she called "embarrassingly geeky" with their thick rims and huge lenses. I thought she looked adorable because they made her prominently beautiful nose stand out even more while at the same time making her brilliant blue eyes larger and cuter. Her bangs were brushed to her right as usual but kept getting in her eyes because she had been putting off getting a haircut on a dare. I wanted to brush aside her hair while going in for a kiss but thought it was too soon to make a pass. Upon entering the restaurant, we both gasped at the warm glow of the interior with its high vaulted ceilings and pastoral wall paintings.

After we finished eating, she probed my mind to get to the core of who I was with questions upon questions in an attempt to break down the complex conversational defenses I had spent years building up. Everything from what I was like when I was younger, to my relationship with my parents, most especially my father, to how I dealt with Edward at Festival Graphics, and why I never went into comics or animation as a career. For every detail I gave up, I insisted she give up something about her past. There was no way I was going to roll over and let her have her way with me mentally without getting something in return. She obliged in kind with stories about what she was like when she was younger, her relationship with her parents, and why she never went into the arts for a career.

As the night wore on, she found me "maddeningly random," but stayed focused and determined on getting me to open up more about my deepest self beyond what I had ever told anyone previously. The sheer force of her personality was enough to keep me glued to that seat. I did the same with her, matching her every inquiry with my own. At a certain point, it wasn't so much a conversation, but a battle of wills between two very stubborn personalities with a strong desire to learn more about the person across the table. After several hours of verbal jabbing and witty banter, we found ourselves alone, as the last patrons there, still wanting more from each other. The rest of the staff left us to our own devices by hanging out at a table on the other side of the room, lost in their own conversation.

"What is your major internal conflict?" she asked, unwilling to end the evening despite the late hour. I thought it was too soon to jump into a heavy discussion on my misgivings with Mormonism, plus I was still stinging from the combative conversation I had with Calvin. It was only our third date and I didn't want to drive her away.

"It's the fight between living a creative life versus a regular life and the desire for the mental purity I have when at an autocross, dancing, making art, writing, or any of the other positive ways I have learned to reach that state of being."

"Wow, that's a good answer," she said with a look of satisfaction. "Okay, you get one final question."

"Just one?"

"One only. No secondary questions or tangents," she warned.

We had already talked about her passions, family, favorite books and movies, plus hobbies and interests, but I didn't know the story of who she was underneath all that.

"This is hard. I keep wanting to ask more than one question."

"Nope. You only get one and it had better be a good one because you're being judged on its quality," she said with a smile.

The problem was I didn't know how to consolidate all my thoughts about her religious beliefs into a single question. I wanted to see how strongly she believed in her faith. Was it a literal truth for her or an extended metaphor? Did her faith affect how she lived her life? More specifically, the people she met and her relations with friends and family, the political beliefs she had, and how she viewed other faiths in relation to her own. Part of me didn't want to ask because I dreaded the answer, even though I didn't know what that might encompass.

"You're really having a problem with this. Let me help you," she said, showing patience and resolve.

"Is it something about my past?"

"No."

"Is it something about my parents?"

"No."

"My childhood?"

"No."

"My adulthood?"

"No."

"My education."

"No."

A long pause.

"Is it something about me?"

"Sort of."

"So, ask then."

Minutes passed with Zoe patiently watching me from across the table before I successfully whittled my thoughts down to a single question.

"What does Mormonism mean to you?" I asked. With that, I got up and went to the restroom to give her time to think about it, fully expecting a positive response talking about the joy of being Mormon.

When I returned, instead of the bright, young chipper woman in complete control of the conversation the past few hours, I found a dark, morose shadow of that self, full of self-loathing and insecurity, cornered and under the spotlight.

From the way she looked, the question went straight to the heart of who she was. She confirmed this while I watched and listened across the table from her with worried fascination.

"It isn't just going to church for me. It permeates my very being from dawn until dusk to the clothes I wear, how I act around people, and with whom I interact," she said.

Tears rolled down her face as she admitted to having fallen in love with a man outside of her faith, a Buddhist, earlier in the year and how it fell apart over religious and cultural differences. They tried remaining friends for a while and she unsuccessfully helped him look for a new love. The day she and I met at the art show was the day she ended their friendship after he told her he had sex with the new woman he was seeing. I thought of the art show where we met, the self-portrait she made in faceplant pose, and the moment when I discovered her alone, makeup slightly ruined from the tears. It all made sense.

"I'm not perfect. I'm not completely good. I have had my failings, and I hate myself for them. Being Mormon is truth, and every time I have strayed from that, things have gone awry."

I had been hoping for a more positive take on Mormonism from Zoe so I could dismiss the damaged psyches all over *Exmormon.org*. This confession of hers was so honest and heartfelt I wanted to save her from the excruciating mental torture she was putting herself through living up to Mormonism's ideals. I wanted to embrace her and tell her everything would be okay, but I couldn't. She wouldn't let me.

The rhetorical question she asked me, after revealing her real self underneath the charming facade she put up for the world to see, was "Why did you have to be so smart?" I couldn't tell if it was because I could get to the heart of something with a single question or if being around me was making it hard for her to be away from me. I was hoping for the latter.

Before my question, things were going well. I had been planning on kissing her at the end of an evening full of great conversation. I found her attractive, inside and out, and wanted to hold her in my arms again as we had done on that park bench weeks earlier. Now, things were all wrong as the tears had become sobs while she answered my question. I tried salvaging the evening by livening things back up with witty one-liners, but nothing worked.

I kept hoping for more conversation on the drive back to her place, but all that greeted me was the disappointing sound of silence. I parked my car in the driveway, and we embraced.

"When can I see you again?" I whispered. There was no way I was letting the morose mood ruin the possibility of spending more time with this beautiful person.

"I think I want to be just friends, but I do want to see you again," she whispered back.

NO! Those were the last words I wanted to hear after an evening of intimate conversation because I wanted to be more than a friend.

"I'll think about it," I said, trying my best to save face by remaining perfectly still, hoping I wouldn't disintegrate on the spot and she couldn't see my look of horror and dejection.

Based on everything I had learned about the Mormon religion and culture over the past weeks since our last date, it shouldn't have been a surprise, but I was still shocked by the rejection. It wasn't how I wanted this to end when our relationship was so promising. We had been getting along better than I would have hoped or guessed based on what I had read on Mormonism. Our open-ended conversations had me thinking we could be one of those interfaith couples who could work past our differences and find a happy compromise. I wanted to lash out at her in a useless tantrum but decided it would be better for both of us if I retreated to the familiar comforts of my apartment to lick my emotional wounds.

Halloween Party

Caleb texted me the next day and asked if I was interested in going to a Halloween party with him. It was an LDS party, and I knew Zoe would be there based on her Facebook page, but thought the chances of running into Zoe were slim because of the high number of attendees. I didn't like the idea of being in the same room with her again so soon, but getting out of the apartment sounded like a much better plan than staying in and sulking over being rejected. There would be plenty of opportunities to meet new women there. Hopefully, ones that were as charming, intelligent, and funny as Zoe. Besides, it had been three days since she dropped the F-word on me, and I needed a pick-me-up.

Since it was an LDS party, the rules for costumes were pretty conservative. You couldn't wear a full-face mask and sexy, revealing costumes were out. Also, there would be no alcohol, though I didn't see it as a big deal. If anything, it was nice to know I wouldn't have to worry about driving home drunk from the party.

I decided not to dress up because I hadn't thought of a costume to wear. I simply wasn't in a festive mood. However, my need to get out of the apartment and meet new people was far greater than my embarrassment over not having a costume. If asked, I could say I was dressed as a serial killer because they looked like anyone else dressed in normal, everyday clothes.

I arrived earlier at the party than Caleb planned and waited out in the parking lot until he arrived before going inside to people watch. After he arrived dressed as an android, we got in line.

After paying the entry fee, I scoped out the place on my own while Caleb went to grab a hand tool out of his car for a friend. The church building had long, cramped hallways, low ceilings, and was packed wall-to-wall with people dressed in costume. I walked right by the makeshift speed dating room and into the dance hall, which was a combined-use area with a gym and stage. Inside were a DJ and dance area with a huge lighting display. The floor was packed with costumed revelers bouncing to the beat. It was weird being around a bunch of young people excited to be in a non-partner dance setting without alcohol.

Were Mormons so repressed that this was a rare opportunity to cut loose all that pent-up energy? Then again, most swing dancing venues I attended didn't serve alcohol either. Maybe I could relate to them after all.

I hadn't been there more than a minute when Zoe ran right by me in a Robin costume, doing a double take as she passed while dressed as Batman's sidekick. I knew of that costume from a conversation we had on one of our dates. She had told me the last time she wore it she found it embarrassingly revealing without tights on. This time, she had on tights per the rules of the party. I let her pass then walked the other direction without looking at her, trying frantically to get a hold of Caleb on my cell phone. I wanted him to find me so I wouldn't have to face Zoe alone. I cursed myself for my stupidity and wished I hadn't come.

The moment I stopped, Zoe approached. "Hi!" she shouted above the music with a huge smile on her face as she tenderly touched my left arm. That simple gesture of friendship sent my head spinning. I wanted to reach out and kiss her to put myself right again, but I was still reeling mentally from the other night. I kept my cool, smiled, and waved back.

"What are you doing here?!?" she asked above the loud music.

Think fast.

"Caleb invited me. In fact, I'm trying to find him right now," I shouted back while tightening my grip on my phone in hopes Caleb would show up sooner rather than later.

Seconds later, Caleb found us and we left Zoe. He showed me around the dance area and guided me to a group he was meeting up with to introduce me to his friends. The group left the dance floor shortly after we met up with them but didn't make much of an effort to hold a conversation with me. I wasn't sure why they were so standoffish toward me unless it was because I wasn't Mormon, though I didn't remember Caleb mentioning to them whether I was or not. I walked with them for 20 minutes, but I was overwhelmed by the crowd and noise. Feeling unwanted by Caleb's friends didn't help either. I went outdoors—where the non-alcoholic drinks and candy were being served—and sat down, a strong desire to retreat to the quiet comforts of my apartment invading my thoughts as I did so.

I caught sight of Zoe with her friends across the crowd and approached her with caution. It took all my strength to walk those 10 feet. I didn't want to just be her friend, but I didn't want to leave without talking to her either.

"Zoe, you wouldn't mind if I hang out with you, would you? I don't know anyone else here."

"Yes, of course!" she said, her winning smile brightening my mood.

We found a spot to sit then sat and talked. We were interrupted frequently because everyone she knew kept wanting to say hello. I didn't care, though. I was just glad to spend time with her. Zoe alternated between keeping me company, talking to her friends, bringing me back candy, talking to me more, and saying hello to strangers whose costume she liked. One poor fellow had no clue who Robin was and an incredulous Zoe gave him a hard time over his ignorance for several minutes. Each time she got up, I saved her seat for her return. And, like a boomerang, she kept coming back.

Watching her make the social rounds, I could see how much she cared for this community. She belonged there. She introduced me to several of her friends, but I failed to connect with them because I couldn't relate to them. Caleb was wrong. I was not fitting in with this crowd. I was sure my lack of a costume for a conversation starter didn't help.

Sitting next to Zoe, I found a ticklish spot on her knee and played with it. She made a cute face; I made a cute face back. And we talked. And talked. Just as we had done ever since we met. At some point, we were going to run out of stuff to talk about. I was glad it wasn't going to be this night.

With my eyes heavy from the lateness of the hour, I checked my phone for the time, hoping it wasn't too late. "Zoe, I have to leave soon. I'm getting up at 5 a.m. to drive down to San Diego to teach at an autocross school."

"Don't leave without saying goodbye!" she ordered as she walked over to talk to a friend she hadn't seen in a while.

"I won't."

"You promise?" she said, her finger pointed at me for emphasis.

"I promise." I didn't want to cross her. Not yet.

A few minutes later, she returned.

"The DJ is cutting off all the inappropriate songs so he doesn't violate the strict rules of the dance," she said with a laugh. "Listen."

Sure enough, the DJ stopped a song barely seconds in, then put on another.

"I know many of the songs he keeps turning off because I listen to a lot of 'normal' music," she said. "What kind of music do you like?"

I rattled off names of bands I enjoyed: The Beatles, Big Star, They Might Be Giants, and several others.

"Sing a song to me," she ordered with authority.

"What? Why?" I didn't want to embarrass myself in front of her with my futile attempts at warbling through a song.

"I want to hear your singing voice. Sing something to me," she said with urgency. There was no way she was going to take no for an answer.

Looking into those insistent blue eyes of hers, I took a deep breath and gave in to her demand and sung her Big Star's "Thirteen."

Won't you let me walk you home from school?

Won't you let me meet you at the pool?
Maybe Friday I can get tickets for the dance
And I'll take you.

Once I was finished singing those words of longing, taking care not to make my voice crack, she beamed me a look of sheer joy.

"Yay! More!" she said with a round of rousing claps.

Encouraged by her enthusiasm, I continued with several They Might Be Giants songs I knew: "Lucky Ball and Chain," "The End of the Tour," and ended with "New York City," a cover of a song by Canadian female-rockers Cub about being young and in love while in The Big Apple.

"Your turn."

"What? No. There is no way I am singing to you."

"Look, I sang for you, so it's only polite you return the favor," I said, calling her bluff.

"Fine. I will sing to you, but you get one song and one song only," she declared.

She didn't tell me the title, but it was an exquisite, moving piece that started off slow, then gradually soared majestically into the night air. My heart skipped a beat as it rose with her voice.

"You have a wonderful singing voice," I told her after she finished.

"I'm not that good of a singer. My voice has a lot of flaws," she said with a head shake.

I was tempted to tell her she should smile and say, "thank you," but I didn't want to ruin the moment by making her uncomfortable with being herself. It was the first time a woman had sung to me in five years. And the first time I had sung to a woman in 13.

When it was time for me to go, we embraced. I didn't care if she wanted to just be friends. The only thing I cared about was being with her and holding her close as long as possible.

"You should thank Caleb for bringing you," she said. There was a tenderness to her voice that melted away any doubts she liked me.

"You should thank him, too," I replied, hoping she understood I enjoyed my time with her too.

Don't Die

Zoe had a rough day, a so-so week at work, and was tired from lack of sleep. And yet, she was perky through the evening with me, our fourth "date."

At an amusement park in the Valley, we played a round of miniature golf. She was beating me pretty handily because I was having difficulty hitting the ball in a straight line. Putting my ball into the mini river next to the course made it worse.

"Whoops," I said.

"Nice job, dear," she said with a laugh.

"I should go grab it," I said as I began to straddle myself across a couple of rocks.

"That's what she said."

"Cute."

"Thanks!" she beamed.

"Ha."

"If you fall in, I am totally going to laugh at you, dear. Just don't get me wet if you do."

"That won't happen, honey," I said with confidence. I began to reach down but had to give up when I started to lose my balance and nerve. She held out her hand to help me back to solid ground, then we continued our game with a new ball.

There were times during the rest of our game where we were physically affectionate toward each other in addition to the quick-witted verbal repartee that was our relationship. Nothing overtly sexual or suggestive. Just innocent, flirty fun. Our personalities were working well together and I believed somehow, some way we would work out as a couple and I would be an idiot to walk away from this.

After she beat me at miniature golf, we went inside the arcade for a round of air hockey, where we were evenly matched.

"You've done this before," she said. "I can tell by the way you hold the mallet, dear."

"Just one of the skills I picked up in college, honey."

In the end, it didn't matter if we were evenly matched. She still won, but barely.

After we finished playing air hockey, I took her to a nearby 24-hour French cafe.

"This place is too cool for me," she said with worry as she looked around at all the hipsters seated at the tables. "But I'm glad I'm here with you." She pulled me toward her and we walked arm and arm to the first open table we found in the packed cafe.

We each did napkin drawings before eating a dinner consisting of a panini for me and a quiche lorraine for her. I did a napkin sketch of my webcomic characters while she drew a portrait of me she kept for her collection of napkin drawings.

She had been trying to pry more information about me from Caleb during Family Home Evening, a night when Mormons spend social bonding time with friends and family, but he didn't know me well enough to satisfy her curiosity. My lack of Facebook status updates and photos frustrated her efforts to learn about me. Once-a-week updates weren't enough for her. She wanted more.

"I want to see your place. I want to know everything about you." I wasn't sure that was a good idea because I thought it was too much too fast.

At the end of the evening, I took her by my apartment since it was close. Zoe called the short distance between our places "destiny." I didn't believe our getting together was destiny, but I did believe we both wanted to be there, making any sense of destiny a self-fulfilling prophecy.

Once we arrived, it was a quarter after midnight, past when I planned to have her home. I parked the car in the driveway between my apartment and Carrie's former place then told her Carrie's story while gazing at that now-empty window, fondly remembering her Southern twang.

"She must have liked you," she said with sadness.

I took a deep breath and sighed.

"I know she did," I replied.

I drove to the parking lot behind my apartment building, stopped, then looked at Zoe and said, "We're not going in, not tonight. Place is a mess."

"Thank you," she said without explaining why she was thanking me. I turned the car around and took her home.

When we arrived at her place, I parked the car in the driveway and Zoe reached over and embraced me. "You are SO good. I would do anything to keep you happy," she whispered in my ear as she held me cheek to cheek. Did she understand the implications of that statement to an emotionally needy artistic type?

As she got out of the car to go into her apartment, she told me, "DON'T DIE," as we promised to see each other again. What an odd thing to tell someone.

When she texted me later, she described our time together as "talking and teasing." It warmed me to see she had as good of a time as I did. Two weeks later, we fulfilled our promise.

Crossing the Line

Zoe had commented in an e-mail earlier in the week we would be "hanging out." While we were out, her dad called and she said she was "out with a friend." I suspected by her words if I didn't make a move that night, I would be stuck in the 'just friends' position indefinitely, and there was no way I was going to let that happen. I had been in too many situations where I didn't make a move and regretted it later. I had to step up my game.

She took me to a well-decorated vintage diner I hadn't been to in seven years. It had been one of the many places the swing dance crowd visited after a night of dancing. She had been there earlier in the year for her birthday because it was one of her favorite places in LA. She had a BLT while I had a salmon and onion bagel concoction. Having the onion bagel was not the best idea for a date, but she did say this was an outing between friends.

After we finished eating, we played a few rounds of Connect4 and Uno, two of the games she played with her acting troupe.

Our first game of Connect4 was pretty close. I couldn't tell if she was taking it easy on me or if I was that good. Our second and third games were a different story.

"Ugh, are you even paying attention?" she asked with a look of disdain as she beat me a second straight time.

I decided to try harder to win the next game, but it didn't work.

"Leonard, you're not even trying!" she exclaimed with a look of exasperation as she won easily. I did my best not to show any emotion, which caused her to frown. "Do you even care how bad I'm beating you?" she said as she stuck her tongue out at me while I pretended to be unimpressed.

"How about we play Uno instead?" I offered.

Her well-practiced hand won again rather easily. I didn't care, though. The more indifference I showed toward her winning our games, the more expressive her face became. I could have teased her all night just to watch her make faces. After we left the diner, Zoe and I went for a walk around the block, stopping by a dessert shop to check out the various confections through the window.

"I want my wedding to be lit with Christmas lights," she said while admiring the wedding cakes.

"White or colored?" I asked.

"White, but colored would be good, too." I couldn't help but think she was talking about our wedding plans. I could see myself lifting the veil of her wedding dress for our first kiss as husband and wife, those beautiful blue eyes lovingly gazing back at me.

When we finished our walk, we went back to my car. I hadn't told her where we were going, but she had a pretty good idea once we arrived at the bright lights at the edge of my neighborhood.

"You should have told me we were coming here beforehand," she said without explaining why.

Once inside my apartment, I gave her a short, guided tour, but what grabbed her attention was my bookshelves.

"One thing is for sure, you are definitely well read," she said as her face lit up at the sight of all my books. She pored over all my science-fiction and fantasy books, graphic novels, art reference books, my binders full of music CDs, and comic books. "I see you have a lot of art and fiction books and you like female writers and music." She moved over to my shelf full of classic literature books that included many of the novels I read as an English lit major, then latched onto a book of 17th-century verse, absorbing herself in a poem. When she finished reading, I plugged in the homemade multi-colored Christmas light disco ball I had won at a swing dance raffle. She squealed and jumped with delight at the sight of the blinking lights as their rays bounced off the plastic cups that made up the disco ball, bathing the room in a rainbow of colors. It was a thrill to see her so happy over something so simple.

"Are those your old yearbooks?" she asked as she knelt down to get a closer look at the last shelf, which had accumulated several layers of dust since dating Emma. I watched as she took out all of my elementary yearbooks. "Aw, you were so cute. What happened?"

"Haha, very funny," I said.

She started to grab my junior high and high school yearbooks, but I pulled them away from her before she could get to them.

"Uh-uh. I don't want you to look through those." I didn't want her to see the photos taken of my Jimmy Connors-inspired bowl-shaped haircuts to go with my plastic-framed eyeglasses with their huge lenses that covered half my face.

"Why not? You've brought me this far. I want to see everything."

"No, I don't want you to look at them." I didn't want Zoe to see them because I didn't want to shatter her view of my being "manly."

"Aw, c'mon. They can't be that bad."

"You have no idea."

"You're right, I don't, and I won't unless you let me look at them," she said as she tried to yank them out of my hands.

"I said 'no' and I meant 'no.' What part of 'no' aren't you getting?" I said as I shielded the books from her prying hands.

She then started poking at me with her fingers in an attempt to tickle the books away from me, but after several minutes I refused to yield.

"Are you scared I'm going to make fun of you?"

"Maybe." She gave me a pleading look with those beautiful blue eyes that made my heart melt. "Well, yes."

"How about if I promise not to laugh?"

"Not good enough." I had to admit, though, I was enjoying every second of the attention. "Promises can be broken."

"Look, you cannot possibly be any nerdier than I was in high school!" she exclaimed.

Knowing the hour was getting late and realizing she wasn't going to leave without looking through those yearbooks, I sighed and let her have a look. When she finally came across my photos, she laughed at them for several minutes.

"I was wrong, you really were nerdier than I was," she said between laughs.

Hearing her laugh made the flush of disappointment over her broken promise easier to take.

"I'm immature for my age," she declared after she calmed down.

"If you're immature, what does that make me?"

"It means you're really, really immature."

"Thanks," I replied under my breath, insulted she would call me immature.

"So ... how is it working out dating a 25-year-old?" she asked with confidence, surprising me pleasantly with her candor over calling our actions dating.

"Mmm ... so-so," I said without hesitation. I didn't want her to think too highly of herself.

"A real response," she gasped. She was shocked I hadn't given her my usual response of "sure," which she had determined in Leonard-speak meant "whatever."

"You know, you can be pretty predictable sometimes, but other times a complete mystery. I can't tell if I have won you over or not," she said. The truth was, she had me from the start.

I admitted I had searched for her dating blog for three days without much success and had given up. "I figured if I couldn't find it, it wasn't worth worrying about." She went into an uncomfortable silence after I told her that. Now I had to find it so I could see what she wrote about me.

The conversation then drifted over to my cancer experience and the ways I dealt with Dad's drunkenness. "You were so undramatic about bringing me over here. People who are undramatic have had a lot of drama in their lives," she said. I didn't believe my life qualified as dramatic, but it was an interesting observation born from having spoken to a lot of people in her short life.

"I don't talk to you as often as I do with my other friends on purpose," she said without explaining why. Funny thing was I did the same to her and our relationship was the least I had interacted with someone I had been dating.

"You know, this relationship between us could end at any time in the future—maybe a couple months, maybe longer," she said. I didn't like the direction she was taking the conversation.

"It could end tonight," I replied, following her train of thought.

Another uncomfortable silence followed. I wasn't sure how to respond and took her home.

It was 3 a.m. when I walked her to her door, wanting to kiss her but expecting a hug. When we reached her door, she placed her right hand on my left elbow and looked expectantly at me with those big, beautiful blue eyes of hers. My head went spinning as my body went light with excitement. I leaned in toward her, closed my eyes, tilted my head, and our lips met. After a few moments of sheer bliss, I pulled away and she kissed me back. She stopped, looked down, and started crying.

In a small voice, she asked, "Do you like me?"

I whispered "yes" into her ear without hesitation.

"Are you sure?"

I couldn't have been more sure about anything in my entire life.

"Yes," I whispered back.

"I'm scared."

I didn't care about the implications of kissing her. I didn't care if she was

Mormon. All I cared about was being with her at that moment. There was no one else whom I wanted to be with and no other place I wanted to be. If this was going to be the first and last time I got a chance to touch her, I wanted to remember every last bit of it.

"Don't be," I said to reassure her.

We kissed again.

When we pulled away from each other, Zoe wouldn't look me in the eyes, choosing to stare at the ground instead. Time stood still as I waited for her to do something. Anything.

"Are you sure?" she whispered.

"Yes," I said, matching her whisper with assured confidence.

We embraced again before one last kiss, then I let her go.

"Have a happy Thanksgiving," I said.

"You too," she said as she opened her door.

"And get some rest." It was late and she had to teach a scripture class in the morning.

"I will," she said before disappearing into her apartment.

It was the first time we had been out on a weekend, the first time she planned it out, the first time we had stayed out well past midnight, the first time I brought her to my apartment, and the first time I walked her to her door.

I had crossed the line from friendship into unknown territory and had no idea what to expect next.

The Chats

Zoe had shut off all contact with everyone who wasn't family during Thanksgiving, including me. I succeeded in finding her dating blog with a few simple keywords. In it, she talked at length about dates she had been on with other guys, as I had suspected, but also at serious length about our own dates. I found it very well-written and took in every word. In it, she laid bare both my dating strengths and weaknesses and admitted fondness and admiration for me, though she couldn't ultimately be with me for reasons not fully explained.

It was the first time I had ever dated anyone who went into such extensive detail on what it was like to date me. It was fascinating to read about myself from someone else's point of view but scary to see my weaknesses laid bare. I suspected she couldn't be with me because I wasn't Mormon, but the only way to be sure was to ask her myself. I contacted her to see if we could talk about it over dinner but had to leave a message to call me.

When she returned to LA, she posted on her Facebook status she was none too happy I and several others had found her blog. So, she made it private. I didn't understand why, after posting in a public forum for so long, having people find the blog was such a big deal. I would have been elated to have readers. Hurt by her need for control, I was confused as to the reasons behind the sudden need for privacy. If she didn't want to talk about personal experiences in a public forum, then she shouldn't have been posting publicly in the first place, pseudonym or not.

"How did you find my blog? I want to know," she demanded when she gave me a call.

"It was easy. Just a few simple keywords."

"Well, that won't happen again."

"Yeah, I saw your Facebook post. If it's any consolation, you write very well."

"No, it's nothing." She couldn't have been further from the truth. Her detailed writing was full of life and verve. It was frustrating to hear how little she thought of herself. I suspected her religion had something to do with this idea of diminishing her talents and skill, but it was difficult to tell the exact reasons why.

"Leonard, I can't be what you want, and I don't want to have dinner with you again." The firmness in her voice indicated there would be no compromise, but I wasn't sure what she meant by what I wanted, and she wasn't providing any clues, leaving me in the dark. It didn't help I wasn't self-aware enough to figure it out myself.

"It's a shame because I really liked you," she said with a sob. For me, the fact we were still talking meant there was a possibility she would change her mind and we would become a couple. I liked her too much to give up.

"You were so awesome the way you asked me out. I thought so highly of you I bragged about you to my friends for days," she said with a combination of pride and sadness.

I was flattered. Nobody had ever talked me up like that before, and her saying so gave me pride and confidence I never previously had. It was like she was building me up to be like a god.

As the conversation wore on, it took on a deeper, more intimate quality.

We wove through difficult subjects, like dealing with internal psychological conflicts between career and family, with ease. The longer we talked, the more I liked her for her company, even if it was just on the phone. I didn't need to be in her presence that night to know from the way we were talking to each other this was far from over.

The next day, I started pulling Zoe into chat on Facebook every chance I could. I would greet her in the morning, and we would chat until lunch. When she got back from lunch, I would greet her again, and we would chat until we couldn't. We spent hours a day getting to know each other better with stories of past exploits, present experiences, and future hopes and dreams.

"I want a copy of your old blog entries," she ordered during one of our chats. "It's only fair. You've seen my blog, now I should see yours."

"Why do you want them?" I asked. I had taken them down from the Internet years ago because I didn't want strangers reading them, mirroring her desire to keep her blog private.

"Insight into how the male mind works?" she replied, unsure herself.

I mulled over her request for a week, then gave in to her demands because I didn't have anything to lose by doing so.

I made a list of pluses and minuses of Zoe and me being together. After reflecting on this list for a couple of days, I deleted it. Zoe was well aware of her shortcomings and didn't need me pointing them out to her. I then made another list. This one was exclusively about things I liked about her. I read it several times before putting it in an e-mail and sending it. She replied immediately, her joy shining through each word of the message.

After that, our Facebook chats became more flirty again. More intimate. More serious. She called me cute for the first time since we had known each other. Yet, every time I asked for time together in person, I was turned down for another day.

"What is it going to take to see you again?" I asked in one of our chats, frustrated by the lack of physical contact. "If we're not going to go out, then what's the point of all these long talks?"

"I'm sorry for putting you in a tough spot," she said.

I didn't like how she kept letting me in mentally yet pushing me away physically, but I understood she was doing it to preserve the sanctity of her vows to God—though I couldn't stop. Couldn't stop thinking about her. Couldn't stop talking to her. Couldn't stop wanting her.

The chats continued.

She talked about being trapped and depressed in her life as a result of her job and hobbies.

At her job, her boss had been refusing to recognize the economic benefit of the work she had been doing that was above and beyond her duties. All her attempts to make her boss see the value she brought to her work were met with indifference. Much like me with Festival Graphics, she wanted out of a job situation that didn't respect her. Having been in a similar situation allowed me an opportunity to give her an understanding ear to confide in while giving her support and encouragement.

The acting troupe she had talked so fondly of during our first meeting was falling apart because the founder and leader wanted to disband it due to personal reasons. Such a move would have been devastating to participants and audience alike because of the joy the troupe brought to them. Zoe offered to take over as the leader, not out of any sense of personal gain, but to keep a program going for the greater good of the community, much as I had done as novice coordinator for our autocross group. In her desire to lead, I saw a kindred spirit.

We talked about her passions for costumes and graphic storytelling and discovered we could spontaneously create imaginary stories full of adventure and romance together in chat. I could see a future where we were writing together like partners in crime. It didn't matter to me if we made any money at it. All that mattered was being with her and enjoying the beauty of her self-expression. I had never considered writing with anyone in any kind of partnership before. But I could see doing it with her.

Anytime I thought about ending it because most relationships between Mormons and non-Mormons lead to nothing but heartache, she would say something charming, flirty, and inviting toward me, and I would get sucked right back into her world. It was like I was an emotional yo-yo being constantly thrown against a wall. And yet ... I was enjoying every minute of it, and it scared me.

"I get nervous with you sometimes," she said during one of our many chats. "I'm emotionally vulnerable around you, and that makes you dangerous."

It was good to know the feeling was mutual.

The Word of God

As I delved more and more into Mormonism, two of my closest friends encouraged me to turn that critical eye onto Christianity. Why not? The Bible was the word of God and should stand up to scrutiny, right?

After my fallout with Emma, I started reading the Bible hoping all of God's rules and commandments would be laid out in an easy-to-read, organized fashion broken down into questions, answers, and rules, but the Bible wasn't like that at all. In those ancient words, I discovered a God whose knowledge of science wasn't good and whose will wasn't always clear.

For example, Genesis with its six days of creation and the garden of Eden creationist stories run counter to what I had learned from science and its theories of evolution and the Big Bang. In the Bible, the six days of creation began with what I could only presume to be a depiction of a flat earth with its separation of light and darkness, and I couldn't get past the idea the stars weren't put in the sky until day four. If there were already light, where was it coming from? After all, the sun is a star and is what gives us light. If there are no stars, there is no sun. If there is no sun, there is no light. Also, without the sun having been created until day four, why were plants dependent on the sun to survive created on day three? It was as if the sun was a project God added on a whim when all his plants died. It was obvious the writer(s) of Genesis were working with what limited knowledge they had of the world.

As I continued to read more of the Bible, I got the impression the God in the Old Testament didn't do a good job of keeping to his own commandment of "Thou shalt not kill." This angry, jealous God continually sent his people off to fight other people and their gods and punished minor infractions rather harshly. This wasn't a moral standard to live by as Christian apologetics touted, this was hypocrisy at its worst.

Also, I found it odd there was more than one god mentioned in the Bible in its early stories. By the time you reached the end, all those other gods had disappeared in favor of the one. It was as if the storytellers and editors got tired of keeping track of all the different gods and decided one angry, petulant god was more than enough.

The story of Jesus Christ and the New Testament was appealing as anyone who believed in Christ would be saved from the wrath of this angry, jealous God. Throw in miracles that were written decades later so no one could dispute them and offer up some historical stories to back it up, and you've got a recipe for a whole new religion for all willing to accept it as truth. On top of Old Testament miracles like burning bushes that speak, talking snakes, men who can part seas, worldwide floods, believers who can drink poison without dying, men who lived for hundreds of years, and a guy who survived three days in the belly of a fish, the New Testament added miracles like a man who came back from the dead, could walk on water, turn water into wine, and literally ascended into heaven. These were all incredible events any person with a high school science education could easily dismiss as fiction due to the unchanging laws of nature.

I could see how using such story devices could make an indelible impression on children, like any story would at that age. Once children latch onto a story, they never let it go, carrying it with them the rest of their lives. I thought of Emma and how she embraced the idea Jesus was by her side at all times, guiding her through thick and thin. As comforting and inspiring as the idea of the Son of God speaking to me sounded, it wasn't for me because the only voice I ever heard in my head sounds remarkably similar to my own, though with a hint of baritone so it has authority. Also, although effective at inspiring followers, the idea of God sacrificing a part of himself in the name of himself to show he could relate to our suffering was disturbing and made little sense when rationally sorted out.

"You're not supposed to take it literally. It's all one big metaphor," a friend at church told me after I confronted him with my issues with the Bible.

I wasn't satisfied with the Bible as a metaphor because I wanted something more concrete to believe in with relatable rules instead of stories up for interpretation. Leaving the Bible, or any work of scripture for that matter, up to interpretation leads to all sorts of conflicts the authors probably never intended. Hence, the existence of more than 30,000 different Christian denominations—each with their own interpretations—that keep growing in number with each passing generation.

Dan Barker's *Losing Faith in Faith* enlightened me due to his studious approach to the Bible. Barker was an evangelical priest and Christian songwriter who converted to atheism and was considered one of the United States' most prominent freethinkers. In his book, Barker challenged believers to tell the story of Easter based on the books of Matthew, Mark, Luke, John, and Acts in chronological order without leaving anything out. He introduced the challenge because the story is impossible to tell if you include every line of scripture. There are too many conflicting or missing details depending on the account. According to Barker, no one has succeeded at his Easter challenge, though many have tried. I was glad he put that challenge in his book because it was one of many discrepancies I noticed while reading the New Testament.

I found many believers, both in person and online, had never read the Bible in its entirety. How could anyone willfully remain ignorant of a book they were supposedly following? Yet, I did the exact same thing for years for the sake of happiness among friends. I did it because the message delivered from the pulpit and the devout was good, and I liked that it was good. It didn't matter if the Bible was a factually correct account of history or not. All that mattered was my happiness and willingness to help others when needed.

For me, the final nail in the coffin for the Bible as the true word of God was Thomas Paine's *Age of Reason*. Paine was a Deist and his *Age of Reason* was the cornerstone of both the Deism movement of the late 18th century and the New Deism movement of the early 21st century. In it, Paine used the Bible against itself by pointing out passages giving clues to their authorship and period when they were written. In almost every case, the stories in the Bible were written long after the events were supposed to have occurred, throwing doubt onto the veracity of these stories. The implication was if the stories aren't the word of God, then they are nothing but fabrications and not to be trusted as a guidebook for living. At one point in his book, Paine called theology "the study of nothing," an attitude I liked the more I read about religions based on scripture.

Paine's idea theology was the study of nothing may have rung true for me, but I could see the stories within the Bible contained universal truths about the way men think and it would take a lifetime of study to grasp all its nuances. If you wanted to understand the psyche of man—all men—you read scripture. For some reason, women get the short end of the stick in the Bible, as if the writers and editors were all men who never bothered to learn about the opposite sex beyond their existing for man's benefit or downfall. However, I couldn't get behind the idea of using the Bible, or any body of scripture, as a basis for a religion because there was too much room for interpretation in it. The more room for interpretation, the more likely there would be conflict and divisiveness. I didn't want a world divided, I wanted a world united as one, free from the barriers created by scripture.

I was glad to be in a church that wasn't all fire and brimstone because not all of my areligious friends had the positive experiences I had. As long as I didn't think too much about scripture, my experiences had been welcoming and friendly. When I told fellow parishioners I was looking at atheist texts, I received the same response from them all.

"It's good you're testing your faith," they said.

The Gift

"You bought me a gift so you could see me," Zoe said as she opened the Christmas gift I had given her. Zoe hadn't heard of the irreverent science-fiction comic strip *Brewster Rockit* before but was happy for the peppermint-covered chocolate cookies.

"Yes, and it worked," I said, relieved she was there in my apartment. It had been weeks since we last saw each other.

"I wasn't going to make you drop it off," she replied.

"You could have backed out, but you didn't."

I was worried she wasn't going to show but knew if she didn't I could go out swing dancing. So, there wasn't anything for me to stress over. Either way, I was going to have a full evening. Zoe took a seat at the other end of my futon, tucking her legs under her as she did.

We started off by talking about music, which led to us singing songs together. She closed with a beautiful rendition of "My Favorite Things," one of my favorite songs from *The Sound of Music*.

She then asked me to show her flirt and seduction techniques I learned from David D'Angelo's book *Sex Secrets* I had mentioned in passing during one of our many Facebook chats. I promised to teach them to her the next time we saw each other and happily obliged her request, breaking the physical barrier between us early in the evening.

She told me about her new iPad, a Christmas gift from her father. She had bought several books of scripture, texts, and magazines for the class she was teaching. Not having to carry an armful of books made her happy. Watching her face light up while she spoke of them filled me with joy.

As I told her the story of a failed relationship when I first moved to LA, I laid down next to her in an attempt to bridge the physical space between us. She looked down at me, softened the look in her eyes, then ran her fingers through my hair, smiling as she did. Then her cell phone rang, putting an abrupt end to the moment. She was supposed to meet a friend at her place after meeting up with me. I was disappointed she had already made plans to cut our evening short. While she was talking, I reached up and stroked the soft spot underneath her chin.

"Is that what you like?" she said as she reciprocated my tender touch in kind after hanging up the phone.

Then she stopped and stared off into the distance, inner conflict consuming her face. Visions of her faceplant painting and standing there alone in the tunnel at the art show flashed before my eyes.

"I need to leave, but you're going to have to help me," she said as her voice went weak.

I didn't want her to go but respected her desire to leave. With that, I got up and escorted her to her car. When we reached it, my body wouldn't stop shivering from the cold as she embraced me tightly, pinning my back to the driver's side door. The embrace lasted quite a while as it took some time for my body to adjust to the evening chill. She didn't want to let go. I lightly brushed her face with my nose and lips, deliberately avoiding her mouth.

"I'm sorry. I can't reciprocate. I just can't," she said with a worried tone. But she didn't move to leave.

I continued for several minutes, her breathing becoming heavier with each passing moment. When she gave in, she shoved me against the door as we locked lips, her hands running through my hair as she did. I equaled her forceful display of passion, the weeks apart falling away while our tongues danced.

"I want to make a New Year's Resolution to be less dirty, and you're not helping," she said as we kissed, much to her chagrin and enjoyment. In between kisses, she told me, "Don't kiss me for my sake," and "You are a really good kisser and tease." And, finally, she said, "Quit being so cute."

"I want to ask you something, but I'm worried you might think less of me," she said after breaking away.

I shook my head. "What is it?"

"I was wondering if you wouldn't mind stroking my ego?" she said while looking down at the ground.

"Go ahead."

She looked up at me with those bright eyes of hers full of worry and asked: "Do you think I'm cute?"

"Yes," I said with confidence. She wasn't just cute, she was beautiful.

She leaned in and we kissed again. Every now and then, she would pull away and catch my face in a state of confusion, unsure if our making out was a good idea. "Is this making you happy?" she asked several times with a look of concern. Each time she asked, she would tell me to smile to show I enjoyed being with her. Though I was enjoying kissing her, I was

214

more troubled over Zoe's worries than my own happiness because each kiss drained her of energy. Every time I thought we were done, we would start up again.

At one point, she stopped and looked down as hurt and anguish consumed her face. She then grabbed my jacket and yanked me to her, looked up at me with wildly frustrated eyes, and yelled "HOW IS THIS GOING TO WORK?!? HOW?!?"

"I don't know," I replied in a small, doubting voice.

"You are SO different!" she cried.

"I know. You'll never meet another guy like me."

"I can't keep kissing you every time I see you!" she exclaimed.

"But we've only kissed the last two times we've seen each other," I replied.

"I KNOW! I can't keep doing this!"

The hurt on her face told me we were through, but before I could end it, she pulled me close for another embrace. I kept pushing her buttons again until she gave in for another round of kissing. When we stopped, I wished her a happy new year into her ear, then licked and nibbled it while she giggled and cringed.

"You're enjoying this, aren't you?"

"Of course."

Zoe then had me put her in her car to send her off, but she didn't drive away. By the expectant look in her eyes, I could see she wasn't ready to leave. I leaned in and we continued kissing.

"What am I going to tell my friend? He knows I'm here with you. I talk about you to him all the time," she said when she pulled away for a brief respite.

As she spoke, I punctuated each of her sentences with a kiss and on her last one I held back while lightly brushing her lips until she couldn't help but kiss me back.

"I HATE YOU! I HATE YOU! I HATE YOU!"

I shook my head and laughed. I knew it wasn't true.

"Come here. I want to give you a proper kiss," she said with a huge sigh.

I closed my eyes and leaned in, her hands cradling my cheeks as I did. If I could have stayed in that tender moment for the rest of eternity, I would have. After we pulled away from each other, I told her I would call her.

"YOU NEVER CALL ME. You say you will, but YOU NEVER DO!"

"That's not true, I called you twice this week!"

"But not once the week before or the week before that OR the week

215

before THAT!"

It drove me wild to see her so emotional over me.

"Yes, but I made a 200 percent increase in phone calls this week," I said with pride. I then closed her door and sent her on her way without knowing when I would see her again.

Child of God

"I'm not afraid of you," Zoe said as I used Facebook chat to jokingly threaten to stalk her by waiting at her place so I could see her. I wanted us to go on a walk together as the sun set, my romantic side kicking in.

It had been more than two weeks since we kissed. Every time I requested to see her, she blew it off, pushing our next date further back. What she was thinking? If she liked me so much, why was she being so coy?

"We can go on a picnic when it gets warm," she promised.

"It will be warm this weekend," I told her after checking the weather online, but she didn't respond. I decided not to make a big deal out of it and backed off.

I got off work early and decided, in spite of my threats, an hour waiting for Zoe to arrive at her place wasn't a good plan. Worried I was being too emotionally needy, I went home instead. An hour after I settled in my apartment for the evening, Zoe surprised me with a text message.

"You know, stalking only works if you show up."

It was the biggest opening she had given me in weeks, and I wasn't going to let the opportunity slide. I grabbed my keys, jumped in the car, drove the 20 minutes to her place, then walked up and knocked on her door.

She opened the door, her sketchbook clearly visible on her couch, and shot me a look that said, "Go away! You're interrupting me!"

I almost walked away. Fighting that impulse with everything I had, I invited her out for a walk.

"Okay," she said, going back in to grab a sweater. I wasn't expecting her to accept the invitation so readily.

The walk through the neighborhood was filled with her talking about her high school and college friends, where they were, and her experiences at both schools. Earlier that day, she had related to me her academic history, skills, and accomplishments. She dismissed them all like ancient history, much as she liked to dismiss her drawing and singing skills. Had I attended the same school, I would have been intimidated by the many ways she exhibited her talents.

As we walked, we looked at houses and would stop to watch families getting ready for dinner. It was the day before the Jewish Sabbath, and we playfully imagined what their conversations were like and how the people we observed were related to each other. I made us do one too many turns around the neighborhood, and we became lost for a while.

"I used to deliver pizzas, so I have a good sense of direction," I declared with confidence and bravado.

"Not necessarily. It just means you don't mind getting lost," she said, deflating my ego. She had a comeback for every situation, and her sharp attentiveness was a big reason I enjoyed being around her so much.

At one point, we stopped to admire a large tree with a huge knot in it. We put our hands on it, feeling its aged texture, then sat beneath it and looked up at the moon, basking in its gentle glow.

At various points throughout our walk, she would hop onto curbs and walk on elevated walls like a kid at play. Watching her gave me visions of a childhood we never spent with each other. With her boundless imagination and love of stories, she would have been a lot of fun to be around.

Like me, she had been too busy in college to date. She didn't start dating until after she graduated, which was when guys took an interest in her. As I suspected, she had been out on several dates while we had been together, but I was the only one she had kissed. I was honored but embarrassed. I didn't realize how aggressive I had been toward her until she said that.

"You know ... you got everything right on your list but one thing," she said, referring to the list I had made of things I liked about her.

"What's that?"

"I hate going on walks. The only reason I went on walks with you was so I could spend time with you," she said. While I was glad she moved beyond her comfort zone to spend time with me, she made being with me sound like a happy inconvenience. I wasn't sure whether or not to take that as a compliment.

When we reached a clearing, we found ourselves at the outskirts of a park. She got her bearings and had us sit down on a bench. We held each other close while admiring the lighted fountain at the park's center. She leaned in toward me, and we were cheek to cheek, enjoying the changing colored lighting of the fountain, when I started nibbling at her ear. After several minutes, I affectionately brushed my nose against her forehead, face, and neck, making sure to avoid touching lips for several minutes.

"Leonard, what are you DOING to me?" she said as her breathing became heavy with excitement. She gathered her resolve, turned around, and told me, "This is the third and last time I'm going to tell you. We can't be together, and I can't ever see you again."

Those were the last words I expected out of her mouth at such a tender moment. Fear and panic over the end of a relationship I had been wanting with every ounce of my being for months took hold. I mentally froze as she straddled me. Whatever her intentions were at that moment, I could tell she was going to make this a memorable night for both of us.

"Why not?" I asked as she put her arms on my shoulders and faced me directly.

"I can't be what you want," she said in a more serious tone.

Again with that damn statement. I was frustrated with her failing to fully express her thoughts yet again. I wanted an explanation, and if this was the end, I wanted to know why now. More importantly, I wanted to know from her directly. I didn't want to grow old, look back, and not know what went horribly wrong years later, when wistfully remembering the time I tried to win over a Mormon whom I wanted more than anyone else in my life.

"What is it? What is it I want? Say it. I want you to tell me out loud," I said, raising my voice.

"Me."

It wasn't enough. There had to be more to it than that. There had to.

"Why not?," I demanded. "Say it. I want you to tell me out loud."

"I want to marry a Mormon."

The words drove a wedge right through my heart and tore it right open. All these months of wanting to be with her led all the way back to the first question she ever asked of me. I should have known to walk away then and there, but I didn't know any better.

I knew from all I had read on Mormonism these past few months that Caleb had been wrong. My skepticism was not a good fit in Mormonism. I wasn't even a good fit for Christianity. I didn't know what I was. I did know this, though. I was not a Mormon, and Zoe, this woman whom I had been obsessing over every detail for months, was never going to be with me.

It hurt to hear her voice my fears out loud so directly. It hurt to hear her reject me over something I had no control over. It hurt to know neither of us could be what the other wanted despite all our long, intimate conversations.

It hurt to know all that buildup these past few months had been for naught.

I used every ounce of that bitterness, anger, and desire to drive her crazy to the point of her trying to stuff her tongue down my throat. I returned the favor, equaling her passion and zeal. I wanted to ensure this night made a lasting impression on both of us. The weather was cold, but I scarcely noticed as we kissed as if we were at war.

She requested I call out her name to make sure I was thinking only of her as her tongue lovingly massaged my ear. It was an easy request to keep. She did the same for me, calling out my name, turning me on as much as I was turning her on. It was a lot of tongue. A lot of lip. A lot of grabbing, groping, scratching, petting, and caressing as weeks of teasing and pent-up passion exploded in an intensely emotional non-committal makeout session.

Whenever we took a break, we would talk about us. About the dates we had been on together, the few times we had seen each other, and shared each other's side of our story. It was great to have the opportunity to compare notes with her in person. We also talked about past relationships, turn-ons, and what we liked in our partners. She had nothing but compliments for me as she called me funny, poignant, smart, passionate, understanding, talented, gentlemanly, and everything else I had always wanted someone to say about me.

"I don't want you to hate me," she said.

I didn't. I couldn't. I wouldn't.

And, more importantly, she liked me. She liked how I made her FEEL pretty and special instead of saying she was.

"I know you like me beyond the kissing because we haven't done it much," she said.

"You know, you would have been able to make the relationship last a lot longer had you not been so aggressive, but it wouldn't have been anywhere near as much fun," she continued.

Disappointment over my lack of self-control took hold. I wanted to throw myself off the tallest cliff I could find because the thought of missing out on a future with her was too much to bear. As if on cue, the tell-tale sign of flashing orange lights breaking the dark of night signaled to us security wanted us out of the park.

"I wonder what tonight would have been like had we been at your apartment," she said as we got up and fled before security could get out of their vehicle.

Visions of us in the throes of passion in my tiny apartment flashed in my head.

"We could still go," I suggested.

We never went.

She pulled me to her and we walked hand in hand with arms locked before arriving at a bench a few addresses down from her apartment. Despite the late hour, the cold stillness of the air, and our growing fatigue, neither of us was willing or ready to let the other go yet, prisoners to each other's desires. One of us would start kissing the other, and then we would go at it for minutes on end building to as far as we were willing to take it while keeping our clothes on. I respected her too much to go any further.

When our kisses came to an end, we snuggled together on that uncomfortably hard, wooden bench. Our eyes locked for several minutes. I couldn't believe we were going to walk away from this, and this would be the last time she would let me see her. With our bodies spent after several intense hours of making out, I got up and escorted her back to her apartment. I didn't want to make that final walk back, but one of us had to move this evening to its proper conclusion.

As we stood outside her front door, we held each other and kissed a few more times, gradually slipping into a loose embrace, gazing lovingly into one another's weary eyes with our fatigued countenances.

I told her to go grab the book I lent her. I didn't want to come back to her place if I didn't have a good reason. Also, I didn't want to know what time it was, knowing full well I should go home and sleep to be somewhat fresh for autocross practice in the morning. I knew from experience racing a car on little sleep would bring nothing but frustration. When she returned with my book, we embraced.

She pulled away and waved her right hand as if she was casting a spell. "I release you," she said.

I grabbed onto her and held her tightly, hoping beyond hope she would somehow change her mind and we would be together forever.

"I know you're conflicted, but I also know you are a Child of God, and I'm glad I got to know you," she said. It comforted me to hear her say that because it helped ease the pain knowing she didn't think ill of me and our time together.

"You're not making this easy," I said.

She pulled away slightly, keeping her hands on me. We looked at each other with tear-filled, longing eyes. She never looked more beautiful to me than at that moment, right at her saddest.

I slid over to the building's exterior door, then paused to whisper in her ear, "I want you to remember something. I LOVE you, you crazy girl. I love you, I love you, I love you." I had nothing to lose, and with this being the last time I would see her, I didn't see another way of saying farewell.

"Goodbye, my Leonard," she whispered.

"Goodbye, my love," I said as I turned to walk off into the night, head held high, never looking back.

When I arrived back at my car, I noticed the tell-tale white and red envelope placed neatly underneath my passenger side windshield wiper: a parking ticket for $63. Maybe there was something to this angry, vengeful God after all. Noting the time stamp on the ticket, it happened around the time we fled the park.

Upon getting into my car, I noticed my cell phone wasn't in its usual spot in the cup holder. I thought I might have left it at home, so I drove there to look for it. Driving proved difficult because I could barely feel my numbed feet push down on the pedals after having been in the cold the entire evening. Failing to find the phone in the usual places, I came to the conclusion I must have dropped it while with Zoe. I didn't like the idea of my cell phone being picked up and used without my knowledge, but I hated the idea of going through the trouble of canceling the account and replacing the phone even more.

I ran through the entire evening in my head, skipping past the emotional parts, in an attempt to figure out where it could have been. I hoped I hadn't dropped it earlier when we had been wandering around, lost in the neighborhood. There was no way I would be able to retrace my steps because I had been too involved in my conversation with Zoe to keep track of them. It must have either been at the bench down the street from her place or at the park. So, I got back into my car and made the short drive back to her neighborhood.

I almost stopped by Zoe's to see if she would help me find it but thought better of it since it was 2:50 a.m. Seeing her would have been awkward at best. I checked the bench where we were last and could see us there holding each other, our sad eyes forever locked, but there was no sign of my phone. Was God punishing me for crossing unseen lines? I dismissed that question because all these problems were results of my own actions. With only myself to blame for my stupidity, I concentrated on the task at hand and got back into the car.

I drove back to the park, stopped the car, grabbed my flashlight from the trunk, and lo and behold, there was my cell phone, lying on the grass underneath the bench where Zoe and I had started making out, the painful vision of her telling me we could never be together chilling me to the bone. I reached down, picked up the phone, and drove back home.

By the time I arrived home, it was well past 3 a.m. I had to be up in two hours for an autocross, but all I could think of was Zoe. Lying there on my bed, I committed to memory every detail of the love I couldn't have because I wasn't the right faith.

Into the Void

One of the most memorable moments of the perennial Halloween TV special *It's the Great Pumpkin, Charlie Brown* is when Linus and Sally are sitting in the most sincere pumpkin patch Linus could find, waiting for The Great Pumpkin to show up. When he does show up, Linus faints as Sally learns the shocking truth: there is no Great Pumpkin, only a beagle dressed as a World War I flying ace. The next morning Linus declares he still believes in The Great Pumpkin and will find a more sincere pumpkin patch next year as the credits begin to roll.

Zoe told me she wouldn't see or talk to me anymore and was going to unfriend me from Facebook after she released me. I didn't like she was being so controlling, not giving me much say in the matter. Despite her words, she kept us as Facebook friends. I saw it as a ray of hope and concluded I only had one opening left with Zoe and that was convert to Mormonism. Though she never brought it up as an option, she hadn't left me with any other choice if I wanted to see her again. And, truth be known, I did. Losing Zoe wasn't just losing a potential lover and partner, it was losing an important building block for my present and future self. Zoe gave me a sense of self-worth I never previously had because she made every single aspect of me important to her, much as Carrie had done, only better because Zoe didn't have alcohol or drugs to cloud her judgment.

When I told Matthew about my relationship with Zoe, he recognized it mirrored his own relationship with his wife before they married. Like Zoe and me, they were both dating outside their religion. Matthew was a devout Episcopalian and his wife was Jewish. Also, Zoe and I were in the same emotional space, and it was driving our attraction to each other as it did with Matthew and his wife when they started dating.

Matthew told me, "Make sure you have something more than attraction to keep you together once the emotions die down. Otherwise, you will be miserable."

Listening carefully to his words, I could hear the voice of wisdom born from hard-earned experience. It was a voice I found impossible to ignore.

I asked Zoe if I could go to church with her, just as I had done with Emma, and sent her a lengthy e-mail asking questions about her faith. It took me a week to write. It took her two weeks to craft a response. Even then, it took a lot of convincing on my end to get her to send me her reply. She was too much of a perfectionist to let it go, making sure every word was just right. It was an honor and privilege to see how much care she was putting into it.

When I received her e-mail, it was full of detail, most of it doctrine-related, but what gave me hope was both of our e-mails ended with us talking about our mutual attraction for each other. That hope was dashed when she shot down the idea I go to church with her or attend her scripture class, saying doing so would hurt both her spiritual growth and my own.

"I don't want you to convert to Mormonism for me and there is no way I would be with someone who did," she said in her reply.

She did, however, encourage me to ask her more questions about Mormonism to help her figure out which Mormon church would be a good fit for me. It hurt to see she didn't want to be with me while on this journey and closed off my idea we would grow a partnership together under the watchful eyes of God.

Since all you had to do to become a Mormon was say you believed the *Book of Mormon* and the Bible were the true word of God, converting to Mormonism wouldn't be difficult. However, it wasn't a decision I could take lightly because the lifestyle changes that came with it would affect every aspect of my life. It wasn't just the undergarments Mormons wore to signify their covenant with God, it was turning my back on alcohol and caffeinated drinks, vowing to abstain from sex until marriage, ending autocross on Sundays, paying a 10-percent tithe, and giving my life over to good works handed down by revelation from men higher up in the church hierarchy. Some aspects of the change, like giving up alcohol and autocross, would be easier to accomplish than others, like believing in others' revelations as a guiding force in my life.

Mormonism was worth a serious look because I wanted to see if it was possible to become a better version of myself within the confines of its rules.

Following a religion like Mormonism wasn't different from the dedication involved with doing a four-panel daily comic strip, much like I had done with my webcomic. Within the format's limitations are infinite creative possibilities allowing you to do whatever you want as long as you stayed within the given parameters. In other words, you could be who you wanted to be within Mormonism as long as you adhered to the rules of the religion.

The skeptic in me wondered if converting to Mormonism to become a better version of myself was such a good idea, especially after having picked up Dan Barker's *Losing Faith in Faith*. I couldn't get over Barker's idea it was possible to be good without God. Curious as to what a life without God was like, I went to an atheist meetup at a popular bowling alley across town. When I walked into the alley, I caught sight of a folded sign sitting on a table in front of a pair of lanes closest to the front door and walked over. I was surprised the people there looked like anyone else you met on the street in LA: skinny, fat, tall, short, blonde, brunette, redhead, dressed in T-shirt, jeans, dresses, and everything in between. There must have been more than 30 people at the meetup hanging out among four lanes.

"Have you been to one of these meetups before?" an attractive brunette in her mid-20s asked.

"First time," I said, noting the engagement ring on her finger.

"Are you an atheist, agnostic, or just curious?"

"Just curious," I replied. "I'm currently reading the Bible, Dan Barker's *Losing Faith in Faith,* and looking into Mormonism."

"I think Mormonism is cool," she said as her face lit up.

"Why's that?" I asked. Weren't atheists supposed to be anti-religious?

"Because you get your own planet! Who wouldn't want their own planet? I could do so much with my own planet!" she said with enthusiasm bordering on reverential.

I could see her point. I should have been thrilled at the idea of running my own planet in the afterlife, not shaking my head in disbelief at the ridiculousness of it all.

In addition to talking about Mormonism, we discussed Christian apologetics and their extensive use of circular logic to defend their beliefs. Gaining an understanding of apologetics' straw man arguments in an attempt to discredit nonbelievers was invaluable.

After the meetup, the organizer, a fit 30-something Middle-Eastern looking man, walked me out to the parking lot.

"I hear you're still clinging to a higher power," he started.

"Um ... yes, I guess I am," I said with uncertainty.

"Why do you still believe?" I could tell by the well-practiced delivery he had asked this question many times before.

"I believe the laws of nature in all their complexity and rules had to be created by a higher power," I replied.

"I see. Many of us here have been through the same exploration and questioning you've been through. All you have to do is ask around, and you'll find the truth you're seeking."

"Thanks, I'll keep that in mind," I said.

While I wasn't convinced by the group God didn't exist, their logical approach to arguments mirrored my own. One of the members of the group suggested I read the Reddit atheism forum for more answers. In one discussion thread, I found a link to a *South Park* episode making fun of Mormonism. The poignant message at the end taught me each religion was true for its followers because it pointed to a common belief there was a God. I could convert to any religion I wanted, including Mormonism, because they all said the same thing and it had nothing to do with God. I could even choose bits and pieces of other religions to create my own religion because it was all about the one, true religious message: be nice.

Inspired by this idea I could convert to any religion I wanted, I sent Zoe a lengthy e-mail detailing both my positive and negative thoughts on Mormonism. My hope was she could help me find a Mormon church I could fit my questioning self with. Shortly after, another thought crossed my mind. "Would you date me if I were a Mormon?" I asked in a shorter e-mail. She responded by refusing to acknowledge any of my chat requests and logged off every time I logged on to Facebook. I didn't understand why she was shutting me off, especially after having been so open to my previous questions on Mormonism. Was it something I said?

Looking back over my e-mail, I was pretty certain I had crossed the line on questioning her religion and not in a good way. I called to apologize, but she never returned it. She did, however, stop logging off every time I got on Facebook. I was thankful she stopped avoiding me, but I took the hint and quit talking to her because I didn't know how to approach her anymore. The open communication between us I had prized when we were dating had disintegrated because of a wrong question and e-mail. Zoe then posted a Facebook status saying she desperately needed a boyfriend now—a Mormon boyfriend.

Hoping I could become the Mormon boyfriend Zoe wanted so I could see her again, I took it upon myself to read the three scriptures Mormons followed in addition to the Bible: the *Book of Mormon*, *Doctrine and Covenants*, and *Pearl of Great Price*.

It took several weeks to go through all the Mormon scriptures while finishing up the Bible and Dan Barker's *Losing Faith in Faith* at the same time. As I closed in on completing all my reading, my hopes of converting to Mormonism faded because all the contradictions and false claims I had detected in the Bible were evident in the Mormon scriptures as well.

It wasn't just the concept of dark skin being used as a curse from God for the sins of our forefathers since I have dark skin myself, it was the stories of an ancient American culture and civilization that flourished with periods of extraordinary growth. According to the *Book of Mormon*, this culture became so proud of its success it would turn away from God and descend into sin. Once it did, God would turn his wrath upon it, destroying all it had built, and the cycle would begin all over again. The idea God would destroy a civilization if it didn't follow his commandments was central to understanding why Mormons were so predominantly conservative as a group. The main problem I had with these stories was there was no evidence of this culture and civilization ever existing outside of the *Book of Mormon*, Mormon apologetics, LDS scholarly journals, and the faith of its believers. Without any verification from outside sources, the literal truth of these stories was difficult to swallow for this skeptic.

Then there was Jesus's coming to America following his crucifixion marked by death, destruction, a voice heard across the earth, and all sorts of unnatural phenomena possible only through the combined power of pen and imagination. In fact, there was not one single line in the Bible that corroborated Jesus's coming to America as depicted in the *Book of Mormon*. Piggybacking one book of myths onto another wasn't "Another Testament of Jesus Christ," as the *Book of Mormon* said on its spine, it was fan fiction.

And, yet, by the end of the book, my skeptical self was supposed to pray to the Holy Ghost to see if the *Book of Mormon* was the true word of God. When it came right down to it, I was too much of a literalist to buy into either Christianity or Mormonism because the scriptures were full of logical fallacies and contradictions. Talk of believing as a matter of faith rang hollow, not because I needed evidence to believe, but because I couldn't believe in something that didn't ring true for me.

I looked more closely at Deism with its belief in an absent God. I went back over Thomas Paine's *Age of Reason* and its vitriolic attacks on the Bible. In Paine's words, I found a like-minded individual whose beliefs I could agree with, even if his attitude toward the source material was less than ideal. Benjamin Franklin, one of our country's founding fathers and close friend of Paine's, was opposed to its publication because it would make a lot of people angry. Franklin saw it as an attempt to destroy an institution that gave followers hope and purpose. For me, the idea of an absent God had its appeal because I could hold on to my belief in a higher power and keep attending the Episcopal church to see my friends there.

After she again posted her need for a boyfriend, I snail-mailed Zoe a Valentine's Day card reminding her there was someone who cared for her. Zoe spent the next couple of weeks occasionally checking my Facebook statuses. I knew because she would hit the "Like" button and Facebook would tell me when she did, even when she retracted it. She sent me an e-mail after I lost my job at the satellite television company, telling me I wasn't a bad person because of my e-mail on Mormonism.

"Thanks for giving me space. Please tell me when you find your next spectacular job," she said.

I replied two days later saying it was good she asked for space even though I knew she didn't. Shutting someone off to get your way isn't the same thing as asking for space. It is emotional blackmail.

I avoided challenging myself with difficult questions because of what they might mean to my beliefs. Staying in Christianity meant conformity in a country where more than three-fourths of the population sees themselves as some form of Christian. It was the safe choice even if I didn't believe in it whole-heartedly. Moving into Mormonism meant giving over my life to a religion with a set of rules seen as odd by those outside of the faith. Neither was as risky as becoming an atheist, where studies have shown atheists are the least trusted group in the United States. I wanted to be liked and trusted, not a societal outcast to be feared and shunned because I didn't believe.

Lying there on my bed alone in my apartment, I relaxed and let my mind wander. If God set the rules and left the universe to its own devices as in Deism, what was the difference between an absent god and no god? With an absent god, prayers would go unanswered and miracles would never happen. The same would happen if there were no god. In my experience, prayer was as effective as a coin toss and miracles were nothing more than natural phenomena we attributed to a higher power. Thus, there was no difference between an absent god and no god. There might as well have been no god at all.

I still believed something must have created the universe and that something was God. The problem I saw with the concept of having an external creator to the universe such as God was that something must have created God. If God could have come out of nothing, couldn't the universe also come out of nothing? I came to the conclusion if God could have come from nothing, then the universe could have as well. Thus, God wasn't necessary for the creation of the universe and didn't exist in any place other than our own minds.

The implications of that epiphany left me unable to return to the Episcopal church—or any Christian church for that matter. With the cloak of divinity removed from God, life's meaning diminished. Work was no longer a gift from God so I could be happy because it made him happy, but a job I did because it would ensure I would remain a content cog in an economic machine that cared little for my personal well-being. No longer was I a Child of God, but just another speck stranded on a remote planet moving through the vast emptiness of space. Christianity and Mormonism were no longer inspiring guidebooks on how to live; they were now mind-control methods using the threat of an angry, petulant Creator to keep us intellectually and emotionally enthralled so we would gladly hand over our lives and, most especially, money to them.

Like Sally and The Great Pumpkin, I had been played for a fool. I couldn't stand being around believers anymore because my version of reality didn't match theirs. The whole idea of converting to Mormonism was gone, too, as was any hope of seeing Zoe again. She was too much of a true-believing Mormon for any relationship between her and a non-believer to work. I wanted to believe, not only for her, but because if so many people in the world believed, why couldn't I?

The reason I couldn't believe was self-evident. I had failed. Failed in my quest to honor my father through God. Failed in my desire to find a good, God-fearing Christian woman to marry to honor my father's memory. Failed in my quest to fit in with the rest of society. Failed to live up to the religious-born ideals Zoe and Emma desired out of their mates. With so many fails, I concluded Dad was right to call me stupid all those years after all.

I sent Zoe a message over Facebook telling her I wasn't going to convert, briefly saying why: I no longer believed in God. I was nervous about hitting send, unsure of what to expect from her. We weren't talking anymore, so what did I have to lose? When I returned home that night, I discovered her smiling mug missing from my list of Facebook friends. My failure with her had run its course. It was a void I didn't know how to fill.

Homecoming

When the tsunami and earthquake that killed almost 16,000 people and damaged more than a million structures hit Japan on March 11, 2011, in the hours after I sent Zoe that Facebook message, I couldn't help but think God had punished Japan, a nation of secularists, for turning their backs on him. An irrational fear God would turn that wrath on me for turning my back on him by giving me cancer again kept crowding my thoughts, though I didn't believe that would happen since all my test results had come up negative so far.

Part of me wanted to give up a life many believers would deem worthless without God. After all, why continue living a life without meaning? Had I been armed with a gun, I would have killed myself and saved the world the trouble of figuring out how to get rid of another godless heathen. During my time at the Episcopal church, I had once been told Jesus would save you in your deepest, darkest hour, but I no longer believed in Jesus.

Looking for a ray of hope, I thought of my positive experiences with a community at the Episcopal church, my early days with the staff at Festival Graphics, the people I met through swing dancing and cartooning, and my autocross experiences. If I could get a fraction of those positive feelings in a place more attuned to my non-belief, I could rebuild myself.

I took the *Belief.net* quiz to determine which religion would fit me best and Unitarian Universalism was at the top of the results. In UU, you didn't have to believe in a higher power to be a member. That fact alone was enough for me to give it a try because it was a place where I could be accepted for who I was. With a sense of optimism for the future, I stepped into the sanctuary and took a seat for the 11 a.m. service at the nearby Unitarian Universalist church the Sunday after Zoe unfriended me from Facebook.

When I first walked into the cozy building, I noticed there were many faces from opposite ends of the age spectrum in the pews. I wasn't surprised because many people my age have gotten married, started families, and continued to practice whatever religion they either grew up in or weren't practicing at all due to their busy lives. Also, most single people my age were spending their Sunday mornings recovering from a night out at clubs and bars, having drinks and dating, or living a lifestyle suited to their interests. Here I was, starting over with a new religion.

As I took a seat in a pew, I looked up at the banners mounted on the walls above representing several of the world's major religions, showing people of all faiths were accepted there. After the opening hymn, musical prelude, and minister's words of welcome, the covenant the congregation recited from the Order of Service handout was a statement I could see myself repeating over and over again, not out of any sense of obligation or duty, but because it represented values I could hold dear:

Love is the doctrine of this church.
The quest for truth is its sacrament,
And service is its prayer.
To dwell together in peace,
To seek knowledge in freedom,
To serve humankind in fellowship,
Thus do we covenant with each other.

The structure of the service was similar to ones I was familiar with in the Episcopal and Catholic churches, but without all that talk of the angry, jealous God, Christ, salvation, resurrection, heaven, or hell. It was filled with a short children's story, community announcements, silent devotional time, and beautiful songs—some sung by the choir and some played by the resident jazz pianist. The sermon itself was built from the same inspiring language as the covenant and was friendly to my new view of the universe because of its emphasis on love: Love for the world around you. Love for your fellow human. And, most important of all, love of yourself.

After the service, I attended the newcomer's orientation, where I met up with both the director of religious education and minister. After the handful of us visitors in attendance introduced ourselves and talked about why we were there, the minister gave us a brief rundown of the history of Unitarian Universalism. I was pleasantly surprised the happy heretics of UU had been around in one form or another as long as Christianity had existed.

A member of the membership and leadership committee talked about how she took the same *Belief.net* test I had taken to see what religion would work for her. Like me, UU was on the top of her list. She tried it out, liked it, and never looked back. Her happiness over having found UU gave me hope.

The director of religious education spoke about the UU church's youth education program and how it taught about different religions. Throughout the year the program would have the youth visit neighboring faiths — on that particular morning, they had gone to visit a Mormon congregation. I smiled at the coincidence. It was the type of early education that would have saved me a whole lot of grief later on in life.

Though religions I had looked at over the years talked about uniting everyone and being friendly toward each other, they also served to frustratingly divide us with each claiming to be the one, true religion. By contrast, UU was not only welcoming persons of both faith and non-faith into its fold, but it was also educating about other religions without any exclusionary practices or claims of superiority. It was a message I could truly believe in.

Over the course of the next several months, I became a more active member of the UU community, attending services when autocross didn't conflict and doing the time-honored UU tradition of joining a committee. I took every opportunity I could to attend their many social gatherings and liked it was an active congregation because it was easy to meet new people. I found a few were lifelong UUs, but many were converts who left other religions because they disagreed with dogma or had problems with scripture as I had. In UU, we were welcome to question all dogma. It was a stark contrast with Mormonism, where questioning the veracity of the religion could get you excommunicated.

I joined their young adult group made up of congregants in their 20s and 30s and found like-minded people closer to my age with an intellectual curiosity and skeptical nature that mirrored my own. Some of the congregants even had similar stories to mine and were sympathetic toward my having had a failed courtship with a devout Mormon.

Looking back, I could see my journey to UU's religious humanism with clarity that matched my beliefs. My surviving cancer hadn't been because of any wishful thinking through prayer, but because of my will to survive by seeking and getting treatment from the right people at the right time. Likewise, the deaths of my father and my childhood friend Kevin had not been the result of intervention from a higher power on my behalf, but a part of the natural order of the circle of life. Seeing them in heaven was no longer something to aspire to, they were part of memories that could be cherished today. Emma and Zoe were no longer women of God, but ordinary people whose company I enjoyed because I found them attractive. Autocross was no longer a God-given directive for doing his work, but a hobby I loved doing because it brought me joy and happiness. The stories contained within the Bible and *Book of Mormon* weren't the word of God, but the words of men of the past with lessons to impart to future generations. And, finally, God was no longer a higher power to be worshiped or feared, but a symbol of hope, a belief in a better world, and an aspiration to be the best version of myself.

Epilogue

Eight Years

March 10, 2013.

The entire day had passed before I remembered the significance of the date. It should have been etched into my memory after celebrating the same date every year for the past eight years. Previously, I had marked the date of my orchiectomy with a Facebook status like a second birthday. This time around, my cancerversary, a phrase we used in the young adult cancer survivor group I attended to indicate the date we became tumor-free, had slipped my mind.

Two months later, I had my annual surveillance checkup at the nearby hospital, my time with Dr. C having long since past due to changing insurances and employers. I drove to the facility from work and easily found parking in the extremely busy structure. I made my way along the friendly, wooden floor through the well-labeled corridors to the urology department to see Dr. P, the tall, dark man with large hands and easy-going demeanor in charge of my surveillance for the past two years. After giving me a brief physical examination, he sat me down.

"I have news for you, Leonard," he said with a serious, unflinching gaze.

I expected the worst.

"You've been cancer-free for eight years now. I want you to have a blood test done today so we can check your tumor markers. If you pass, you're done with tests," he said with a confident smile.

A wave of relief nearly knocked me to the floor as my eyes welled up with tears.

"I can't do the test today, but I'll do it first thing in the morning," I said, unable to control my grin.

"You won't forget, will you?" he asked, raising an eyebrow.

"Doctor, I have been doing this for eight years and have only been late for one blood test: I won't forget this one."

"Good."

I didn't forget.

And, best of all.

I passed.

Acknowledgments

Thanks go out to Amy, Carrie, Becky, Emma, and Zoe for giving me the opportunity to get to know them better. To Dr. H, Dr. K, Dr. C, Dr. P, and their wonderful staffs—I wouldn't be here without their expertise and care. To the Thrive/Survive young adult cancer survivor group for helping me learn how to cope emotionally with my Big C experience many years after the fact. To the Unitarian Universalist religious exploration program for their inspiration, love, and support. Without the *Build Your Own Theology* class to provide the basic framework for this book, there would be no book. To the Writer's Group at the UU church for their input and encouragement. And to all of my friends who gave me their time and input. You're all wonderful and I am glad to have you as part of my life.

Most especially, huge thanks go out to Melanie Melancon for her time and dedication editing this project. I know she would have loved to see this book to completion, but she passed away before she finished her work. Huge thanks also go out to Ben Loory, Christa Percival, Leslie Schipa, Greg Machlin, and Dan Patterson for giving me the push I needed to make this book better. Without them, this book would be nothing but several hundred journal entries in search of a story.

Finally, I thank Mom and Dad for encouraging my creative expression through writing and drawing. Without their love and support, this book would not have been possible.

About the Author

Leonard Cachola is a graphic designer living and working in the Los Angeles area. His hobbies include autocross, choral singing, watching movies, reading books, swing dancing, photography, cartooning, and writing. He has been the novice coordinator for Sports Car Club of America's CalClub region autocross division since 2008. *The Truth Within: A Humanist's Memoir* is his fourth book and first memoir.

Made in the USA
Columbia, SC
09 January 2024

29444167R00145